Restoring and Prot

The Role of Engineering and Technology

Committee on the Role of Technology in
Marine Habitat Protection and Enhancement

Marine Board

Commission on Engineering and Technical Systems

National Research Council

National Academy Press
Washington, D.C. 1994

NOTICE: The project that is the subject of this report was approved by the Governing Board of the National Research Council, whose members are drawn from the councils of the National Academy of Sciences (NAS), the National Academy of Engineering (NAE), and the Institute of Medicine (IOM). The members of the panel responsible for the report were chosen for their special competencies and with regard for appropriate balance.

This report has been reviewed by a group other than the authors according to procedures approved by a Report Review Committee consisting of members of the National Academy of Sciences, the National Academy of Engineering, and the Institute of Medicine.

The program described in this report is supported by Cooperative Agreement No. 14-35-0001-30475 between the Minerals Management Service of the U.S. Department of Interior and the National Academy of Sciences.

Limited copies are available from:

Marine Board
Commission on Engineering and Technical Systems
National Research Council
2101 Constitution Avenue
Washington, DC 20418

Additional copies are available for sale from:

National Academy Press
2101 Constitution Avenue
Box 285
Washington, D.C. 20055
800-624-6242 or 202-334-3313 (in the Washington metropolitan area)

Library of Congress Catalog Card Number 94-66886
International Standard Book Number 0-309-04843-5

B-064

Copyright 1994 by the National Academy of Sciences. All rights reserved.

Printed in the United States of America

Dedication

Dr. William E. Odum, a distinguished expert in ecology, was a member of the committee until his death in 1991. His contributions to the committee and commitment to the ecology discipline and his students were substantial. His sudden, untimely death touched each committee member deeply. We have lost a good friend; the scientific and academic communities have lost a respected leader.

The National Academy of Sciences is a private, nonprofit, self-perpetuating society of distinguished scholars engaged in scientific and engineering research, dedicated to the furtherance of science and technology and to their use for the general welfare. Upon the authority of the charter granted to it by the Congress in 1863, the Academy has a mandate that requires it to advise the federal government on scientific and technical matters. Dr. Bruce M. Alberts is president of the National Academy of Sciences.

The National Academy of Engineering was established in 1964, under the charter of the National Academy of Sciences, as a parallel organization of outstanding engineers. It is autonomous in its administration and in the selection of its members, sharing with the National Academy of Sciences the responsibility for advising the federal government. The National Academy of Engineering also sponsors engineering programs aimed at meeting national needs, encourages education and research, and recognizes the superior achievements of engineers. Dr. Robert M. White is president of the National Academy of Engineering.

The Institute of Medicine was established in 1970 by the National Academy of Sciences to secure the services of eminent members of appropriate professions in the examination of policy matters pertaining to the health of the public. The Institute acts under the responsibility given to the National Academy of Sciences by its congressional charter to be an adviser to the federal government and, upon its own initiative, to identify issues of medical care, research, and education. Dr. Kenneth Shine is president of the Institute of Medicine.

The National Research Council was organized by the National Academy of Sciences in 1916 to associate the broad community of science and technology with the Academy's purposes of furthering knowledge and advising the federal government. Functioning in accordance with general policies determined by the Academy, the Council has become the principal operating agency of both the National Academy of Sciences and the National Academy of Engineering in providing services to the government, the public, and the scientific and engineering communities. The Council is administered jointly by both Academies and the Institute of Medicine. Dr. Bruce M. Alberts and Dr. Robert M. White are chairman and vice-chairman, respectively, of the National Research Council.

iv

COMMITTEE ON THE ROLE OF TECHNOLOGY IN MARINE HABITAT PROTECTION AND ENHANCEMENT

THOMAS A. SANDS, Adams and Reese, New Orleans, Louisiana
DEWITT D. BARLOW, III, Great Lakes Dredge and Dock Company, Oak Brook, Illinois
JOHN MARK DEAN, University of South Carolina, Columbia
OLIVER HOUCK, Tulane Law School, New Orleans, Louisiana
MARY C. LANDIN, U.S. Army Engineer Waterways Experiment Station, Vicksburg, Mississippi
ROY R. LEWIS, III, Lewis Environmental Services, Inc., Tampa, Florida
ASHISH J. MEHTA, University of Florida, Gainesville
JOHN M. NICHOL, Consultant, Long Beach, California
WILLIAM E. ODUM, University of Virginia, Charlottesville, Virginia (until April, 1991)
RUTH PATRICK, **NAS,** Academy of Natural Sciences, Philadelphia, Pennsylvania
R. EUGENE TURNER, Louisiana State University, Baton Rouge

Liaison Representatives

JOHN HALL, National Oceanic and Atmospheric Administration
WILLIAM KLESCH, U.S. Army Corps of Engineers
KAREN S. KLIMA, Environmental Protection Agency
LAVERNE SMITH, U.S. Fish and Wildlife Service

Staff

Wayne Young, Project Officer (from August 1990)
Paul M. Scholz (until August 1990)
Delphine D. Glaze, Administrative Assistant
Brooks Moriarty, Research Assistant
Sheila Mulvihill, Editorial Consultant

MARINE BOARD

JERRY R. SCHUBEL, *Chairman*, State University of New York at Stony Brook

JERRY A. ASPLAND, Arco Marine, Inc., Long Beach, California

ANNE D. AYLWARD, National Commission on Intermodal Transporation, Alexandria, Virginia

ROBERT G. BEA, **NAE**, University of California at Berkeley

MARK Y. BERMAN, Amoco Production Company, Houston, Texas

JOHN W. BOYLSTON, Argent Marine Operations, Inc., Solomons, Maryland

JAMES M. COLEMAN, **NAE**, Louisiana State University, Baton Rouge, Louisiana

WILLIAM M. EICHBAUM, World Wildlife Fund, Washington, D.C.

EDWARD D. GOLDBERG, **NAS**, Scripps Institution of Oceanography, LaJolla, California

MARTHA GRABOWSKI, Lemoyne College and Rennselaer Polytechnic Institute, Cazenovia, New York

ROBERT W. KNECHT, University of Delaware, Newark

HENRY S. MARCUS, Massachusetts Institute of Technology, Cambridge

ASHISH J. MEHTA, University of Florida, Gainesville

J. BRADFORD MOONEY, **NAE**, Consultant to Ocean Engineering and Research Management, Fort Pierce, Florida

STEPHEN F. SCHMIDT, American President Lines, Ltd., Oakland, California

STEPHANIE R. THORNTON, Coastal Resources Center, San Francisco, California

JUDITH S. WEIS, Rutgers University, Newark, New Jersey

ALAN G. YOUNG, Fugro-McClelland BV, Houston, Texas

Staff

CHARLES A. BOOKMAN, Director

DONALD W. PERKINS, Associate Director

DORIS C. HOLMES, Staff Associate

Foreword

This report addresses the role of technology in protecting and restoring marine habitat. The report finds that coastal engineering can and should play a positive role in protection and restoration work. However, the use of technology for these purposes is not a substitute for prudent and wise stewardship of marine resources. At the rate that coastal areas are being developed for industrial, commercial, and residential uses, and with significant losses from natural erosion and subsidence, there is no offsetting engineering fix to achieve "no net loss" of marine habitat. The positive role that the report envisions for coastal engineering can only fully develop as part of a larger national strategy for protection and preservation of marine habitats as vital natural resources.

Sound ecological principles need to be applied in measures to protect or restore marine habitats. Because of the complexity of natural ecosystems, full restoration of natural functions at altered or disturbed sites can take years, and is feasible in only some situations. Nevertheless, coastal engineering techniques and technology, including structures and equipment, can be applied at suitable sites to protect them, establish the physical conditions essential for enhancement or restoration, or assist in recolonization.

All these factors need to be considered in planning decisions to develop, and to protect marine habitat. In sum, technology has an important role to play in protecting and restoring marine habitats as one element of a national strategy to improve the management of these essential natural resources.

Thomas A. Sands, Chairman

vii

Preface

BACKGROUND

The nation's estuaries, coastal wetlands, and nearshore submerged areas are precious national resources. They provide marine habitats that are critical not only to the production and replenishment of living marine resources generally, but also to commercial and recreational fisheries, non-consumptive recreation in the coastal zone, and natural protection against an advancing sea. Despite their value and government controls and programs, these habitats are being degraded at an alarming rate. They are altered by natural processes such as erosion and subsidence and are directly or indirectly threatened by human activity, including acceleration of natural phenomena associated with human-related alteration of physical processes. A substantial national effort is being directed to understand these losses and effects through research and to correct them through regulation as a management strategy. Scientific knowledge and engineering efforts are being applied to the problem as well, but not always harmoniously. Although much has been learned from pilot projects, and there is considerable experience in the use of dredged material and other areas, more could be done with existing knowledge and expertise to enhance, protect, restore, and create marine habitats. Advancing the state of practice involves creating an institutional and academic climate for advancing policy and procedural change, establishing goals and objectives, developing cooperation among involved organizations, enlisting collaboration among involved scientific and engineering disciplines, adapting technology and facilitating innovation through experimentation, transferring information

THE NRC STUDY

within and among disciplines, implementing incentive-based solutions, and measuring performance.

On its own initiative and as a result of informal discussions with the U.S. Army Corps of Engineers, the National Oceanic and Atmospheric Administration (NOAA), the Environmental Protection Agency (EPA), and the U.S. Fish and Wildlife Service (USFWS), the Marine Board determined the need to explore the role of coastal engineering in enhancing and restoring marine and estuarine habitats and contiguous shorelines within the coastal zone. These areas include marine wetlands such as tidal marshes, emergent wetlands, sea grass beds, kelp forests, and mangrove swamps. Also included are beaches, shallow inshore and near-shore submerged environments, and tidal and intertidal flats. Offshore marine habitat is outside the boundaries of this assessment except for artificial reefs and offshore berms on the continental shelf. The National Research Council (NRC) convened the Committee on the Role of Technology in Marine Habitat Protection and Enhancement under the auspices of the Marine Board of the Commission on Engineering and Technical Systems.

Committee members were selected for their expertise and their wide range of experience and viewpoints. The principle guiding the constitution of the committee and its work, consistent with NRC policy, was not to exclude members with potential biases that might accompany expertise vital to the study, but to seek balance and fair treatment. Committee members were selected for their expertise in coastal engineering, coastal and estuarine science, wetlands mitigation and restoration, dredging technology, policy for and management of living marine resources, and environmental law. Academic, industrial, government, scientific, and engineering perspectives are also reflected in the committee's composition. Biographies of committee members are provided in Appendix A.

The committee was assisted by the National Marine Fisheries Service of NOAA, the Army Corps of Engineers, the EPA, and the USFWS, all of which designated liaison representatives.

The committee was asked by the NRC to conduct a multidisciplinary assessment of the needs for a coastal engineering strategy to preserve, protect, enhance, restore, and, where necessary, create marine habitats to mitigate or reverse coastal marine habitat losses. Included in the scope of study are:

• the state of coastal engineering practice in marine habitat management and the potential for protection, enhancement, creation, and restoration of marine habitats;

• future needs and opportunities to restore and enhance habitat through engineering approaches and innovative applications of technology (including projects that combine other engineering objectives with habitat enhancement);

PREFACE   xi

• a definition of engineering community, scientific community, and government roles in advancing technical and innovative approaches to the protection and restoration of these habitats;

• environmental conflicts, such as those surrounding dredged material placement and water pollution control from nonpoint and uncontrolled sources, which may directly affect marine habitats;

• management and maintenance needs for natural and reconstructed marine habitats; and

• the need for collaboration between coastal and ecological sciences and coastal engineering.

The assessment is an initial examination of the application of coastal engineering technology in marine habitat management. Emphasis is given to the broad suite of dredging and marine sediment placement issues because of their importance to the nation, the wealth of available information on this topic, dredging and dredged material responsibilities of project sponsors, and the disposal of large quantities of nontoxic dredged marine sediments as a waste in lieu of their use in marine habitat restoration work. Marine wetlands include marshes, emergent wetlands, seagrass beds, mangrove swamps, and kelp forests. Some of these are not commonly recognized as wetlands by the public, but are emphasized in the report because of their biological importance. Marshes were given special treatment because of their importance as nurseries for many species and their fragile nature. However, as much attention was given to other aspects of marine habitat management as supported by the available information. The report does not provide a detailed technical analysis of individual technologies, nor does it provide an assessment of scientific theory. Rather, it provides a scientifically and technically based examination of the issues and a strategic vision for advancing the state of practice.

The committee reviewed available data and literature and conducted site visits to determine the state of practice of marine habitat management. The committee also solicited data and views and met with expert practitioners and researchers in federal, regional, state and local government agencies; research institutions; public interest groups; and professional societies. This activity was supplemented by visits to the Gulf Coast and the San Francisco Bay Area to examine individual projects. Case studies of specific projects and technologies are included as Appendix B. A source reference table (Appendix C) and an extensive bibliography are included to facilitate identification and practical use of these materials.

REPORT ORGANIZATION

The audience for which this report was prepared consists of policy and project decisionmakers; members of the technical community associated with *xii*   *PREFACE*

waterway and coastal design, construction, and maintenance; scientists and engineers concerned with design, construction, and maintenance of marine habitat projects; and the general public. Understanding the role of coastal engineering in marine habitat management requires an understanding of both the science and the physical processes of marine systems.

Chapter 1 frames the loss and degradation of marine habitats in the context of natural and human processes and identifies the need for engineering and science to work together to expand and enhance marine habitat management.

Chapter 2 provides scientific and engineering perspectives on marine habitat management.

Chapter 3 discusses engineering practices in the coastal zone as they pertain to the protection, enhancement, restoration and creation of marine habitats.

Chapter 4 discusses lessons learned from committee-prepared case studies of marine habitat projects.

Chapter 5 discusses institutional factors that inhibit project decisionmaking and implementation and suggests ways to overcome these obstacles.

Chapter 6 examines the criteria used to assess marine habitat projects. It offers a multidisciplinary approach for achieving project objectives through improved planning and implementation.

Chapter 7 identifies research needed to improve the scientific basis and engineering capabilities for application to marine habitat protection and restoration.

Chapter 8 presents the committee's conclusions regarding the state of practice and recommendations to foster and enhance the interdisciplinary teamwork needed to improve the role of coastal engineering in marine habitat management.

Acknowledgments

The committee gratefully acknowledges the contributions of time and information provide by liaison representatives, their agencies, and the many individuals within and outside government who are interested in the role of engineering and technology in protecting and improving marine habitat. The committee is especially indebted to the many practitioners in the restoration industry, permitting and resource agencies, academia, and environmental organizations who provided detailed descriptions of projects and technologies as well as a wealth of reference materials not widely available.

John Hall, National Marine Fisheries Service, participated in West Coast site visits and provided technical support and reference materials throughout the study. William R. Murden, NAE, Murden Marine, provided valuable insight on dredging technology, underwater berms, and use of dredged materials in habitat protection and restoration and contributed to development of underwater water berm case study material. Michael N. Josselyn, Tiburon Center for Environmental Studies, helped in organizing the committee's West Coast meeting and field trips, served as panel moderator, and hosted site visits. The support of the Mississippi Valley Commission for assessment of Gulf Coast marine habitat needs is also greatly appreciated.

Special thanks are extended to the many members of the scientific, engineering, and academic communities and public interest groups who met with the committee and provided scientific, technical, and policy advice on the state of practice of habitat protection and restoration. The extraordinary cooperation and interest of so many knowledgeable individuals were both gratifying and essential.

xiii

Contents

Executive Summary   1

1   INTRODUCTION   9
    Marine Habitat—A National Treasure in Decline, 9
    The Challenge for Coastal Engineering, 14

2   SCIENTIFIC AND ENGINEERING PERSPECTIVES   18
    Ecological Setting, 18
    The Scope of Coastal Engineering, 21
    Impacts of Technology in the Coastal Zone, 26
    Observations on the Implications of Sea Level Rise to the
        Application of Protection and Restoration Technology, 27
    Defining Success, 28
    Summary, 29

3   THE STATE OF ENGINEERING PRACTICE IN
   MARINE HABITAT MANAGEMENT   31
    Restoration Technical Issues, 31
    Applying Technology, 35
    Dredging and Dredged Material Placement, 49
    Alternative Approaches and Technologies for Minimizing or
        Avoiding Impacts to Marine Habitat, 53
    Implementation Factors Affecting Use of Technology, 58
    Summary, 61

4   THE APPLICATION OF PROTECTION AND RESTORATION
   TECHNOLOGY IN MARINE HABITAT MANAGEMENT   63
    Case Study Findings, 64
    Summary, 70

xv

5 INSTITUTIONAL ISSUES AFFECTING MARINE HABITAT
  MANAGEMENT   71
     Institutional Issues, 72
     Summary, 88

6 IMPROVING PROJECT PERFORMANCE   90
     Project Performance, 90
     The Decision Process, 92
     Summary, 100

7 RESEARCH NEEDS   102
     Research Programs Relevant to Marine Habitat Management, 102
     Multidisciplinary Research, 106
     Environmental Technology Needs, 106
     Engineering Technology Needs, 109
     Summary, 112

8 CONCLUSIONS AND RECOMMENDATIONS   113
     Do Habitat Protection, Enhancement, Restoration, and Creation
        Technologies Work?, 115
     What Institutional Improvements are Needed?, 118
     What Research is Needed to Advance the State of Practice?, 123

APPENDICES:

A. BIOGRAPHICAL SKETCHES   125

B. CASE STUDIES   129

C. SOURCE REFERENCE TABLE   154

D. SUMMARY OF SOLICITED EXPERT ACCOUNTS   169

REFERENCES   173

CONTENTS *xvii*

BOXES, FIGURES, AND TABLES, USED IN THIS REPORT

Box 1-1	Terms Used in This Report	11
Box 1-2	The Meaning of Restoration of Marine Habitats and Relationship to the Sediment Stream and Dredged Material	12
Box 3-1	Composition of Dredged Material	33
Box 3-2	The Army Corps of Engineers Approach to Using Dredged Material	34
Box 3-3	Intertidal Marsh Functions	42
Box 5-1	Professional Regulation and Certification Terms	85
Figure 2-1	The domain and role of coastal engineering.	22
Figure 3-1	Status in 1978 of three selected splays totaling 559 acres in Lower Mississippi River Delta following levee breaches.	45
Figure 3-2	Status in 1988 of selected splay development of lower Mississippi River delta after 10 years. Intertidal wetlands acreage increased from 559 to 1,756 acres.	46
Figure 4-1	General locations of habitat protection and restoration projects and applications of technology examined in Chapter 4.	65
Figure 6-1	Decision model for achieving success in marine habitat protection and restoration projects.	92
Figure B-1	Site of shrimp habitat destruction and completed and active Surface Water Improvement and Management Act restoration sites in Tampa Bay.	132
Figure B-2	Sites of Chesapeake Bay restoration and protection projects.	135
Figure B-3	Locations of San Francisco restorations sites visited where dredged material was used or planned.	140
Table C	Source Reference Table	155
Table D-1	Research Needs Derived on Reported Gaps in the Coastal Engineering State of Practice	170
Table D-2	Reported Barriers to Successful Implementation of Beneficial Technology in Marine Habitat Projects	171

Executive Summary

Extraordinary changes have occurred during this century in the nation's coastal habitats, the way society views them, and how and what management is attempted. The most striking changes placed great pressure on marine and estuarine ecosystems. Conversion, alteration, and loss of marine habitat are both a consequence and symptom of coincidental developments that include:

- a concentration and continuing growth of human populations in the coastal zone;
- a proliferation of industrial and residential shoreline development;
- human activities that degrade water quality;
- increasing commercial and recreational use of marine and estuarine areas;
- development of natural resources in the coastal zone;
- physical changes in the environment, including subsidence, elevation, and sea level changes; and
- construction and maintenance of port and waterways systems and operation of associated commercial vessels.

Although changes may be gradual or episodic, prodigious cumulative losses have led to great uncertainties over physical and biological dependencies within coastal ecosystems, and coastal development has had profound adverse effects on the functioning of marine habitat and coastal processes. These facts are all the more alarming because marine habitats are critical to the production and replenishment of living marine resources and to the vitality of commercial fisheries, recreation in the coastal zone, and natural protection of coastal areas from an advancing sea and storm damage. The degree to which marine habitats can survive further pressure is not certain. Thus the management of marine habitats, including marine and estuarine habitats and contiguous shorelines to the top of the intertidal zone, has reached a critical point. Urgent action is required not only to arrest but also to reverse the loss and conversion of marine habitat. Active measures to protect and preserve coastal wetlands are especially needed because of their critical role in the natural functioning of marine ecosystems. However, national, regional, and local policies tend to constrain rather than instigate effective stewardship. Establishment of a proactive national policy to protect, improve, and enlarge marine habitat acreage cannot wait for the resolution of scientific uncertainties; the rate of loss and conversion is too great and the potential consequences of no action too severe to be ignored. Much more could be done with existing habitat knowledge and engineering expertise to enhance, protect, restore, and create marine habitats. But scientific and engineering capabilities cannot achieve their full potential in the absence of a focused policy to guide their application as an important element of a broad-based approach to protecting, preserving, and enlarging marine habitats.

Considerable scientific and engineering effort is already being applied, although not always harmoniously. Engineering technologies and structures are employed to maintain a tenuous balance with nature, often adversely altering the physical processes that form and reform coastal features, threatening human habitat and activities in the process. At the same time, many habitat enhancement, restoration, and creation projects are performing well. Much has been learned from them. Many other habitat projects may be functioning according to design but lack the monitoring necessary to document performance. It is time to rethink the role of coastal engineering in serving both human and environmental objectives. An integrated, holistic approach that recognizes engineering practices and capabilities as well as the functions of marine ecosystems and their habitats is especially important.

Civil engineers practicing in the coastal zone are increasingly faced with seemingly contradictory objectives: habitat conversion versus restoration; structural versus nonstructural shore protection, use of dredged material as a resource rather than a waste by-product, and commercial versus ecological values. The engineering profession, in cooperation and collaboration with the scientific community, has a growing opportunity to accommodate these competing objectives. It can do so through research and development, education and continuing professional development, innovative application of engineering knowledge and capabilities, and refinement of the general rules of marine habitat management.

The principal obstacles to wider use of coastal engineering capabilities in habitat protection, enhancement, restoration, and creation are the institutional, regulatory, and management barriers to using the best available technologies and practices. Decisionmaking options in current regulatory processes lack the flexi-

EXECUTIVE SUMMARY   3

bility necessary to engender innovative engineering and management solutions. There are few economic incentives for marine habitat protection and restoration by the private and industrial sectors. Regulators and practitioners are often not sufficiently qualified to guide effective application of habitat protection and restoration technologies.

A history of successful projects is necessary for building and sustaining public and private support for more widespread use of habitat protection and restoration technology. However, there are no universally accepted measures on which to gauge performance or direct the evolving state of practice. One approach to habitat restoration espouses a strong ecological perspective defining success principally in terms of the ability to recreate nature. Although return of a disturbed or totally altered natural area or ecosystem to its predisturbed condition is generally preferred, it is not usually practical or even possible: the understanding of all of the physiological processes and interactions to maintain the functioning of a natural system is not complete. Enhancement of existing sites or partial restoration is often feasible. A determination needs to be made about which natural processes can probably be restored at prospective restoration sites. Another approach, the one endorsed by this report, is that success is defined as achieving well-defined project goals and objectives. This viewpoint deems the ability to replicate nature as very important but not necessarily an exclusive criterion for success; it thus provides the flexibility necessary to accommodate environmental and social (including economic) objectives and allows for partial restoration as a viable alternative where full restoration is infeasible or not possible.

Substantial restoration research has been undertaken but often on a project-by-project, opportunistic basis rather than through a systematic program designed to fill gaps in knowledge and technology. Valuable basic and applied (project-specific) research has been performed by the National Marine Fisheries Service (NMFS), the U.S. Army Corps of Engineers, the U.S. Fish and Wildlife Service (USFWS), and academic research stations, particularly the research sponsored by the National Oceanographic and Atmospheric Administration's Sea Grant Program and the Army Corps of Engineers' dredging and wetlands research programs. Yet, these national research efforts have not been coordinated to conserve and maximize the use of research resources. In addition, availability of research literature is constrained by the lack of information on research documents and their acquisition and costs of procurement or reproduction.

Advancing the state of practice will involve creating a climate for

- developing a better understanding of how an ecosystem functions;
- promoting policy and procedural change;
- establishing restoration goals and objectives;
- cooperation among involved organizations, including integrated and collaborative actions;

- collaboration of relevant scientific and engineering disciplines;
- technology adaptation and innovation through experimentation;
- information transfer;
- incentive-based solutions; and
- performance measurement.

This study addresses three questions about the role of technology in protecting and improving marine habitats:

- Do protection, enhancement, restoration, and creation technologies work?
- What institutional improvements are needed?
- What research is needed to advance the state of practice?

The answers to these questions apply to habitat degradation and loss from both human-induced and natural causes. Whether attempts should be made to reverse natural conditions, and if so, who should pay for this work are important issues, but their analysis is beyond the scope of this report.

DO PROTECTION, ENHANCEMENT, RESTORATION, AND CREATION TECHNOLOGIES WORK?

Scientific and coastal engineering capabilities can be effectively used to protect, enhance, restore, and create marine habitats, but their application is not a substitute for prudent stewardship of these natural resources. Substantial technology exists for protection and restoration of emergent marshes and intertidal habitat, primarily through dredging and placement of dredged materials. This technology is well developed in coastal engineering practice. Restoration technologies and techniques have been developed to varying degrees for other marine habitat types. Less developed, however, is the technology to ensure restoration of many natural functions of these habitats.

Existing knowledge and technology provide a strong foundation from which a credible coastal engineering program could be launched to arrest habitat loss and degradation. Existing engineering capabilities are capable of supporting a program to achieve a net gain in high-quality marine habitat acreage through well-planned and well-executed protection and restoration projects, if such a goal were to be established as national policy.

The most favorable results are obtained in protection and restoration projects with multidisciplinary collaboration among scientists and engineers. Multidisciplinary teamwork should be required by federal and state agencies, project sponsors, and practitioners of marine habitat protection and restoration projects.

Building widespread acceptance of restoration technologies as a viable means to arrest and reverse habitat loss will require practical demonstration of successful applications under varying site-specific and regional conditions, including restoration of natural functions. A practical definition of success that establishes performance criteria specific to the project should be used instead of a strict comparison to natural conditions that existed at a site prior to disturbance or alteration, unless restoration to former conditions is the project objective. Performance criteria should be sound but reasonable from both scientific (including ecological) and engineering perspectives, and project performance should be measurable through effective monitoring during and after the effort. The criteria should be determined by authorities responsible for approving marine habitat projects in consultation with scientists, engineers, and interested parties. A practical measure of project performance relevant to natural functions may sometimes be obtained by determining how nearly a project mimics an undisturbed natural habitat of the type being restored nearby in the same ecosystem. Environmental and engineering monitoring should be conducted to establish that quality control objectives are being met, and where feasible, to advance the state of engineering and scientific knowledge about the application of habitat protection and restoration technology. This monitoring should be carried out at frequencies matched to performance objectives and physical and ecological conditions affecting each project site. To the degree that restoration of natural functions is a project objective, monitoring should encompass the organisms that contribute to the processes on which ecosystem health depends. Approving authorities should require that project sponsors commit to long-term maintenance and monitoring sufficient to provide the data necessary for determining project performance, indicate any necessary corrective, and encourage accountability. Insofar as practical, monitoring regimes should be designed and performed to contribute to the advancement of scientific and engineering knowledge about

- physical and ecological processes and their interaction, and
- restoration technologies and techniques.

Although essential to advancing the state of practice and determining long-term project performance, long-term maintenance and monitoring are likely to increase overall project costs. However, effective monitoring coupled with timely corrective action could help avoid or mitigate future problems and could result in a long-term cost savings.

WHAT INSTITUTIONAL IMPROVEMENTS ARE NEEDED?

Degradation and loss of marine habitats will continue unless a firm policy to preserve and protect them is established and backed by a commitment to execute that policy. The executive and legislative branches of the federal government should establish a national policy to prevent or, where development is considered in the national interest, offset, the further degradation, conversion, and loss of marine habitat. The policy should specify goals and establish a time frame for achieving them. Each federal and state agency with marine habitat management responsibilities should develop compatible and quantitative goals supporting this national policy and establish milestones for their attainment. Emphasis should be placed on protection and sound management of existing resources first, followed by restoration and creation projects where feasible.

Institutional policies, regulations, and procedures need to be changed to

- provide incentives rather than disincentives to invest in marine habitat protection and restoration, especially marine sediments, in marine habitat management;
- expand options for more effective use of natural resources;
- increase the opportunities for pilot, demonstration, and experimental habitat protection and restoration programs and projects;
- remove procedural barriers to advancing the state of practice of marine habitat restoration;
- improve understanding of the multiple facets of marine habitat management, including physical processes, natural functions of ecosystems, impacts of human origin, and restoration capabilities; and
- motivate widespread evaluation, documentation, and publication of lessons learned.

Substantial action will be required to effect these changes. All federal, state, and local agencies with jurisdiction over or responsibility for marine habitat management should

- individually and collectively revise policies and procedures to improve opportunities for use of suitable restoration technologies, taking into account which natural functions can be restored or facilitated;
- encourage and support the innovative application of available and emerging restoration technologies;
- improve intra- and interorganizational coordination to accommodate competing interests in marine resources;
- include environmental and economic benefits derived from nonstructural measures in benefit/cost ratios of marine habitat projects; and
- examine the feasibility of improving economic incentives for marine habitat restoration in their areas of responsibility.

The U.S. Army Corps of Engineers should specifically revise its policies to facilitate more effective transportation and use of dredged material as a habitat restoration resource, even when its use is more expensive than disposal in the *least costly environmentally acceptable* manner. This change should be emphasized nationwide. The Corps of Engineers and the NMFS should establish a funding agreement (comparable to the Corps' agreement with the USFWS) for

EXECUTIVE SUMMARY 7

an interagency transfer of funds to NMFS to enhance execution of its obligations under the U.S. Fish and Wildlife Coordination Act. All federal agencies should review existing projects to determine whether they can initiate improvements beneficial to marine habitats. If necessary, they should seek enabling legislation from Congress. All agencies responsible for marine habitat management should document and broadly distribute information on their experience with the projects that they undertake or oversee.

Improvement is needed in scientific and engineering knowledge by all who are involved with marine habitat management, particularly those in the restoration industry and in regulatory bodies. Specifically, multidisciplinary training for coastal engineers needs to address effective responses to the wide range of engineering, ecological, and social issues attending the planning, design, implementation, and operation of marine habitat projects. Voluntary certification from credible organizations is one indicator of professional qualifications; it also improves an individual's perceived potential to perform effectively. This procedure should be encouraged. Continued professional development should be required as a means for building and maintaining a credible base of restoration expertise.

WHAT RESEARCH IS NEEDED TO ADVANCE THE STATE OF PRACTICE?

Although existing engineering capabilities can be applied to habitat protection and restoration, basic research is needed to complete the scientific knowledge of marine habitat functions and processes. Basic research is also needed in scientific and engineering predictive capabilities relative to marine habitat and coastal processes. A better way of quantifying the value of marine habitat needs to be developed. A systematic, coordinated national program of dedicated research is needed to address

- Natural functions in restored or created marine habitats;
- Hydrology and hydraulics of marine ecosystems;
- Sediment properties that influence the physical and biological performance of restoration projects;
- Sediment transport by natural energy;
- Use of dredged material in full and partial restoration;
- Use of new and innovative dredging equipment for habitat restoration;
- Habitat utilization by biota in marine ecosystems;
- Recruitment mechanisms for marine intertidal biota;
- Structures and functions of artificial reefs; and
- Methodologies for economic valuation of marine habitats.

The executive branch should designate an appropriate federal agency to convene an interagency committee to develop and coordinate a national research program that balances research needs, competing agency interests, and available resources. This effort should include representatives of the Departments of the Army, Commerce, and Interior and the EPA. Advice from experts from the scientific and engineering communities should be used to establish specific research needs in each of the aforementioned areas as well as in additional areas identified as the state of practice evolves.

1

Introduction

MARINE HABITAT—A NATIONAL TREASURE IN DECLINE

This century has seen vast changes in the nation's coastal zone management practices, in societal views of marine habitats, and in marine habitats. The most striking changes, a consequence of several often-coincidental developments, include

- a concentration of population in coastal areas approaching 50 percent of the total U.S. population and projected population growth;
- a proliferation of shoreline development;
- increased water-dependent recreation;
- water quality degradation from the introduction of pollutants, excess nutrients, and sediments into coastal waters from nonpoint and point-sources and from soil erosion affecting upland areas;
- damage to seagrass beds from degradation of water quality and from the operation of recreational and commercial vessels in shallow waters;
- declining fish and shellfish stocks and harvests;
- degradation of scenic and cultural assets; and
- permanent habitat loss, especially coastal wetlands.

The evolution of these changes may have been gradual, but it has now reached a critical threshold if habitat losses are to be arrested and reversed. If a goal of "no net loss" of coastal wetlands, is to be achieved, then new, and innovative measures will need to be applied.

9

Substantial scientific and engineering knowledge and practical experience that could be used to improve the management the nation's marine resources if these capabilities can be effectively brought to bear for this purpose. Indeed, *engineers and scientists have already developed and shared expertise and technology to counter the trend of marine habitat degradation and loss to some extent,* but these capabilities have not been guided by national policy or objectives. Available technology provides opportunities to protect, enhance, restore, and create marine and estuarine habitats and, subsequently, to protect some fishery resources and wildlife, including endangered species. But, existing methods do not address these issues adequately; nor do they adequately address the effects of large-scale subsidence, land use in the coastal plain, sea level rise, extensive erosion, and massive and continuous salt water intrusion into freshwater surface and groundwater systems.

This report examines the role of coastal engineering in countering these trends through the application of technology to protect and restore marine habita (see Box 1-1 for terms used in this report). But, the issue is far greater than applying engineering capabilities to a environmentally beneficial purpose in the marine environment. A larger national strategy for protection and preservation of ecosystems is needed (NRC, 1992a). Without such a development, the underlying pressure on marine natural resources will continue.

Scope of Marine Habitat Degradation and Loss

As residential, industrial, and recreational development continues to encroach upon the ocean's edge, the sea relentlessly shapes and reshapes the coastal zone. Humankind and the land are greatly affected by this interplay (Culliton et al., 1990; NRC, 1990a; Platt et al., 1992; Williams et al., 1990). About 30 square miles of Louisiana disappear into the sea each year, depending on the estimate used, although the rate of loss is decreasing. Through this process, shallow water and intertidal marine habitat with high biological activity critical to the ecological balance is transformed into subtidal water, generally unvegetated habitat. Although deep water habitat is also important and is threatened by pollutants and not an inexhaustible resource, the more immediate and noticeable problems are the loss of critical breeding, nursery, and feeding habitats in estuarine, near shore, and intercoastal areas. The cumulative habitat losses resulting from erosion, natural subsidence, sea level rise, altered natural sediment movement caused by flood control and navigation projects, and changes in hydrology and salinity from oil and gas exploration and from episodic storms are no less certain unless local changes occur in these processes (Boesch et al., 1983; Brown and Watson, 1988; Clark, 1990; Mendelssohn, 1982; Mendelssohn et al., 1983; Turner and Cahoon, 1988).

Similar losses affect other regions as well, although on a less grand scale than in coastal Louisiana. For example, in San Francisco Bay and the Sacramen-

INTRODUCTION   *11*

BOX 1-1
TERMS USED IN THIS REPORT

Coastal zone Coastal waters and adjacent shorelands which are strongly influenced by each other and uses of which have a direct and significant impact on coastal waters.

Creation Construction or formation of a habitat of a different type than existed before a site was disturbed or conversion of one habitat form to another. The principal differences between restoration and creation are the condition and status of the habitat acreage rather than the technologies used. Because the technology is essentially the same, creation is treated as a subset of restoration as an approach to improving marine habitat.

Enhancement Improvement of one or more of the values of an existing habitat, usually one that has been degraded or disturbed. May result in a decline of other values.

Improvement General result, if beneficial, of one or a combination of protection, enhancement, restoration, and creation initiatives.

Marine habitat Marine and estuarine habitats and contiguous shorelines within the coastal zone. These areas include marine wetlands such as tidal marshes, emergent wetlands, sea grass beds, kelp forests, and mangrove swamps. Also included are beaches, shallow inshore and near shore submerged environments, and tidal and intertidal flats. Offshore marine habitat is outside the boundaries of this assessment except for artificial reefs and offshore berms on the continental shelf.

Marine habitat management A comprehensive approach to stewardship of marine habitat including protection, enhancement, restoration, creation, and administration.

Mitigation Measures taken to reduce adverse impacts. A regulatory approach that, in effect, permits conversion of habitat in return for compensation in the form of enhancement, restoration, or creation of other habitat.

Monitoring The collection of data to aid project planning and design and to enable evaluation of project performance.

Partial restoration Return of a degraded or altered natural area as close as possible to its condition prior to disturbance if full restoration is not feasible (Box 1-2).

Protection Use of structural and nonstructural means, including regulation, to minimize or prevent harm to existing habitats.

Restoration Return of a degraded or altered natural area or ecosystem to a close approximation of its condition prior to disturbance (Box 1-2).

SOURCES: Cairns (1988), Lewis (1990b), NRC (1992a).

---

to–San Joaquin River delta, intense development of shorelines and inland areas, and use and diversion of fresh water within the watershed are causing or contributing to hypersalinity subsidence and erosion problems (Bay Institute of San Francisco, 1987; EPA, 1992; Josselyn and Buchholz, 1984; McCreary et al., 1992; NRC, 1990a). Along much of the Atlantic and Gulf coasts, engineered

BOX 1-2
**THE MEANING OF RESTORATION OF MARINE HABITATS
AND RELATIONSHIP TO THE SEDIMENT STREAM AND
DREDGED MATERIAL**

In this report, *restoration* is defined as the return of a marine natural area or ecosystem to a close approximation of its condition prior to disturbance. In restoration, ecological damage to the resource is repaired. Both the structure and the functions of the natural area are improved or recreated. Merely recreating the form without the functions, or the functions in an artificial configuration bearing little resemblance to a natural resource, does not constitute restoration. The goal is to emulate a natural, functioning, self-regulating system that is integrated with the ecological landscape in which it occurs.

In practical application, since ecosystems are the cumulative result of a sequence of climatological and biological events, full ecological restoration is rarely achieved. Therefore, efforts to restore habitat may necessarily consist of various measures to enhance or partially restore natural functions depending on site-specific conditions, habitat improvement objectives, and other factors. In some cases, the ecological landscape may have been so altered as to preclude a return to a predisturbed condition. In these cases, partial restoration may be feasible, recognizing that all natural functions may not be completely restored and that assisted regulation may be necessary, such as control of water and sediment flows.

Marine ecosystems typically involve dynamic forces including substantial physical energy in the form of currents and waves, local or global changes in relative mean sea level, and sediment streams that can lead to rapid changes in the characteristics of a natural area. Therefore, defining what constitutes a predisturbed condition can be problematic. In such cases, the characteristics of a natural, functioning, self-regulating system that is integrated into its ecological landscape and which emulates nearby undisturbed natural areas is an alternative frame reference.

Although use of dredged material does not constitute restoration, per se, restoration can be accomplished using dredged material *in its native environment* to achieve general parameters which will aid in natural marsh evolution in those locations where marine sediments would normally form essential substrates for intertidal and emergent wetlands habitat. Placing marine sediments so as to mimic natural deposition of sediment at sites where conditions otherwise favor restoration would preclude the chemical changes that occur when marine sediments are exposed to air in upland areas or in wetlands above appropriate intertidal elevations. Further, natural deposition of sediments to form intertidal flats and emergent wetlands can occur over relatively short time spans in deltas and estuaries, depending on such factors as hydraulic conditions and sediment loads. The rapid placement of suitable dredged material at appropriate locations and elevations in an estuary or delta approximates natural deposition and can be an important, but not exclusive, element of a marine habitat restoration project.

INTRODUCTION   13

protective structures and sand replacement activities are used to try to stabilize
the shorelines of otherwise dynamic and resilient barrier islands (Charlier et al.,
1989; NRC, 1990a). Engineering technologies and structures maintain an increasingly tentative balance with nature in every coastal state.

Throughout the coastal zone, habitat is continually lost to human development; what remains is under constant threat of degradation or further loss (EPA,
1992). The causes of the decline in marine habitat quality and quantity may be
traced to several factors. Human activities have altered natural current action and
sedimentation patterns; degraded water quality by introducing excess nutrients,
toxins, and sediments into coastal waters as a result of nonpoint and point-source
pollutants; altered estuarine inflow and outflow patterns; and changed other physical, chemical, and biological processes. Protecting finfish and shellfish habitats
is a concern, as are sedimentation starvation and excess sedimentation in deltaic
and other fragile wetland systems. Scientific concern has also arisen regarding
the effects of beach stabilization measures, whether physical structures or placement of beach-quality sands, on biotic communities for which beaches provide
habitat. Considerations include the fate of biota in the nearshore borrow area,
impacts on biota using the changed shoreline, changes in sedimentation patterns
and shoreline stability beyond the project boundaries, and project stability.
Sweeping changes in the policies and practices of all parties involved in marine
habitat protection and enhancement are needed to arrest and reverse these trends
(NRC, 1992a).

Finding Balance Among Competing Objectives

Institutional, political, and sociological factors that have made it difficult to
strike a balance among competing objectives for the use of coastal sites include:

- the fragmented structure of existing management regimes and legal in-
struments related to marine habitat management;
- fragmented and overlapping authority, complicated by competing agency
objectives;
- conflicting or self-serving project goals;
- limited cross-training among scientific and engineering disciplines;
- an incomplete scientific and engineering understanding of the functional
relationships among marine habitat, marine life, and coastal processes;
- an established trend of human overexploitation of coastal resources for
developmental and recreational purposes; and
- the lack of a holistic approach to managing end use so that the natural
functions of ecosystems are not abused.

Despite these constraints, engineers working in the coastal zone and using the
technologies and practices they develop can contribute to better management of

marine resources by working hand in hand with coastal scientists and policy-makers and managers on projects that benefit marine habitat. Where feasible, these capabilities can be put to use for the protection of natural marine habitats before they are degraded or lost or for after-the-fact enhancement or restoration.

THE CHALLENGE FOR COASTAL ENGINEERING

It is time to rethink the role of coastal engineering in serving both human and environmental objectives. An integrated, holistic approach that encompasses engineering practices and capabilities and understands the functions of marine ecosystems and their habitat is especially important. Engineers are faced with seemingly contradictory objectives: habitat conversion versus enhancement, restoration, and creation; traditional structural ("hard") protection, such as seawalls, versus enhanced natural ("soft") shore protection, such as beach nourishment and underwater berms; use of dredged material as a resource rather than as spoil (that is, waste by-product); economic versus ecological returns to the national welfare; and prevention of pollution versus cleanup and restoration. Through research and development, education, and the innovative application of engineering knowledge, the engineering profession has the opportunity to accommodate these competing objectives. A comprehensive understanding of engineering practices and capabilities and their relationship to the ecology of marine habitats is as important to informed decisionmaking over habitat use as are economic considerations. A positive role for the engineering profession can be developed in cooperation with the scientific community to protect and enhance marine habitat and contribute information essential to the formation and refinement of national policy and management objectives.

Overview of Scientific and Engineering Capabilities

Although examples of successful applied engineering capabilities to accomplish environmental objectives are numerous, traditional engineering practices have not always recognized and dealt fully with the varied needs of marine habitats. New territory for the engineering profession includes methods to protect habitats, especially from contaminants, erosion, and subsidence, while preserving or retaining their natural attributes. An ecosystem approach to project design and implementation that recognizes the ecological interdependencies of marine systems is seldom applied. Further development of the potential for coastal engineering to protect, enhance, restore, and create marine habitats therefore depends in part on further collaboration between the coastal sciences and engineering.

Status of Science and Engineering

Scientists and engineers concerned with marine systems share many interests and have a wide variety of tools at their disposal. Some technology transfer has occurred, demonstrating the fact that science and engineering can be complementary. For example, marine turtles returned to historical beach nesting areas after well-timed deposition of beach-quality dredged material. Knowledge of habitat requirements, when the turtles came ashore to nest, and the capability to place beach-quality material prior to turtle arrival were required. Applied research has demonstrated that beach nourishment can be timed to accommodate environmental, stabilization, and aesthetic objectives. This measure is now widely used in Florida (Higgins and Fisher, 1993; Hodgin et al., 1993; Montague, 1993; Nelson, 1993; Nelson and Dickerson, 1988). Although there are still gaps in knowledge about turtle nesting, the approach used shows the potential benefits from cooperative application of scientific knowledge and coastal engineering technology.

Fisheries biologists and navigation project design engineers (interested in successful construction and maintenance of navigation channels) are both concerned with hydraulic and hydrologic conditions, water quality, sedimentation patterns, salinity and temperature, and other physical and chemical factors. Although discipline perspectives differ, each group is vitally interested in the effects of physical modifications to an existing system. For example, changes to an estuary's tidal prism that do not maintain hydraulic balance within the system can greatly affect sedimentation rates and salinity, benefiting either navigation, biota, both, or neither. The full potential of scientific and engineering contributions to marine habitat protection, creation, restoration, and enhancement has yet to be realized despite the advances that have been made.

Scientific Tools and Techniques

Over the past three decades, the scientific community's understanding of marine habitats has advanced greatly. Science produced monitoring, sampling, and analytical techniques that help detect and respond to problems affecting marine habitats. The rapid advances in the computation power of computers, computer modelling, and graphic representations has significantly advanced the capability to analyze, interpret, and apply the data that are collected. This understanding and monitoring capabilities have been instrumental in decisionmaking to set environmental quality objectives (NRC, 1990b,c).

Science recognizes the importance of a holistic approach to understanding the interrelationships of species and how they function to consume and change the chemical composition of wastes such as sewage, buffer the system against shock, and secure the health and reproductive capacities of species forming the ecosystem. This recognition requires an understanding of the chemical and physical characteristics of the environment that promote the success of or harm to the species. Density-dependent interactions as well as the effects of density-independent factors such as temperature, light, heat, precipitation, wave actions, and pollutants of various types, must also be understood. Understanding the geology, hydrology, and chemical characteristics (such as salinity) of the system enables description of physical and chemical processes that are important in determining sensitive land forms, sediment transport regimes, and the quality of sediment and water. Understanding the formation of substrates in estuaries and the material composing them is not fully developed. Likewise, the effects of organic matter and contaminants such as pesticides in substrates as they pertain to restoration of natural functions in and performance of habitat restoration projects are not thoroughly understood and are a concern. This is an important consideration because the substrates are the foundation materials for marine habitats. Nevertheless, the holistic approach is an integrated one that enables human activities to fortify rather than destroy fragile and complex coastal ecosystems.

National concerns about the relationship of human activities and natural marine systems involve economic and social sciences, as well as natural sciences. Assessment of economic and social values of natural marine systems is marked by controversy because of uncertainties in scientific knowledge about the functioning of marine ecosystems and the contribution of marine habitat to commercial fisheries, recreational activities, and other activities. These factors make it difficult to establish economic values of marine habitat in natural uses. Economic sciences can be employed to assess the costs and benefits of alternate uses, residential development, for example (Bell, 1989; Costanza and Wainger, 1990; Smith, 1990). The social sciences can address the range of variables and help identify interested parties whose participation in planning and implementation is needed to ensure project acceptability and success, examine social attitudes and changes, and address quality-of-life issues (Caldwell, 1991; Davos, 1988; Dwivedi, 1988; Hickman and Cocklin, 1992; McCreary et al., 1992). The disparity in the ability to quantify the value of marine habitat as a natural resource places these attributes at a disadvantage when determining their fate— whether they should be preserved and improved or converted.

Coastal Engineering Tools and Techniques

Various engineering disciplines, including civil, hydraulic, sediment, geotechnical, environmental, biological, mechanical, and sanitary engineering, are involved in coastal zone projects. All are experienced with project design, implementation, evaluation, equipment, and structures. Their experience contributes to an understanding of and methods to prepare construction plans, documents, and cost estimates; evaluate and recommend contractor engagements; and develop and implement project monitoring techniques and performance evaluations.

INTRODUCTION

A substantial body of engineering knowledge and tools has been developed and applied in the coastal zone to design, construct, and maintain waterways and port facilities; protect and stabilize shorelines, entrances, and channels; control flooding and lessen storm-driven energy; improve water quality and lessen pollution; monitor, calibrate, analyze, and adjust physical aspects of hydraulic and sediment systems; and lessen or mitigate the environmental impacts of water-related projects. Over the past three decades, various diagnostic procedures have been developed for examining coastal processes and impacts of structures and other restorative measures. These procedures rely on field and laboratory studies and advanced mathematical modeling. These same techniques are then extended for prediction of anticipated impacts. Laboratory capabilities include physical scale models and wave tanks. Advances in coastal engineering capabilities are regularly published in the proceedings of national and international conferences, handbooks, and professional journals and magazines. Engineering techniques developed by the USACE are usually well documented in official reports which are generally accessible to practitioners.

A great many coastal engineering projects involve the transport and placement of dredged sediment and sands (Bruun, 1989a,b; Dyer, 1986; Herbich, 1990, 1991, 1992a; NRC, 1983a, 1983b, 1985d, 1987b, 1989b; Vanoni, 1975). The use of dredged material to restore or create marine habitats is an accepted practice in many world ports and estuaries, some in the United States, as discussed in this report. Herbich (1992b) and the Permanent International Association of Navigation Congresses (PIANC, 1989, 1992a) describe dredging technologies and practices, including the constructive use of dredged material to support environmental objectives. The environmental benefits of dredged material have sometimes been learned by accident. For example, practitioners learned that artificial islands created with dredged material from operations to maintain shipping channels often provide a primary habitat for sea birds and wading birds and a refuge for species displaced from other sites by human activity. Eroded natural islands can be restored for these purposes. Such habitats are now being routinely designed and constructed (Landin, 1992b; James F. Parnell, personal communication, December 13, 1990). Successful habitat protection, enhancement, restoration, and creation programs, as elements of coastal engineering works, are growing in number and significance, but interdisciplinary principles of natural resource management are not fully utilized.

2

Scientific and Engineering Perspectives

To assess coastal engineering practice in marine habitat management, a scientific understanding of marine habitats as ecosystems and as components of larger ecosystems is essential. Just as essential are the engineer's tools, practices, and techniques through which this scientific knowledge can be intelligently applied. These two broad fields—science and engineering—each multidisciplinary, come together as the twin pillars of effective and environmentally sound practice in marine habitat management. The social sciences, including law, economics, and management are also important, but sound science and engineering is fundamental to a habitat project's actual performance. The term multidisciplinary, as used here, includes all the disciplines that contribute to either understanding the ecological setting or providing the techniques used in engineering in the coastal zone.

The first two sections of this chapter introduce basic themes from these two fields that resonate through the rest of the report. The third section sketches the too frequent situation where technology, including engineering technology, has intruded on marine habitats, uninformed or unconcerned about the consequences for their ecological functioning.

ECOLOGICAL SETTING

An ecosystem has numerous components that are all interdependent to some degree. Coastal habitats and ecosystems are prime areas for marine and estuarine organisms. Some of these organisms are fixed in place for some or all of their life cycle; others are capable of spontaneous movement, moving from one habi-

18

SCIENTIFIC AND ENGINEERING PERSPECTIVES

tat to another between birth and their juvenile and adult stages. Both types of organisms are present within any marine habitat. The basic underlying questions relate to the degree to which one component of the ecosystem affects or depends on the others and to the density-independent environmental variables necessary for an ecosystem to function.

Interrelationships among biological and physical processes are particularly apparent for marine and estuarine ecosystems. Water is a transport medium for plants, larvae, animals, nutrients, and pollutants. Because of this, there are no closed or isolated ecosystems. Some fish, for example, may spawn offshore and move in and out of coastal areas at various frequencies. Some shrimp species spawn within 50 kilometers of the coast, migrate to the estuary mouth, and then move within the estuary for several months before migrating offshore again. Commonly, larval and juvenile fishes migrate into an estuary for further development after spawning offshore. Some fishes also move into estuaries to spawn. Seasonal migrations and changes in habitat use patterns also occur, such as over wintering in bottom sediments by non-migrating shrimp in some estuaries. Organism movement within an estuary may also include daily travels among sea-grass beds, muddy bottoms, salt marshes, and other coastal habitats. For birds and other terrestrial animals, coastal habitat includes brackish marsh, maritime forests, and coastal islands. Such movements represent the evolutionary adaptations of species for optimal growth, survival, and reproduction as affected by competition, predation, and food limitations.

Adult population size is often determined during the posthatching stage of a species' life cycle. The movements from one habitat to another often depend on physical factors including salinity gradients, tidal movement, wind and wave energy, and temperature. These factors can help or hinder an organism's ability to optimize or balance energy expenditures for food capture during early life history stages and during old age or sickness. For example, fisheries populations are sometimes dependent on estuarine conditions, such as salinity, temperature, and currents, during the early life history stages. Natural processes and human activities that affect commercially valuable fish and shellfish species also affect the less conspicuous species that provide food, influence habitat, and decompose and recycle nutrients in a given system. With the interdependencies of ecosystems in mind, it is clear that human activities that degrade or destroy any marine habitat affect the whole marine ecosystem in the area that is influenced. At the same time, it is difficult to detect the effect caused by incremental degradation and cumulative loss, even while it is occurring. A degraded salt marsh, for example, may appear healthy while its biological production has been severely disrupted. Water quality degradation below the water's surface is difficult to detect without sophisticated analysis or continuing monitoring programs. Overall, the cumulative effect on the ecosystem can be substantial.

The stresses that challenge an organism's growth, survival, and reproductive potential can sometimes bring about adaptive change over time. Organisms live in an environment that changes each year through the accumulation or loss of sediments, seasonal variation in climate, and changes in hydrology. Yet all can survive as long as these changes are within their range of tolerance. For example, the rate of global sea level rise has been slow, and impacts are not readily discernible in the near term, except where relative sea level rise has been accelerated, as when subsidence is also occurring. The effects are cumulative over a prolonged period. Complicating these ecological stresses are the increased human uses of the coastal zone, uses that sometimes exceed the ability of some marine organisms to adjust. Human activity has modified marine habitats in ways that science is just beginning to understand; the most conspicuous is habitat loss. For example, eutrophication has altered algal communities or species, increased occurrences of algal blooms, and created oxygen deficits in some waters. These changes may greatly decrease the shellfish population or make them unfit for human consumption.

Although much is known, the effectiveness of management of the coastal zone is still limited by an incomplete understanding of the habitat requirements of species. The EPA and the NOAA have undertaken research monitoring programs to identify and assess indicators of ecological health. Nevertheless, it is very difficult to establish definitive cause and effect relationships, especially for marine ecosystems. Comprehensive ecosystem-based predictors of the effect of change on catches of commercially important fisheries species are generally absent or underdeveloped. The best predictors are often based on a hindsight system measured in previous landings, fishing effort, or surveys of abundance. This problem is widespread, making the success of coastal engineering projects dependent on less-than-certain environmental assessments. Science cannot predict with much certainty, for example, the consequences of seagrass losses or gains to sea trout, shrimp, and oysters in any estuary of the northern Gulf of Mexico. Further, most widely used population models exclude interactions between competing species (USFWS, 1980). The present distribution and abundance of species are not understood in sufficient detail to answer many key management questions. The management of a species often focuses on specific habitats rather than on a comprehensive evaluation of the range of habitats used by a species over its life cycle. This approach could adversely affect successful management of the target species as well as policy and management decisions regarding the importance of marine habitat and the funding of protection and restoration work.

It is widely recognized that natural habitats serve society in a variety of ways. Less recognized is the broader alternative view that human society and these habitats are already functioning together. As a result of heightened environmental consciousness, society has begun to embrace this alternative view and improve its management of natural ecosystems, but public appreciation of the extent to which society and the natural world depend upon one another is limited. The importance of these ecological relationships is not clearly defined in

SCIENTIFIC AND ENGINEERING PERSPECTIVES

terms of goods and services. For example, although the important role of wetlands in supporting commercial shrimp populations is frequently cited as a clearly valuable function, other benefits are not well appreciated. These include the capacity of wetlands to control greenhouse gases that contribute to global warming, act as critical components of the life cycles of animals and fish, buffer storm surges, improve water quality, reduce flooding, and reduce the national export-import debt by supporting valuable fisheries. The adverse impacts on fishery resources caused by habitat degradation and loss are further complicated by overexploitation of some fish stocks by recreational and commercial fishing (Stroud, 1992). When species diversity and abundance change as a result of habitat degradation and loss or from over exploitation, it logically follows that human society will need to change its approach to prevent habitat and species losses. Modern society does not understand or fully appreciate the degree of destruction and alteration that is occurring and does not realize what changes are needed to prevent loss or how to achieve them.

A particularly important problem lies with not knowing how to assign a precise value, economic or otherwise, to a particular habitat. Establishing a defendable value of habitat in natural versus converted uses is a challenge. This is a daily task for managers of coastal resources. The only value assessments that can be given within the current state of knowledge and practice are incomplete, resulting in highly subjective decisionmaking on the fate of valuable natural resources (Water Quality 2000, 1992). *The lack of acceptable valuation regimes complicates efforts to protect, enhance, restore, and create coastal habitats.* The challenge to scientists and engineers is to overcome the past narrow views about the value of habitats, learn more about what makes them important, and interpret and then communicate that information for intelligent decisionmaking and the public's information.

THE SCOPE OF COASTAL ENGINEERING

Engineering practice in the coastal zone has several general objectives including prediction of sediment transport, movement of surface water and groundwater, and shore evolution and to development and implementation of structural or other means to alter coastal water movement and shore evolution (Mehta, 1990). In addition to engineering activities that are conventionally considered within the domain of coastal engineering, these general objectives encompass relevant aspects of dredging technology, soil and geotechnical engineering, water resource engineering including wastewater treatment and disposal, and civil construction practices related to soils and structures.

Coastal engineering practice is conditioned by six factors:

- habitat management objectives (including physical, chemical, biological, and ecological components);

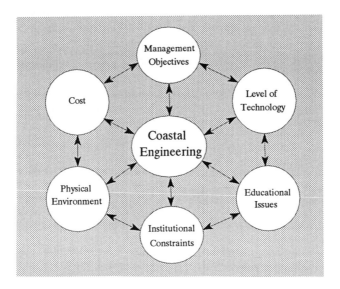

FIGURE 2-1 The domain and role of coastal engineering.

- the physical environment;
- level of technology;
- institutional constraints;
- professional capabilities; and
- cost.

The interactive relations among these factors (Figure 2-1) cannot be overemphasized. Unless the management objectives for a habitat are set in harmony with the other five factors, the overall management program will be missing or incomplete and its efficacy jeopardized.

Of these six factors, habitat management objectives are in the committee's experience the least coordinated and developed but are nonetheless important for coastal engineering applications. In particular, the complexities of natural systems make it difficult to predict accurately the final form and function of habitat in any coastal engineering project. Thus, in addition to engineering considerations, setting habitat management objectives is conditioned by scientific and societal factors as well. These factors are a challenge to the engineer. For example, although the functions of a salt marsh are known (see Box 3-3), there is no consensus on what constitutes a fully functional salt marsh. Incomplete scientific knowledge about the biological processes that characterize the functions of a marsh continues to foment debate (NRC, 1992a). There are also philosophical and practical concerns regarding standards of comparison for physical and ecological factors and the time frame necessary to assess success in habitat restoration. Contentious issues are the preexistent conditions that should serve as standards of comparison and the time scales that should be used to assess whether or to what extent full natural functionality has been achieved. For example, physical alterations within watersheds might preclude restoration to pristine conditions prior to all human activity. If degraded or converted habitat is subsequently reconverted to a form of habitat different or less functional than the habitat that predated human or natural alterations, is the result restoration? Some would say it is not. A related view is that all dredged material is waste and that construction of wetland habitat with such material is not restoration regardless of the result, even when the material is used in its native environment (NRC, 1992a). The view of the committee is that most dredged material is nontoxic in its environment and is a valuable resource that can potentially be effectively used to support habitat protection and restoration. Many completed habitat restoration and creation projects constructed with dredged material are functioning to design specifications (Landin et al., 1989c; USACE, 1986). It is clear, however, that despite the successful use of marine sediments in well-founded marine habitat restoration projects, many marine habitat management projects are likely to stimulate controversy. Substantial debate can be anticipated over definitions, natural functions, and with regard to contaminants, the quality of dredged material. As a consequence, habitat protection and restoration using dredged material may continue to be treated by some individuals and organizations as purely experimental into the foreseeable future, although the potential for effective utilization is appropriate.

Disagreements over definitions do not mean that less than fully functional modifications or restoration, including those involving dredged material, should not be attempted. For example, while it may not be possible to recreate a fully functional natural wetland, it may be possible to create some habitat characteristics of these wetlands that will in turn support colonization by some animal and fish species. In some cases, partially restored natural functions may nevertheless help maintain the functions of the ecosystem of which it is a part.

The diversity of physical settings for habitats requires the use of wide-ranging engineering principles for feasibility studies, design, and application of technology. The physical principles of some coastal processes, such as hydrodynamics and sediment transport, are sufficiently established to enable universal application. However, the technology needed for predicting, developing, and maintaining habitat varies with the physical setting. The maturity and sophistication of technologies for these purposes differ widely and are not as far advanced as the understanding of the underlying physical principles.

The engineering profession typically must conform to institutional constraints; principal among them are time, cost, and project specifications. Institutional culture and accountability can be less obvious but still powerful constraints. The time required to obtain approval for projects affecting marine habitat, particularly those involving dredging and dredged material, can be prolonged (Kagan, 1990; NRC, 1985d). This is attributable to fragmented and multitier decisionmaking and regulatory processes at the state and federal levels as well as competing objectives (and conflict over them) among the interested parties. These factors affect not only the interested parties but also the federal, state, and local agencies responsible for decisionmaking and permitting.

Although conflict over project goals and specifications can result from economic and sociopolitical factors, it can also result from limited scientific knowledge of the effects of various engineering actions. The engineer is responsible for informing the client of the possible risks involved in a particular project and for providing a reasonable success rate. These are daunting tasks considering the fact that it is often difficult to predict the effects of engineering operations on ecological functions. When possible and feasible, a cautious, phased approach to design and implementation in projects involving marine habitat is normally the best option. Engineering technology could benefit from development of techniques that minimize perturbations to natural systems along with careful documentation of the effects through post project monitoring of both physical and ecological parameters. Indefinite approaches are not standard engineering practice; they also add costs to habitat projects, for which funds are always limited. Comprehensive monitoring regimes also drive up project costs and are not a routine practice. Good monitoring regimes have been applied in some of restoration projects (Clarke and Pullen, 1992; Landin, 1991, 1992a; Landin et al., 1989a,c). *However, monitoring is more often cursory and sporadic, failing to provide an opportunity to learn from the successes and failures of the projects being monitored.*

A particular problem with the creation or modification of marine habitats is the lack of consensus on criteria to determine project success (Westman, 1991; Zentner, 1982). Criteria are available (Landin, 1992b,c) and discussed in Chapter 6, although all interested parties may not accept them. The practicing engineer prefers that success be practical and determinant, and not relative to competing perspectives and subjective. Engineering success is defined as meeting project goals and objectives that were agreed on prior to construction. If project goals do not effectively address habitat needs and issues of scale in space and time, the result may or may not be a fully functioning marine habitat or, more realistically, a product positioned to achieve functional objectives over an agreed-to time scale (Risser, 1988; Westman, 1991). The product is also dynamic rather than fixed, a nontraditional engineering result that not only makes determination of success more difficult but also runs counter to predominant engineering approaches to problem solving. To the degree that natural functions and ecosystem needs are project objectives, the involvement of marine biologists, coastal geologists, ecologists, and other scientists in the early stages of project development is fundamental to developing sound project specifications. But again the result may be something less than restoration to natural conditions that preexisted human effects on the environment. Thus, the time factor is a definitional issue in project objectives, and prospective project outcomes can pit theory and philosophy against practical application. Disagreements in these areas might make multidisciplinary collaboration among the scientific and engineering disciplines difficult at times.

Advances in technology and heightened societal concerns mean that team effort is increasingly required to address problems. The need for team effort is well recognized by leading practitioners involved in creation or restoration of coastal wetlands and of shallow water and intertidal marine habitats; the coastal engineer typically works with a wet-soil scientist, a sedimentologist, a hydrologist, a biologist, and a systems ecologist, among others. For engineers specializing in environmental work, the multidisciplinary nature of the work requires general familiarity with a broad range of topics across and outside the engineering disciplines. The growing need for interdisciplinary and multidisciplinary perspectives in engineering work generally is one of the reasons why some schools still offer a 5-year degree as an option and why some 4-year undergraduate engineering curricula in the United States have stretched to almost 5 years (NRC, 1985a,b). Yet, a sense of disciplinary dichotomy between science and engineering continues to exist in academic curricula. The engineer often has limited exposure to other disciplines. On the other hand, coastal scientists often do not take advantage of available coastal engineering expertise. Education that is scientifically and technically more integrated without diluting essential engineering or scientific principles would benefit individuals interested in marine habitat management following undergraduate study. This is difficult to achieve under existing curricula requirements, but could be a long-term objective for engineering schools.

Because coastal engineering principles and practices are rooted in civil engineering, many coastal engineers recognize and understand civil engineering design principles. But on a global scale, coastal engineering design is not always carried out, permitted, or implemented by engineers who are specialists in this field. Civil construction along the shore often suffers from this lack of expertise. Although this issue is perhaps more institutional than educational, the results have been quite positive where coastal construction was carried out with due regard for coastal hazards through improved coastal engineering design practice and its codification. For example, soon after Hurricanes Elena in 1985 (Hine et al., 1987), Hugo in 1989 (Davison, 1991; NRC, 1990a), and Andrew in 1992 (Schmidt and Clark, 1993), fairly extensive field inspections of the coasts of eastern, southern, and western Florida, Cancun in Mexico, South Carolina, and Louisiana were carried out to document erosion and structural damage. Structures built to modern coastal engineering design standards were found to have weathered the storms, generally without major damage (Dean, 1991), although repairs were necessary in a few locations to correct displacement damage (of

26   RESTORING AND PROTECTING MARINE HABITAT

rubblemound groins) and damage to armor stone and foundations [USACE and Florida DNR, 1993].

IMPACTS OF TECHNOLOGY IN THE COASTAL ZONE

Although an activity may be sound from an engineering perspective, it may not be sound for the organisms living in the area affected. Such is the case where engineering practices and technological developments have intensified human habitation and use of the coastal resources. The coastal habitats that existed naturally in the absence of roads, culverts, flood protection, and urban runoff have been stressed in often unpredictable and consequential ways. These responses are frequently unpredictable because methodologies have not yet been developed to predict changes that will occur, particularly those that are subtle or take a long time for their effects to become visible.

The application of engineering and technology in the coastal zone has both directly and indirectly influenced coastal habitats. The visible results, such as habitat conversion or loss caused by port development or oil and gas exploration, can often be readily discerned. Documented examples of habitat destruction and adverse effects of human-related activity include seagrass habitat losses from changes in water quality and from propeller damage from recreational and commercial craft, coral reef damage and loss from ship groundings and propeller strikes; species decline from pollutants and impoundments, wetland losses from disruption of sediment transport and from construction of bulkheads; loss of intertidal flushing, and waterlogging following hydrologic impoundment. The full ecological impacts are usually less obvious, especially in the near term, and are subject to intense debate.

Focusing the debate over ecological impacts is complicated by the limitations of accepted data and analysis, a lack of consensus among decisionmakers and regulators, limited long-term monitoring, and disciplinary perspectives that are too narrow for holistic problem solving. For example, the large-scale physical impacts of constructing navigation channels, underwater berms, and flood protection levees are easier to predict than the ensuing and perhaps long-lasting effects of the hydraulic and hydrologic modifications that affect sedimentation rates and turbidity, water quality, fish and wildlife use, and endangered species. The problems associated with this uncertainty often result in and are compounded by contradictory project objectives. In another example, objectives for the protection of a "client species" may indirectly and unintentionally overlap with objectives affecting a large part of society. In hindsight, project participants may recognize the interdependencies between ecosystems and the human activities that alter them, but it is difficult to incorporate these realizations into project planning. First of all, the relationship between incremental habitat loss and degradation and human activities is difficulty to quantify. Engineering and scientific capabilities to quantify interdependencies in ecosystem functioning and the crit-

SCIENTIFIC AND ENGINEERING PERSPECTIVES

ical nature of natural functions is not fully developed (Cairns and Niederlehner, 1993). Further, those who would convert marine habitat to other uses can bring their resources quickly to bear while the regulators and managers who are the overseers of change and the stewards of natural resources generally have less flexibility and resources.

Less appreciated but substantial roles for technology in coastal habitat management include recently developed capabilities to manage information, habitats, and communications through both remote sensing, both computer simulations and ecologic-economic-physical models, and graphic display capabilities for training and monitoring. Geographic information systems (GIS) are powerful organizers of data. For example, GIS can provide overlays of spatial data sets accumulated in one location for nearly instant analysis of habitat changes and landscapes for use in permit evaluations.

OBSERVATIONS ON THE IMPLICATIONS OF SEA LEVEL RISE TO THE APPLICATION OF PROTECTION AND RESTORATION TECHNOLOGY

Plant and animal communities are generally resilient, being capable of relatively rapid response to ecological changes—if there is a place with suitable conditions that supports migration and there is sufficient time for migration to occur (Daniels et al., 1993; NRC, 1987a; Ross et al., 1994). A global eustatic rise of relative mean sea level (RMSL) at many shores could potentially eliminate vast and presently extant habitat areas while creating new ones upland (NRC, 1987a), and changes in the character of species can occur as compression of habitat takes place (Titus, 1988). Although the full extent of sea level is not known, the apparent eustatic rise in sea level places a demand on the scientist and the coastal engineer to reconsider fundamental approaches to protecting, improving, and creating wetlands (NRC 1987a, 1989b, 1990a, 1990c; Titus, 1988).

Both coastal development and marine habitat management have often assumed a relatively stable RMSL except in coastal Louisiana where the rate of change is obvious and subsidence is also a factor. Even without a drastic eustatic rise, the RMSL rise in coastal Louisiana has created a situation wherein cost considerations may limit engineering responses to protecting those areas that are vital to the state's and the nation's economy. In other areas, an RMSL rise may mean that costs could preclude any defense, and abandonment may be the only outcome. Although abandonment may not be a humanistic policy option, defending the coast at any cost may prove unrealistic (NRC, 1987a; Roy and Connell, 1991).

Shoreline recession is one indicator of sea level rise. A common method of calculating the recession of sandy shoreline owing to sea level rise is a simple mathematical relationship known as the Bruun Rule (Bruun, 1962, 1981, 1988).

The basis for this relationship does not include any net gain or loss of sand from the beach profile but considers only sediment shifted seaward to maintain a profile in equilibrium with the wave climate. This relationship dictates that doubling the rate of sea level rise doubles the rate of recession. Calculations based on this relationship and/or other sources suggest, for example, that the majority of the shoreline of the east coast of Florida is suffering from moderate to severe erosion (Williams et al., 1990). This situation may be a harbinger of what may occur as a result of greater RMSL rise than in the recent past, but careful calculations based on measured shore profiles along Florida's east coast over the past century indicate otherwise. Although the shoreline has indeed receded locally (quite drastically in some places, especially near inlets), on average, the shoreline has actually advanced at the rate of 0.16 meters per year over more than 100 years (Grant, 1992). Further, the application of the Bruun Rule to shorter-term changes in the shoreline to corresponding changes in the sea level for the same shoreline shows no significant correlation (Grant, 1992; SCOR, 1991). Shore processes other than a transitory rise in sea level have evidently had a dominating effect on the shoreline position. Transport of sediment from offshore as well as local biogenic production of carbonaceous sediment may be important factors affecting RMSL. Because simple computational procedures such as the Bruun Rule are often based on basic assumptions and can easily be misapplied, future predictions will depend on carefully defining the applicability of such procedures. On the other hand, computational procedures can be modified, where feasible, to broaden their use (NRC, 1987a).

These facts argue for the initiation of both short- and long-term strategies to perfect restoration technology and apply it aggressively to the problem of historical wetland loss and the future threat of accelerated sea level rise. Further, they dramatize the challenges and limitations of restoration; a system cannot be restored in a context that requires continual, intensive subsidy. Those engaged in enhancement, restoration, and creation efforts need to consider four approaches:

- enhancement or restoration of individual sites that were damaged as the result of human influence;
- large-scale ecosystem approaches (referred to as landscape ecology) to maintain and enhance habitat while remaining cognizant of the implications of sea level rise, including spatial relationships.
- long-term needs for shoreline protection measures; and in the extreme,
- retreat or abandonment.

DEFINING SUCCESS

A successful track record is necessary for building and sustaining public and private support for more widespread use of protection and restoration technology. This record is especially needed to establish the credibility of restoration

SCIENTIFIC AND ENGINEERING PERSPECTIVES 29

technology and of practitioners where protection or restoration is used as mitigation in exchange for coastal development.

Despite the importance of defining and achieving success, there are no universally accepted measures for gauging project performance or guiding evolving practices. One school of thought, the ecological viewpoint, is that success should be principally defined as the ability to fully reproduce natural processes, although social and economic values should be considered to some extent (Cairns, 1988; Erwin, 1990; Josselyn et al., 1990; NRC, 1992a). Goals (that is, expected results) focus on natural functions (Zedler and Weller, 1990) to the exclusion of social (including economic) interests in a restoration project. Determining whether predisturbed natural conditions have been restored requires rigorous, long-term monitoring that can strain the limits of scientific knowledge to interpret the results (D'Avanzo, 1990) and increases project costs. Each can be a problem for project sponsors, engineers, and regulators, who prefer more quantifiable measures.

Returning a disturbed ecosystem to its predisturbed condition is generally preferred but is not always feasible. However, enhancement or partial restoration is often possible (Landin, 1992c; Sheehy and Vik, 1992). Then the environmental or social value can be produced even when nature is not fully replicated. But from a purely ecological perspective, the projects would not be considered successful. A second school of thought, reflected in this report, defines success as achieving project goals and objectives. This viewpoint considers natural functions important but does not give them status as exclusive parameters for defining success (Berger, 1991; Clark, 1990; Garbisch, 1990; Landin, 1992c; Lewis, 1990a; Westman, 1991). Thus both environmental and social (including economic) factors can be accommodated in project goals and objectives. This approach provides a more traditional format for compatibility with regulatory processes, economic reality, and engineering practice. Establishing project goals and objectives, implementing the project, and measuring performance in relation to the objectives remain challenges regardless of how success is defined.

SUMMARY

Concomitant application of scientific knowledge of marine habitats as ecosystems and coastal engineering capabilities is needed to produce effective and environmentally sound human interactions with coastal resources, but this is not common practice. The ecological setting is not widely understood or accommodated in human activities that impact marine habitat. The application of coastal engineering capabilities and technologies may be sound from an engineering perspective but not beneficial to organisms affected by engineering work. Habitat management objectives are not well developed from an engineering perspective and are also conditioned by societal and scientific factors, including the effects of relative sea level rise. Interdependencies in the functions of coastal habitats are not fully understood and are therefore difficult to restore to a natural state. Standards of comparison for determining the performance of habitat restoration projects are a source of substantial debate. Use of dredged material in habitat restoration work, concern over the chemical properties of sediments, and questions over natural functioning stimulate considerable controversy. But some dredged material is also a resource that is needed for constructing habitat projects in coastal ecosystems. Even if not fully functional, habitats based on dredged materials may help maintain the natural functioning of the coastal ecosystems of which they are a part. How well areas restored using dredged material mimic habitats that have been converted is an issue. Controversy over these issues may continue use of dredged material in restoration as an experimental rather than proven application.

Coastal engineers have traditionally not always adequately prepared for multidisciplinary design and construction of protection and restoration projects. Where scientific knowledge and engineering capabilities were not in harmony, the result was often adverse consequences to affected coastal ecosystems. To avoid these consequences, a conservative and multidisciplinary approach is essential whenever engineering activities may impact marine habitat. Project objectives need to adequately incorporate both scientific and engineering principles as well as social factors to enhance their prospects for successful performance and to ensure their broad acceptability. Project performance to these objectives provides a practical measure that can be used to determine success.

3

The State of Engineering Practice in Marine Habitat Management

Whether marine habitats can be protected or restored has stimulated considerable debate; so too has the application of technology in protection and restoration. Major issues include the functioning of habitats following application of protection or restoration technology, dredging impacts, the efficacy of using dredged material in restoration work, and the placement of dredged material. These issues introduce our examination of the state of engineering in marine habitat management, followed by an examination of the application of technology in various marine habitat settings (Box 3-1). Dredging and dredged material placement technologies and their application in marine habitat protection and restoration are reviewed, as are alternative approaches and technologies that have been or could be used to establish marine habitats or to minimize or prevent deleterious impacts from human activities. The chapter concludes with an overview of various factors that affect the use of technology for habitat protection and restoration. A categorized list of major references is included as Appendix C. A summary of regional perspectives on the state of practice is provided in Appendix D.

RESTORATION TECHNICAL ISSUES

Functionality Following the Application of Technology

The technology to enhance, restore, or create the physical or three-dimensional structure of marine habitats is generally well developed. (For marine wetlands see Kirkman, 1992; Kusler and Kentula, 1990; Landin et al., 1989b; Sene-

31

ca and Broome, 1992; Simenstad and Thom, 1992; and Zedler, 1992. For coral reefs see Maragos, 1992. For artificial reefs see Lewis and McKee, 1989; Seaman and Sprague, 1991; Sheehy and Vik, 1992. For shallow water submerged seagrass see Fonseca, 1990, 1992; Lewis, 1987; Lewis et al., 1985. For kelp forests see Schiel and Foster, 1992. For mangrove systems, see Cintron-Molero, 1992; Hamilton et al., 1989; Lewis, 1982.) Technology also exists for shore protection and water quality control, although its application by coastal managers and the engineering community is not uniform (Crewz and Lewis, 1991; Roberts, 1991). Regardless of the technology used, the capacity of enhanced, restored, or created structural components to function as refugia or filter contaminants or to serve as sources of carbon and food for marine organisms is seriously debated (NRC, 1992a). For example, Lewis (1992) and Landin et al. (1989c) support the hypothesis that restored marine habitats can function as if they had not been disturbed or altered from preexisting natural conditions; the Pacific Estuarine Research Laboratory (PERL, 1990) disagrees.

There is a general acknowledgement that use of existing protection and restoration technology and regulatory enforcement to offset or mitigate permitted losses of marine wetlands has not resulted in "no net loss" of ecological functions (Lewis, 1992; Redmond, 1992; Roberts, 1991). In light of continuing loss of aquatic habitat, the NRC encouraged a dedicated program to reverse historical and current loss of wetlands. The NRC recommended that

> inland and coastal wetlands be restored at a rate that offsets any further loss of wetlands and contributes to an overall gain of 10 million wetland acres by the year 2010. . . . In the broadest terms, aquatic ecosystem restoration objectives must be a high priority in a national restoration agenda; such an agenda must provide for restoration of as much of the damaged aquatic resource base as possible, if not to its pre-disturbance condition, then to a superior ecological condition that far surpasses the degraded one, so that valuable ecosystem services will not be lost.
>
> (NRC, 1992a)

Despite of the controversy over how fruitful marine habitat projects are, they continue to be launched and implemented, and technology continues to be applied. From a coastal engineering perspective, capabilities for dredging and placement of dredged material are important resources that may be used in marine habitat management in conjunction with other important engineering capabilities. These include design expertise, predictive tools, and practical experience with a wide array of engineering technologies and structures. These capabilities may be used for integrating marine habitat objectives into coastal development, improving channel design to reduce dredging requirements, control of hydraulic conditions and sedimentation, planting marsh and submerged vegetation, stabilizing and restoring beaches, and designing and operating sewage and other waste disposal facilities to minimize environmental impacts. It is with this range of tools that the coastal engineering profession can aid in the

THE STATE OF ENGINEERING PRACTICE

improved stewardship of vital coastal resources. Dredging and the placement of dredged material, although important, are also the source of much controversy, whether applied in marine habitat management or more traditional coastal engineering work.

Use of Dredging and Dredged Material in Restoration

Dredged material (see Box 3-1) is used in constructing many marine habitat management projects. Thus, in practice, marine habitat management depends heavily on its availability and suitability. Material is obtained either through dredging or water control structures that regulate the natural movement of suspended sediment. In some cases, shore structures have been modified, such as breaching levees (creating artificial crevasses) to reestablish or improve water transport of sediments into areas where they will settle to the bottom and accrete to form emergent wetlands.

Substantial quantities of sediments are dredged to maintain federal navigation projects (shipping channels). Disposal of material dredged from such projects is often complicated by controversy over placement because of potential environmental impacts. Lesser quantities of sediments are moved for private navigation projects, such as maintenance of marinas but can still result in a placement problem. Dredging is also conducted during construction of new navigation projects and port facilities and for some commercial and residential developments in shore areas either to provide or improve water access or for fill, although this latter activity is less common today.

The placement or disposal of dredged material often creates considerable controversy, regardless of its source (Hamons, 1988; Kagan, 1990; Lethbridge,

---

BOX 3-1
COMPOSITION OF DREDGED MATERIAL

Dredged material varies substantially in composition. It may be clean or may contain pollutants (NRC, 1985d, 1989a), affecting its potential use as a resource in marine habitat management. There are five general categories: rock, gravel and sand, consolidated clay, silt and soft clay, and mixtures of the four. Silt and soft clays are of particular interest for use in marine habitat restoration. They form much of the material obtained through maintenance dredging and are potentially useful for habitat development in and out of marine settings. Also of interest are gravel and sands that may be used to stabilize or improve turtle nesting beaches, construct bird nesting islands, and provide elevations necessary for restoring wetlands (Herbich, 1992b; Landin, 1992b; PIANC, 1992a). Rock and consolidated clay obtained through dredging have potential applications as well as construction material for offshore berms and artificial reefs (PIANC, 1992a), for example.

1988; Stromberg, 1988). Dredged material is treated as a resource or a spoil, depending on one's point of view. Concerns over use of dredged material outside its natural marine environment include the chemical changes that occur when marine sediments are exposed to oxygen and contamination of sediments by pollutants (Davies, 1988; Engler et al., 1991a,b; Herbich, 1985; Lee and Jones, 1992; NRC, 1985d, 1989a, 1992a; USACE, 1984). Relatively few navigation project areas are heavily contaminated by pollutants that typically have emanated from nonpoint sources into affected ecosystems. These occur near major coastal cities (Robertson and O'Conner, 1989; Zarba, 1989). About 95 percent of all dredged material is classified by the U.S. Army Corps of Engineers as suitable for open water disposal, although some materials with small amounts of pollutants may require capping, depending on the nature and level of contaminants present. Much of this material is therefore potentially suitable for use as a nourishment and construction resource for habitat enhancement, restoration, and creation projects (Engler, 1988; Landin and Smith, 1987; Murden, 1989b; OTA, 1987) (see Box 3-2) . Another relevant concern is the fact that organic and inorganic materials are lost to the dredged material in varying degrees when

---

BOX 3-2
THE ARMY CORPS OF ENGINEERS APPROACH TO USING DREDGED MATERIAL

Historically, the Army Corps of Engineers was concerned primarily with the disposal of dredged material. In the past two decades, applied research and dredging interests within the Corps have emphasized dredged material as a resource for habitat protection, enhancement, restoration, and creation (Landin et al., 1989c; PIANC, 1992a; USACE, 1986, 1989a). This approach is referred to as the beneficial uses of dredged material. Such uses primarily involve one or more habitat types: upland meadows and woodlands, marshes and wooded wetlands, wildlife islands, and estuarine and marine habitats. For island design and management, all four are often included. The environmental and engineering technology for using dredged material for habitat purposes has been developed, published, examined in conferences, demonstrated through field applications, and monitored since the 1970s by the Corps of Engineers. Landin (1992a) and Landin et al. (1989c) found that the performance of projects using dredged material can be predicted reliably for salt and fresh marshes. Where feasible, USACE regulations now encourage inclusion of wetland restoration and creation in dredging projects under Section 150 of the Water Resources Development Act (WRDA) of 1986, 1990, and 1992. The Corps has not widely implemented regulations based on these acts; the acts authorize regulations but did not include appropriations to enable widespread implementation. Further, the acts only regulation of wetlands, thereby excluding all the other habitats associated with natural progression in a coastal ecosystem. Another limitation on the use of dredged material is the Army Corps of Engineers policy requiring least-cost, environmentally acceptable placement.

THE STATE OF ENGINEERING PRACTICE   35

sediments are disturbed, depending on compaction and local conditions. This affects its quality for use in habitat restoration.

The nation's ports are vast economic engines and access by modern ships is fundamental to their efficient operation. Despite economic and environmental controversy over dredging issues, as discussed in the preceding paragraph (Kagan, 1990; NRC, 1985d, 1992b), past history has shown that bottom sediments will continue to be moved to maintain federally authorized navigation channels as an economic necessity. When this occurs, environmental objectives established by law and regulation need to be met constructively and responsibly (Hamons, 1988; Harr, 1988; Murden, 1989b; NRC, 1985d, 1992b; Rhodes, 1988; Stromberg, 1988). For example, dredging operations could be planned and conducted to disrupt ecosystems as little as possible, such as by maintaining biologically active shallow water and intertidal areas where feasible. In some cases, this might even reduce the amount of material to be moved and the costs of construction and maintenance, all of interest for improving waterway design (NRC, 1992b). Nevertheless, the materials obtained from dredging can provide the very resource needed to reduce or reverse habitat losses. In fact, in the Mississippi River delta region of Louisiana, the controversy is not over whether to use bottom sediments as a resource but about how to overcome federal policy and budgets that constrain wider productive use. Such use, however, may be more costly than least-cost, environmentally acceptable placement options (Landin, 1993a, in press-b). Under current national policy, who should pay for increased costs if use of dredged materials in marine habitat management is not the least-cost alternative becomes an issue.

APPLYING TECHNOLOGY

This section reviews the general ecological settings within which the various technologies are often applied; it is intended to be illustrative but not exhaustive. The discussion begins with an examination of the relationship between the ecology of barrier islands and estuaries and traditional coastal engineering practices and includes problem areas affecting the application of coastal engineering technology. A similar treatment of marine wetlands follows, including seagrass meadows and tidal marshes. The role of coastal engineering is not as well defined for these habitats. The section concludes with a summary of artificial reef technology.

Shoreline Engineering

An almost continuous chain of barrier islands, and in some areas beaches extending from headlands, stretch along the Atlantic and Gulf Coasts. When undisturbed, these areas develop complex, dynamic ecosystems. Barrier islands are especially dynamic, shifting and migrating in response to tidal, wind, wave, and storm energies. These coastal barriers are a first line of defense for back bay areas and uplands against winter storms and hurricanes. The beaches serve to dissipate storm wave energy. The sand dunes protect against storm surges, and when breached, result in overwash that naturally raises upland elevations behind the dune line. The stability and health of barrier island ecosystems depends on this flexibility (Amos and Amos, 1985; Mendelssohn, 1982; Perry, 1985; Platt et al., 1992; Rose et al., 1878; Weber et al., 1990; Williams et al., 1990).

However, human activity has disturbed the physical processes that caused barrier islands to shift and migrate by replacing sand dunes with homes and commercial properties, and through construction of shoreline protection and beach and inlet stabilization structures. Nevertheless, barrier beaches continuously respond to the influence of waves, currents, and wind. The net effect has often been erosion that threatens both fragile barrier island ecosystems and shorefront properties (NRC, 1987a, 1988, 1989a,b).

Faced with a challenge from the sea to coastal development, there is strong public interest in stabilizing eroding shorelines. Several strategies are used in shoreline management. Permanent structures ("hard" projects), such as seawalls, groins, jetties, and offshore parallel breakwaters have been used for many years. They create an effective barrier between the sea and land but interrupt the littoral flow of sediment (Charlier et al., 1989; USACE, 1991, 1992). This change perpetuates erosional problems in some instances and creates new ones in others, such as accelerated erosion on downdrift sides of jetties. In extreme cases where the barrier island is forced landward, marshlands behind the island are lost. Permanent shoreline protection structures, although popular in the past, are used less extensively except to protect harbor entrances and port facilities because of actual and perceived adverse effects on erosion (Charlier et al., 1989; Hall and Pilkey, 1988; Pilkey and Wright, 1988; USACE, 1994). Some coastal engineers have concluded that properly engineered seawalls and revetments can protect the land behind them without adversely affecting the fronting beaches (NRC, 1987a, 1990a). There is evidence that beach change near seawalls is like that on beaches without seawalls in both magnitude and variation (Kraus, 1988; NRC, 1990a). Hardened structures technology is well advanced and could potentially be applied in some circumstances to protect marine habitat (Bruun, 1989a,b; Herbich, 1990, 1991, 1992a; USACE, 1984). For example, breakwaters could be constructed to dissipate wave energy that threatens wetlands in large estuaries. However, effects on sediment transport would need to be considered.

An increasingly popular shoreline engineering technique is to nourish an eroding beach by adding sand of suitable size and quality. In the United States, normally dredged material is used. The main purposes of beach nourishment are to increase the capability of beaches to act as storm buffers to protect structures in the coastal floodplain and on barrier islands and peninsulas and to provide attractive recreational "habitat" (Anderson, 1980). Periodic replenishment is needed to maintain the desired beach platform and profile. Secondary benefits

THE STATE OF ENGINEERING PRACTICE   37

include possible locations for placement of beach-quality material dredged from some navigation channels (presently institutionally constrained) and enhancement of nesting beaches for sea turtles. Improving the performance of beach nourishment projects is sometimes attempted by anchoring the beach with terminal structures such as groins. Some practitioners prefer beach nourishment as a preferred management solution from an environmental perspective; nonstructural ("soft") measures could replace hard structures (Charlier et al., 1989). Beach nourishment is a nonstructural measure with some potential for use in marine habitat management. However, much remains to be learned about the physical performance of these projects, and whether they can be effectively considered a long-term solution to shoreline erosion (USACE, 1994).

Another aggressive approach is to dredge and fill, or dike and pump, thereby altering the configuration and characteristics of estuaries. This approach is practiced most extensively in the Netherlands (Charlier et al., 1989; Verhagen, 1990).

Beach nourishment involves excavating large quantities of sand from one site (usually offshore or from ebb tide shoals, but the source could be sand deposits in an estuary, for example, a flood tide shoal). The sand is placed on an existing beach to advance the shoreline seaward. The beach is essentially moved back in time so that an earlier sequence of shoreline change can be repeated (O'Brien, 1985).

Beach nourishment projects are typically site-specific. Although some projects have covered 10 or more miles of shoreline, most are much smaller. Landscape (regional) perspectives have generally not been employed in planning and design to address effects on downdrift beaches or on sand budgets for long-term maintenance including periodic renourishment. However, it is recognized that the greater the length of the beach segment that is nourished, the longer will be the duration of retention of the placed sand (Dean and Yoo, 1993).

Another approach to beach nourishment is sand bypassing. Sand is artificially transported from one side of a shoreline protection or inlet stabilization structure or from a sand deposit in an inlet to the other side of the structure or inlet in order to restore the sand budget for the downdrift beach. Typically, special pumping systems are installed to dredge the sand and transport it by pipelines to downdrift beaches. The few applications of this technique in the United States have been principally for beach nourishment purposes. The beach nourishment projects have used hydraulic pumping systems for sand transport and are used intermittently as needed. Special pumping systems have recently been developed for continuous bypassing. However, these are currently being tested at only a few locations. Data on their efficiency and effectiveness are minimal (Mehta, 1993). The sand bypassing technique appears to have only very limited potential for application in marine habitat management projects.

The efficacy of beach nourishment projects and their relation to structural protection is controversial; some projects have been considered successful, others not (NRC, 1987a, 1990a; Pilkey, 1989). Success is determined by the volumetric loss, loss rates, planned versus actual renourishment intervals, and project objectives, including whether a project was designed as direct nourishment or to serve as a feeder beach for natural nourishment of other beaches. Some coastal engineers trace failures to inappropriate siting (such as attempting projects where there are high background erosion rates) or inappropriate application of the technology (such as less than optimal design) (NRC, 1990a). Critics attribute failures to gaps in knowledge of shoreline processes and consistent underestimation of the volume of sand required to maintain beaches near their design dimensions (Pilkey, 1989). The technical controversy is fed by the fact that

- shoreline processes are complex, and their effects are highly site specific, making case histories difficult to apply to broader applications;
- data interpretation methods are not consistent, so that what appears to one person as erosion may appear as accretion to another; and
- arguments are sometimes advanced to support a point of view.

Decisionmaking about beach nourishment is undergoing major change. Recent changes include a 50 percent cost-share requirement by local sponsors for shoreline improvements. As a result, states and municipalities now have a substantial and direct interest in the cost and performance of shoreline projects. Further, the Water Resources Development Act (WRDA) of 1990 [Public Law (P.L.) 101-640] linked federal participation in the planning, implementation, or maintenance of any beach stabilization or nourishment project with a state's establishment of or commitment to a beach front management program. The act accentuates the controversy over beach nourishment. The cost-share requirement may hinder use of beach nourishment technology to benefit marine habitat management (in the absence of a residential or commercial tax bases that benefits from a project), except where marine life uses the nourished beaches or the objective is to protect parks or preserves.

Some nourished beaches along the South Atlantic have enhanced sea turtle nesting habitats. This result was effected by placement of dredged sand in advance of turtle migration to the beach for reproduction. Timing is critical so that sorting and settling of materials occur before the migration. Improving turtle habitat was unanticipated but has now been incorporated in beach nourishment project planning and implementation (Nelson, 1985; Nelson and Dickerson, 1988). Typically, material is placed in late fall or early winter to satisfy nesting requirements. Costs of placement may increase if more sturdy equipment is required or if placement is hampered by environmental conditions in the winter months.

Although knowledge of project performance has improved considerably over the past few decades, prediction of the loss rates associated with a beach nourishment project is still probably no better than about 30 percent (NRC, 1990a).

THE STATE OF ENGINEERING PRACTICE   39

However, the associated design methodology and placement technologies continue to evolve in an effort to improve the longevity of fill. Although potentially negative environmental impacts may result from beach nourishment, they may be offset by implementing management techniques, such as relocation of nests, tilling of compacted sand, use of compatible sand, smoothing of scarps, and placement of dredged material prior to the nesting season (Nelson and Dickerson, 1988). These techniques are prime examples of a conscious effort to improve marine habitat management through the use of beach nourishment technology.

Estuaries

The nation's estuaries are of great value as breeding and nursery grounds for post-larval fishes as well as feeding grounds for many young adult oceanic fishes. The estimated value of estuary-based commercial fisheries in the late 1980s was $5–6 billion. The recreational fishing industry generated more than $8 billion in 1986. Recreational fishing activities are believed to have increased an estimated 40 percent since then (Bell et al., 1989; Brown and Watson, 1988; Kelley, 1991; Water Quality 2000, 1992; Weber et al., 1990). The importance of estuaries and the need to preserve and improve those that remain were recognized in 1987 when Congress established the National Estuary Program (NEP) as part of Clean Water Act amendments. The NEP builds on earlier and continuing programs for the Great Lakes and Chesapeake Bay ecosystems. Twenty-one major estuary projects are in progress under the program (EPA, 1992).

Estuarine health depends on complex interactions among physical, chemical, geological, and hydrological factors. These interactions are not fully understood, and they differ among estuaries and within specific locations of an estuary. Process-oriented and empirically based predictive models are available, but not well developed (Bell, 1989; NRC, 1983a).

Salinity gradients are important to marine and estuarine life in associated marshlands. Any engineering practice that alters estuarine salinity patterns can severely impact the functioning of the ecosystem. For example, altered hydraulics and salinity in the Savannah River estuary related to channel maintenance adversely impacted some fish species and invertebrates (Weber et al., 1990). Water diversion (that is, removal from the system) also threatens the health of estuaries. Fresh water removal alters the salinity gradient, making the area that is affected unsuitable for fresh water vegetation, fishes and other organisms that are suited to fresh or low salinity waters. For example, dams and water diversions have eliminated 80–100 percent of fish migration and spawning areas in northern California rivers. In the Sacramento River, Columbia River, and Chesapeake Bay systems, dams have eliminated hundreds of miles of anadromous fish spawning areas in the main streams and eliminated access to tributaries; hatchlings are not able to successfully migrate downstream (NRC, 1992a; Stroud,

1992; Williams and Tuttle, 1992). Effects of water wells and diversions, particularly in times of low rainfall in the watershed, are being felt in the Delaware River system as well. Salinity in the estuary has increased because the salt water wedge penetrates more deeply into groundwater and freshwater marshes. The oxygen content of the estuary water has changed substantially. The severity of effects on marine life depends on the amount of water removed from the system, particularly on a continuing basis.

Flushing time is an important factor in maintaining a favorable oxygen concentrations in an estuary. Any activity that slows the flushing rate probably will decrease the oxygen supply when all plants are macrophytes (that is, large plants), and thus produce conditions deleterious to aquatic life. Restoration efforts require comprehensive assessments of flushing times to ensure that oxygen demands are identified and accommodated.

Seagrass Meadows

Submerged seagrass beds are highly productive habitats that are often found in estuaries and are associated with tidal salt marshes and mangrove swamps (Hamilton et al., 1989; Weber et al., 1990). Eelgrass (a macrophyte) dominates the more northern coasts, and turtle grass dominates the coast of Florida and isolated places on the Gulf Coast. Seagrass beds may develop from coral or rock reefs or from sand and mud substrates. Many species of invertebrates, such as crabs, mollusks, and shrimp, and also larval and juvenile fish, use seagrass beds for habitats and nursery grounds. Turtles also use these areas extensively. Because submerged seagrass beds hold sediments in place, their removal or loss can lead to severe erosion. The restoration of seagrass habitat has grown increasingly important, and considerable experimentation has been attempted (Merkel, 1990a,b, 1991; Phillips, 1990; Thorhaug, 1990). Seagrass restoration includes plantings using plugs, tufts, seeds, grids, or sprigs. Thorhaug (1990) identified the literature available on specific projects. Successes have been achieved with lessons learned reported by Hoffman (1990), Merkel (1990a, 1991), and Nitsos (1990) for seagrass restoration work performed in southern California.

Evidence shows that simply installing seagrass sprigs on an unvegetated bottom or bare spot in an existing seagrass meadow does not usually work (Fonseca, 1990; Lewis, 1987). Seagrass meadows require good water quality characterized by low dissolved nutrient and suspended sediment levels, and high light transparency. The increasingly eutrophic conditions in coastal waters have caused major declines in the areal cover of extant seagrasses in the Chesapeake Bay (Orth and Moore, 1983), Tampa Bay (Lewis et al., 1985), and Galveston Bay (Pulich and White, 1991), among other water bodies. The precise mechanisms causing these losses may vary somewhat among estuaries, but without significant improvements in existing water quality, the planting of seagrasses could fail. Many losses are due to an increase in nutrients and sediments from point

THE STATE OF ENGINEERING PRACTICE   41

and nonpoint sources, causing eutrophication and increased turbidity. The subsequent reduction in light penetration has eliminated many seagrass beds. Dredging activities for developing and maintaining ports and navigation channels have mechanically removed many acres of seagrass beds and increased turbidity. When water quality management improves conditions appropriate for natural seagrass recolonization, planting efforts often succeed (Johansson and Lewis, 1992; Merkel, 1990a).

Intertidal Marshes

Intertidal salt marshes occur along all U.S. coasts, particularly along the Atlantic and Gulf Coasts (Amos and Amos, 1985; McConnaughey and McConnaughey, 1985; Perry, 1985; Weber et al., 1990). Intertidal marshes are among the most productive vegetative areas in the world, supporting abundant fish and wildlife populations. Their great value in protecting the shoreline, providing fish and wildlife habitat, filtering pollutants, and providing nutrients to adjacent estuaries was not generally appreciated until the latter half of this century. Despite their critical importance in providing marine habitat, salt marshes and other coastal wetlands were drained and filled to provide more coastal land for development, an important economic consideration in earlier times when natural areas were far more plentiful and seemingly inexhaustible. Water diversion projects and other activities upstream from estuaries have degraded or destroyed intertidal marshes as well (Brown and Watson, 1988; GAO, 1991; Gooselink and Baumann, 1980; Kusler, 1983; OTA, 1984).

Ecological Considerations

Intertidal marshes usually develop on coasts with low physical (wave and current) energy; accordingly, they are frequently within the protected confines of estuaries or on the landward side of barrier islands or barrier beaches extending from headlands. Mature coastal intertidal marshes have many functions (Box 3-3) and are complex ecosystems that usually developed over long periods. They are the result of a wide range of chemical, biological, and physiological processes, including sediment deposition and erosion, nutrient and other organic cycles, and tidal energies. These forces define the structure of marsh ecosystems. Tidal energies are particularly important. The diversity of species depends a good deal on the individual marsh characteristics and, in the long term, on marsh stability.

Intertidal marsh typically has a much higher primary productivity rate than the higher marsh, which is less frequently inundated. These grassy marshlands are also important in the production and export of detritus to coastal areas, where it comprises a main portion of food available to many invertebrates and fish. These marshes are also effective in removing excess nutrients and in the production of oxygen.

BOX 3-3
INTERTIDAL MARSH FUNCTIONS

- Fish and shellfish habitat
- Wildlife habitat
- Storm protection
- Sediment stabilization
- Water quality improvement
- Containment sinks and purifiers
- Recreation and aesthetics

Coastal marsh, which is regularly inundated and drained by the tides, consists of an expanse of salt-tolerant grasses and a network of tidal creeks. Tidal creeks are excellent breeding, nursery, and feeding grounds for many invertebrates and fish. Each creek has a complex structure with regard to salinity gradient, depth of flow, and type of sediment present. The extent and frequency of tidal rhythms may profoundly effect the value of a marsh as a nursery and breeding ground.

In some marshes, tidal pools known as salt pans maintain water during low tides. While they are inundated with salt water from tides, they may also receive varying amounts of freshwater from groundwater. Thus they support vegetation distinct from the surrounding marsh.

The substrate of a coastal wetland is highly variable in structure because it contains sediments of various-sized particles, a considerable amount of organic matter formed mainly from plant debris, and peat. The marsh may contain some clay as well as larger particulate matter. Extensive mud flats usually appear along the seaward edge of salt marshes and are exposed only by the lowest tides. Nutrients in the soil or substrate of a coastal marsh come mainly from river deposition and tidal action. In some cases, groundwater greatly influences nutrient concentrations. A substrate favorable to plant growth is essential when a wetland is restored or created.

Increasing a marsh's stability, such as by laying down the right mix of different sized sediments and organic material, is important to its ultimate development. Stability depends on a system of accretion and subsidence. The combined effects of accretion and subsidence result in an RMSL for each location that is typically different than the absolute change in sea level. Long-term causes of a rise in the RMSL are

- eustatic (global) rise of world sea level,
- crustal subsidence or uplift due to neotectonics,
- seismic subsidence caused by earthquakes,

THE STATE OF ENGINEERING PRACTICE   43

• subsidence resulting from compaction or consolidation of soft underlying sediments,
• subsidence of human origin caused by oil, gas, and water extraction or structural loading, and
• variations due to climatic fluctuations (Barnett, 1990; NRC, 1987a, 1991).

These factors may work separately or in combination. Salt marshes are relatively stable along the northern Atlantic Coast because accretion is keeping pace with RMSL. In contrast, autosubsidence due to compaction and downwarping of delta sediments along the Gulf Coast is causing the marshes there to subside and disappear (NRC, 1987a, 1991; Saucier, 1992). The possible threat of large-scale sea level rise jeopardizes the future of all coastal wetlands (Brown and Watson, 1988; NRC, 1987a).

Restoring Intertidal Marshes

In creation of a wetland or the alteration of water flow or estuary size, great care is necessary to ensure that the functioning of other processes important to fish and wildlife are not adversely affected. For example, placement of structures could alter the rate of water exchange between areas, affecting salinity and sedimentation, such as that which occurred in modifications to the Savannah River estuary (Appendix B).

Success in establishing vegetation in tidal marshes is quite high when appropriate technology is applied (Broome, 1990; Josselyn et al., 1990; Landin et al., 1989c; Lewis, 1990a; Shisler, 1990). When creating a habitat for organisms that form the basis for fisheries is an objective, success appears to include the need for higher ratios of marsh to open water edge. Many small creeks and channels may be necessary to establish a marsh–water interface that replicates the functions of a natural marsh (Minello et al., 198y). However, in the evaluation of mitigation projects requiring vegetation, credit is often not given for inclusion of small creeks and channels even though they may be more biologically productive than the marsh surface.

Kusler and Kentula (1990) note that for all wetland types in the United States, "in general, the ease with which a project can be constructed and the probability of its success are . . . greatest overall for estuarine marshes." The capability to establish *all* the functions of a natural tidal marsh has been demonstrated; for example, fish utilization of restored or created marshes is generally equal to that in natural marshes in 3–5 years (Landin et al., 1989c; Lewis, 1992). Other functions may lag behind faunal colonization (Zedler and Langis, 1991). Certain approaches, such as creating artificial crevasses in levees, thus diverting riverine sediments to adjacent marshes, rely on nature for the restoration once hydraulic regimes are provided (Brown and Watson, 1988; Fritchey, 1991). There is a localized sediment buildup, referred to as splays, as a consequence of breaks in the levee. These buildups usually take the shape of a small delta. With splays, wetlands accrete in the same manner as if the river had cut a new channel (Figures 3-1 and 3-2), and they appear to achieve equal quality. In some demonstration projects, substantial biological activity approaching that found naturally has been achieved in 5–15 years, depending on conditions at the project site.

Practitioners do not agree on what level of interdependent biological activity constitutes full restoration of natural functions. Nor is there agreement on the baseline criteria for making comparisons. One attribute of full ecological restoration might be the capacity for self-maintenance or self-perpetuation, although measurable attributes that could be robust indicators of the capability for self-maintenance have not been identified (NRC, 1992a). The question becomes whether to wait until research finds solutions or to undertake projects given the present state of knowledge, using the projects to increase scientific and engineering knowledge about marsh restoration. Full functional replacement as a concept is desirable, and it may be mandatory for marsh mitigation projects. Full functionality is not necessarily a limiting factor when restoring wetlands for other objectives, including species-specific goals.

Mangrove Forests

Mangrove forests are coastal wetlands dominated by mangrove trees; they replace tidal salt marshes along both high and low-physical energy tropical coasts. These habitats have high ecological value but have been long unvalued by society. Hamilton et al. (1989) provide a comprehensive description of mangroves and their value as a natural resource.

Most mainland U.S. mangrove forests are in Florida, although they also occur in Louisiana and Texas. The red mangrove typically dominates the intertidal zone because it can tolerate high salt concentrations. The arching prop roots of these trees help hold the substrate in place. Black mangroves appear behind the red mangroves in areas exposed to high tides. Both the black and white mangroves feature special structures in their root systems that serve as respiratory organs. The structures, known as pneumatophores, contain bodies of cells, known as lenticles, which serve as pores for the respiratory system. These morphological features allow mangrove species to live where other plants cannot. The tangled masses of prop roots and pneumatophores are havens for many forms of aquatic life. Important recreational and commercial fish feed in these relatively protected areas as well.

Mangrove swamps export much organic material to adjacent estuaries (Heald, 1969). Mangrove detritus is the primary food source for many estuarine animals and is important to the sport and commercial fisheries in the Gulf of Mexico. Primary consumers that use mangrove swamps as nursery and breeding grounds also serve as prey for game fish, such as tarpon, snook, sheepshead, spotted sea trout, red drum, jack, and jewfish.

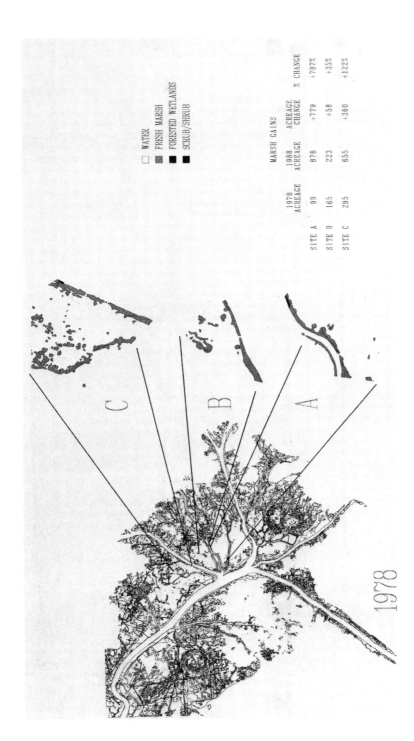

FIGURE 3-1 Status in 1978 of three selected splays totaling 559 acres in Lower Mississippi River Delta following levee breaches (USFWS, 1992, unpublished data).

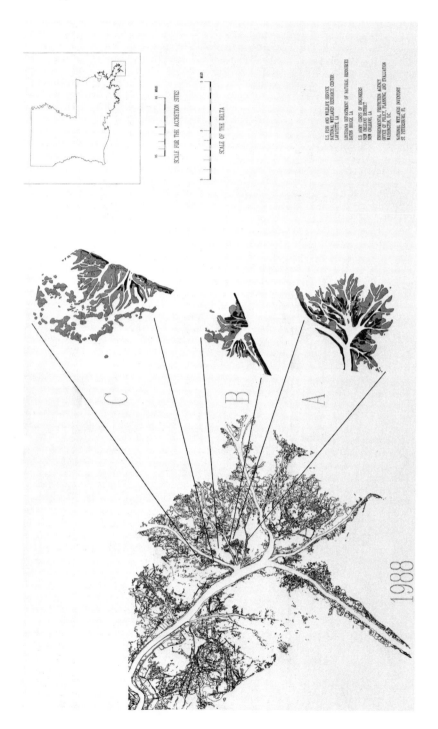

FIGURE 3-2 Status in 1988 of selected splay development of lower Mississippi River Delta after 10 years. Intertidal wetlands acreage increased from 559 to 1,756 acres (USFWS, 1992, unpublished data).

THE STATE OF ENGINEERING PRACTICE   47

Like tidal salt marshes, mangrove wetlands preserve the coastline by mitigating the effects of floods and violent storms. Protection of these coastal wetlands is therefore essential. The general techniques for successful restoration or
creation of the plant community have been demonstrated for mangrove forests
(Cintron-Molero, 1992; Crewz and Lewis, 1991; Lewis, 1982, 1990a). Mature
propagules are harvested directly from the trees, surrounding grounds, or naturally planted propagules. Early maturity of transplanted specimens is a problem
that can be offset by transplanting them at the young tree stage. Relocation of
mature tress is possible, but it requires extensive top and root pruning. Cost is a
constraining factor (Thorhaug, 1990).

The equivalency of all functions has not been demonstrated, but evidence
shows that the potential to restore mangrove habitats and provide good habitat
for fish and epibenthos exists (Roberts, 1989, 1991). Alteration of mangrove
systems often results in unanticipated severe effects because the natural shoreline protection provided by these systems is typically degraded or lost. For example, destroying red mangroves on a high-energy coast will eventually lead to
erosion of the area. It is the active growing of these trees with their root and stem
systems that makes possible the stabilization of the sediments there.

Coral Reefs

Reef corals grow principally in clear tropical waters. Fringing reefs, the only
major type of coral reef in continental U.S. waters, are found only in southern
Florida, primarily off the southeastern keys. Coral heads are scattered elsewhere
off Florida's west coast, and in a few areas off the Texas coast. Coral reefs and
heads consist principally of calcium carbonate deposits from stony corals, and
coralline algae. They are utilized as habitats by a diverse array of other organisms. These creatures require clear, clean water; they tolerate little pollution. The
growing portion of a seaward fringing reef is essential for survival and maintenance of the entire reef system. The coral reefs and the astonishing variety of
marine life that depends on them combine to form a most unique habitat. In
addition, fringing reefs provide highly effective natural protection against waves
generated by hurricanes and other episodic storms (Amos and Amos, 1985;
Guilcher, 1987; Maragos, 1992; Wiens, 1962).

Restoration of coral reefs or heads once damaged or lost relies on natural
restoration, although recolonization can be assisted. Full recovery takes decades
even when local conditions are ideal. Thus it is essential to protect coral reefs
from damage or loss owing to degradation of water quality or human activity,
including recreational boating, commercial vessel operations, and recreational
activity on the reefs themselves.

Various techniques documented by Maragos (1992) for aiding in coral reef
restoration include:

- transplanting reef corals, including cementing reef substrates with reef coral attached in damaged areas;
- construction of artificial reefs to provide both habitat for reef fishes and suitable substrates for recolonization;
- construction of reef quarry holes to provide suitable depths for recolonization;
- placement of rubble mound revetments and breakwaters for recolonization;
- cementation to restore reef frameworks in order to protect adjacent undamaged areas and promote recolonization;
- removal of diseased organisms;
- control of fisheries;
- replanting of seagrasses and mangroves to restore ecosystem links; and
- protective regulations.

Although favorable results have been achieved with these approaches, their application is expensive (Maragos, 1992). Technology can also be applied indirectly to provide conditions more favorable to natural restoration, principally through measures to improve water quality.

Artificial Reefs

The use of artificial reefs or artificial habitat enhancement is defined as the manipulation of natural aquatic habitats through the addition of natural structures or structures of human origin (Seaman and Sprague, 1991). More than 250 artificial reefs have been established in the coastal waters off most states, primarily off the South Atlantic and Gulf coasts. Many of these projects are characterized by placement of old ships, rubble, and other materials of opportunity rather than by specific design and construction for certain fish species. Nevertheless, the technology for artificial reefs is well developed (Bell, 1986; Bell et al., 1989; Lewis and McKee, 1989; McGurrin and Reeff, 1986; McGurrin and ASMFC, 1988, 1989a,b; Sheehy and Vik, 1992; Shieh et al., 1989).

Use of artificial reefs in fisheries management raises serious questions about what constitutes success. Artificial reefs can increase the efficiency of harvesting fish by concentrating them around an easily identifiable site. Less clear is the functional equivalency of artificial reefs compared with natural reefs and their real capability to increase standing stocks rather than attracting those that already exist (Alevizon and Gorham, 1989; Gorham and Alevizon, 1989; Seaman and Sprague, 1991; Wendt et al., 1989). Lack of long-term monitoring and controlled experimental studies are cited as factors limiting understanding of artificial reef ecology (Bohnsack, 1989; Bohnsack et al., 1991).

The United States took a major step in coordinating artificial reef activities through passage of the National Fishing Enhancement Act of 1984 (P.L. 98-

THE STATE OF ENGINEERING PRACTICE   49

623). The act's purpose is to promote and facilitate responsible and effective efforts to establish artificial reefs in specific waters. It provides a formal mechanism for reef development and encourages state activity, and the number of permitted reefs has increased substantially since 1983, but there is only moderate continuity in habitat construction (McGurrin and Reeff, 1986; McGurrin et al., 1989a,b).

In a comparative study of the U.S. and Japanese development of artificial reef technology, Grove and Wilson (in press) concluded that the United States regulates reactively and Japan takes a proactive approach. Both approaches are advancing construction techniques and understanding of artificial habitat. The Japanese are focused much more on carefully engineered structures for commercial production of selected species, and they have conducted considerably more applied research to determine species life histories (Bell, 1986). Japan provides substantial funding yet offers little latitude for experimentation; the United States, in contrast, provides encouragement and great latitude that leads to indecision and works against focused development of reef technology. A further difference is resource ownership. In Japan, fishery resources at private reefs are treated as property of the reef owner. In the United States, coastal and riverine fishery resources are, with few exceptions, treated as public property. Thus there is little incentive for private development of reefs as a fisheries resource.

DREDGING AND DREDGED MATERIAL PLACEMENT

Historical Uses of Dredged Material

Use of dredged material dates back to harbor development and mariculture impoundments by the Chinese, Greeks, and Phoenicians. A substantial body of literature details techniques and methodologies for its application (Landin 1988a,b; Landin and Seda-Sanabria, 1992; Landin and Smith, 1987; Lazor and Medino, 1990; PIANC, 1992a; USACE, 1986).

The United States and Canada have used dredged material since colonial times. It was generally used to fill shallow water and wetland areas for urban, aviation, port, farm, industrial, and other interests. Until recent decades, these uses were acceptable. For example, much of the historic inner city areas of Baltimore, Washington, Newark, New York, Boston, Norfolk, Savannah, Charleston, Portland, San Francisco, and San Diego are built on dredged material. But the use of dredged material as fill for development is no longer common practice because of environmental concerns about the quality of the sediments, possible harm to vegetation from chemical changes when dredged material is exposed to air, and the cumulative losses of remaining coastal wetlands and shallow water and intertidal marine habitat. Today the most extensive use of dredged material as a resource in coastal areas is the placement of beach-quality sands in beach nourishment projects to protect shorelines. Further, the use of

50   RESTORING AND PROTECTING MARINE HABITAT

dredged material to aid in restoring wetlands in areas such as Louisiana, which are experiencing severe changes in wetland character and acreage, is being explored.

Another important use of dredged material in marine habitat management over the past 100 years is the creation of some 2,000 estuarine islands. They have become important to nesting water birds as natural shorelines and islands disappeared under the pressures of coastal population increases and development. More than 1 million water birds nest on these islands each year. These habitats have been studied to determine the best ecological and engineering designs, soil types, configurations, slopes, and other features. Technical guidelines for island creation, additions, enhancement, and protection for wildlife habitats have been published by both the Army Corps of Engineers and the National Park Service (Herbich, 1992a; Landin, 1980, 1992b). When not constrained from doing so by the least-cost environmentally acceptable alternative rule, the Army Corps of Engineers continues to maintain habitats and nourishes eroding both natural islands and those of human origin using dredged material. Nesting islands are an example of restoration and creation in a landscape scale (that is, a category or habitat lost in an ecological landscape is replaced within the landscape, but not necessarily at the site where the loss occurred). Ecological improvements are more likely to persist and to be self-maintaining if they can be carried out in a landscape context.

Dredged material use as a resource has historically included extensive development of recreational facilities and parks throughout the U.S. waterways systems, in Washington, D.C. (much of the Mall was created by filling intertidal wetlands), the Great Lakes, the lower Columbia River, and San Diego. Other historical applications have been shoreline protection, sediment stabilization, beach erosion control, and storm protection, primarily along the Gulf coast, in the Chesapeake Bay, and in the Great Lakes. It has not been used to the fullest extent technically possible where extensive erosion is occurring, however. At the same time, alternative uses have continued to surface in recent decades, such as in the creation of oyster beds, fishing reefs, and clam flats (Landin, 1989, 1992a).

Dredging and Dredged Material Placement Technology

Herbich (1992b) details dredging technology and methods, including their application in environmentally sensitive coastal areas. Generally, specialized dredges and equipment have been developed nationally and internationally for custom placement of dredged material for wildlife islands and other upland habitats, as core material for large placement facilities, berms, wetlands, oyster reefs, clam beds, fishing reefs, and beaches. A broad range of dredging and dredged material placement equipment, such as multihead pipe heads, diffusers (for better dispersement material), perforated pipes, and flexible pipes, is used for (precise) placement of material at intertidal elevations. Booms are used to reach

THE STATE OF ENGINEERING PRACTICE   51

placement locations without traversing sensitive wetlands. Light foot-pressure floating and tracked equipment can "walk" in water up to 6 feet deep and in wetlands with minimal adverse affects. Abandoned oil and gas pipelines have been used experimentally in coastal Louisiana to distribute sediments in coastal wetland restoration sites. Specialized equipment and techniques are used for construction of barrier islands, sediment entrapment to form marshes, substrate stabilization using bioengineering,[1] and planting.

Innovative dredging and dredged material placement technology in the United States is primarily the result of USACE dredging and wetlands research since 1973, and is well documented (USACE reports are generally available from the agency or through the National Technical Information Service). Research areas include dredging equipment, dredged material placement technology, structures, habitat protection and restoration, long-term fate of dredged material, contaminated sediments, and long-term monitoring criteria. The USACE also conducts technical assistance and technology transfer programs. Innovation by the commercial dredging industry is almost exclusively on an as-needed basis for application in marine habitat protection and restoration. The national, privately based dredging industry currently has no ongoing research and development program to support this work further.

Application of Dredged Material to Habitat Protection and Restoration

Dredged material has been used extensively in protection and restoration. Care must be taken to ensure that the dredged material intended for use in restoration work is suitable for this purpose (NRC, 1989a; PTI Environmental Services, 1988). Suitability can be determined through existing risk analysis and sampling techniques. Ecotoxicological evidence that indicates the presence of contaminants needs to be carefully assessed with the objective of minimizing risk. The examples that follow describe some of the more well-known current uses.

Underwater Berms

The USACE has built 23 underwater berms for storm wave attenuation, shoreline nourishment, bottom topographic relief, and fisheries habitat improvement. The Corps periodically monitors the berms for engineering stability and project performance. Only three have been monitored for environmental purposes (Clarke and Pullen, 1992; Hummer, 1988; Murden, 1988, 1989b):

• the deep water and nearshore berms off Mobile Bay as part of a national demonstration project for underwater berms, and

---

[1]Bioengineering is the coupling of traditional engineering technology with living plant material.

52   RESTORING AND PROTECTING MARINE HABITAT

- the offshore underwater berm at Norfolk, Virginia, south of the entrance
of Chesapeake Bay, primarily for its physical performance and, as an adjunct,
for fisheries production (Clarke et al., 1988; Langan, 1988).

To date, data from these three berms indicate that

- the deep water berm off Mobile Bay is stable and, in effect, is providing
artificial reef-like fisheries habitat and a refuge for numerous species of several
age classes;
- the nearshore berm off Mobile Bay, consisting of beach-quality sand, is
slowly moving with the current to nourish the beach; and
- the Norfolk berm is providing habitat to over wintering blue crabs from
the Chesapeake Bay, among other fisheries benefits (Clarke and Pullen, 1992).

Shallow Water Vegetated Habitats

The most difficult habitats to establish using dredged material are shallow
water vegetated habitats, such as seagrass meadows. Seagrass species have precise requirements with respect to current action and water quality. With few
exceptions, mitigation and restoration of seagrasses have not been successful. In
Mission Bay near San Diego, a dredging project provided ideal habitat conditions. Eelgrass plantings there established and multiplied extensively around la-
goons (Merkel, 1991; Merkel and Hoffman, 1990). This area might have recov-
ered on its own over time. Based on observations of seagrass restoration efforts,
a rule of thumb is that seagrasses will become established in areas where they
had previously occurred naturally regardless of whether dredged material is used
(USACE, 1986). Dredged material can be used in seagrass restoration projects to
provide elevations suitable for seagrass recolonization and to construct berms to
provide protection.

Oyster Beds

One recent application of dredged material involves raising bottom elevations and covering the new areas with suitable culch or gravel to provide oyster
beds. These habitats were built both accidentally and intentionally in Galveston
Bay. The USACE and the NMFS cooperated in building similar habitats in Chesapeake Bay. Early findings of ongoing research indicate that intentionally built
oyster bed habitats are achieving project objectives (Earhardt et al., 1988). The
overall effect of these projects on function and balance within the ecosystem has
not been determined.

ALTERNATIVE APPROACHES AND TECHNOLOGIES FOR MINIMIZING OR AVOIDING IMPACTS TO MARINE HABITAT

Adverse impacts on coastal habitats may be minimized or avoided through use of non-traditional and innovative methods for dredging and minerals exploitation. Some alternatives are:

- refinement of channel design and maintenance operations to minimize impacts to marine habitat and, if possible, to improve existing habitat;
- directional drilling (drilling several oil or gas wells from one location instead of dredging individual canal slips for each drilling location);
- spray dredging (spraying the dredged material over the wetland in layers under hydraulic pressure so that no spoil bank is formed);
- hovercraft (use of air-cushion vehicles (ACVs) to lift seismic or drilling equipment over the wetland on a cushion of air, thus eliminating the need for dredging). However, this technique is very expensive in comparison to traditional technology;
- use of oil and gas pipelines to distribute sediment (Suhayda et al., 1991); and
- use of coastal engineering capabilities to assist in the management of wastewater and storm water (including the use of natural marsh functions to treat sewage and wastewater and concurrently develop marine habitat).

Improving Channel Design and Maintenance

The principal objective of channel design is to provide for safe and efficient transits by vessels. The design vessel is, in effect, the largest vessel that the channel is designed to accommodate safely. Channel cross sections are based on engineering guidelines and rules of thumb for design, which are sometimes supplemented by physical scale modeling or computer-based shiphandling simulations. The latter offer more precise channel dimensions required for design vessels. This precision may reduce requirements for dredging and placement of dredged material. Shiphandling simulations are also used to address environmental concerns about channel adequacy for tankers and other large vessels (NRC, 1992b). Potentially, reduced dredging requirements could reduce turbidity and impacts on shallow water and intertidal habitats.

Sedimentation of navigation channels is a continuous process that is traditionally addressed through dredging to maintain project depths necessary to support marine commerce. Each port and waterway system is unique, necessitating site-specific examinations to determine the sources and extent of sedimentation, requirements for channel maintenance, and the potential effects of dredging operations on the local environment. Alternatives that potentially could be used to reduce sedimentation include stopping or diverting sediments before they reach navigation channels or keeping material in suspension as it passes through. These alternatives could be employed to reduce sedimentation from many existing facilities, although such action would be costly. Alternately, sediment management could be incorporated into the site selection, design, construction, and maintenance of new waterway projects and facilities. More complete and accurate hydrographic data would be needed than are normally available (NRC, 1987b). Attempts to manage sedimentation need to be carefully formed to avoid unintended side effects (Appendix B).

Physical scale modeling has been done for both channel design and environmental purposes. Cross sections could be modeled to determine their effects on an estuary's hydraulics. If the cross sections create an area of greater volume than the tidal prism, then the water flow through the system is reduced, changing the salinity, temperature, oxygen content, and sedimentation rates. A better understanding of these effects and their accommodating design could potentially lead to a reduction of impacts on existing marine habitat.

Shiphandling simulation technology has apparently not been used to determine whether equivalent safety performance in maneuvering could be achieved using cross sections designed to (1) mitigate wave or current action on contiguous habitats, (2) serve as habitat for vertebrates and invertebrates, or (3) provide migration routes for various species. It may be possible to provide cross sections that support all three uses. For example, it may be feasible in some areas to provide a substantial deep to shallow water intertidal habitat from the 25-foot depth contour to the shoreline.

Although scale modeling and computer-based shiphandling simulations potentially could be employed to help improve channel design relative to marine habitat needs, counter pressures could reduce design effectiveness for this purpose. For example, channel improvements lag years behind changes in ship technology. The result is that channel configurations are routinely stressed well beyond design ship parameters because of economic pressures and competition between ports. Even where improvements are authorized, there is great pressure to minimize costs because of increased cost sharing responsibilities of local sponsors (NRC, 1992b). Thus, sloping a channel wall to the 25-foot depth contour could increase dredging requirements, increasing project cost. Other alternatives to modify channel design to satisfy habitat objectives would be subject to similar pressures. Another issue is who would pay for the added modeling, simulation, or construction costs associated with the marine habitat objectives.

Alternatives to Access Canals for Mineral Exploration and Production in Coastal Marshes

The construction of access canals for oil and gas exploration and production in coastal marshlands results in significant direct and indirect losses of marine habitat. Canals can also lead to salt water intrusion in estuaries and blockage of

THE STATE OF ENGINEERING PRACTICE   55

natural channels. Alternatives for substantially reducing the need for canals and reducing the impacts of those that are constructed include directional drilling, spray dredging, and the use of air cushion vehicles.

Directional Drilling

Directional drilling is a subsurface mineral-recovery process that usually creates a nonlinear wellbore track from the surface to a recovery zone beneath, occasionally several miles from the drill site. Directional drilling is often used in coastal Louisiana to avoid disturbing sensitive environmental features (such as barrier islands, endangered species, or wetlands). This technology could also reduce the number of drilling sites needed in a given field.

Directional drilling is more complex than drilling straight downward because of the increased and variable pressures on the subsurface equipment, loss of lubricants, and increased chances of well blowout. Drilling angles are usually less than 30° (<2° per 30-meter change in the vertical) for vertical drilling and less than 20° with multiple curvatures (<1.5° per 30-meter drop). Directional drilling is generally 15–70 percent more costly than conventional methods (Louisiana's average cost is 30 percent or more).

The technical feasibility and safety of using directional drilling for certain oil and gas wells have been evaluated in Louisiana since mid-1982; the procedure, known as a geological review, involves a state petroleum geologist and petroleum engineer. Its purpose is to minimize the area and number of dredging access canals and well slips in wetlands (Scaife et al., 1983). A geologic review meeting can reduce adverse impacts on vegetated wetlands by

• shortening access canal or access road lengths by directional drilling to proposed bottom hole locations or to geologically equivalent strata;
• eliminating proposed access canals/well slips and board roads/ring levees by directional drilling from open water or from existing slips or ring levees within the directional drilling radius of the proposed bottom hole location; and
• allowing advance planning of field-wide exploration from one central drilling location instead of random canal or board road dredging to individual locations.

Directional drilling engineering practices succeed because

• an appropriate technology is applied in a mixed institutional setting of environmental managers, geologists, and permit applicants;
• the additional costs of directional drilling assumed by the permit applicant are generally known and acceptable to the applicant; and
• knowledge of the coastal ecosystem affected (primarily wetlands and

56   RESTORING AND PROTECTING MARINE HABITAT

barrier islands) is sufficiently understood to be persuasively applied as a management and regulatory tool.

Spray Dredging

High- and low-pressure spread dredging are the two types of hydraulic dredging being used infrequently in the Louisiana coastal zone to construct oil and gas access canals and well slips. Cahoon and Cowen (1988) provide a comprehensive assessment of these technologies. The advantages of spray dredging over conventional bucket dredging include:

• It creates no spoil banks, resulting in less wetland habitat destruction. In addition, the method maintains the low elevations prevalent in coastal wetlands throughout the life of an active oil and gas well.
• Spray dredging may result in less damaging impacts on localized hydrologic conditions. Sheet flow across vegetated wetlands and tidal interchange through surrounding waterways may be less affected by spray dredging. Further, spray dredge barges are usually smaller and require less draft than bucket dredge barges. More remote and shallower areas may be accessed with less disturbance of water bottoms.
• Spray dredging may result in slower or less compaction of underlying sediments, thereby slowing subsidence rates.

The disadvantages of spray dredging include:

• It is less efficient than conventional dredges, thereby increasing placement costs for dredged material.
• Costs can be 2–14 times higher than bucket dredging.
• Pollution risks increase when an oil spill or well failure occurs (the lack of spoil banks may allow contaminants access into surrounding wetlands).
• It is considerably less effective in aquatic substrates and wetland swamp habitats and where underwater obstructions (such as logs and stumps) are common.
• Equipment breakdowns are frequent, especially where organic materials occur in the sediments.

Options for improving the technology and use of spray dredging include:

• Spray dredging costs reported during geologic review meetings could be evaluated to determine whether the habitat value and acreage of wetlands to be impacted by a proposed project justify the added costs to the applicants.
• Additional funding could be provided for scientific research to examine

THE STATE OF ENGINEERING PRACTICE   57

the elements of projects that use spray dredging for the purpose of developing
data and analysis to better understand the potential of this technique.

- Equipment could be more efficient and cost effective.

Air-Cushion Vehicles

The use of ACVs to avoid long-term impacts on coastal tundra wetlands of
the North Slope arctic oil fields has been discussed in both general and technical
publications (Sikora [1989] is a substantial review). Both drilling barges and
smaller support craft that utilize ACV technology are in regular use in that region. The advantages of the ACV technology are:

- It would eliminate the majority of the dredging for exploratory wells.
- The need for maintenance dredging is likely nil.

The obstacles to their use are:

- No demonstration or field tests in other coastal habitats have been conducted for more expensive alternative equipment.
- No minimal regulatory or economic impetus exists for oil exploration
companies to consider their general use.
- Substantially increased transport and placement costs for the excavated
material (the cost per cubic yard is two to five times that of traditional placement
technology).

Industry practices will likely continue to rely on a proven infrastructure in the
absence of a workable and cost-effective or required alternative.

One option, therefore, is for states or the federal government to provide an
economic incentive grant to a recognized ACV company or petroleum exploration company that would underwrite the costs of drilling and producing an oil or
gas well with ACV equipment where marine habitats could be affected. Some
expenses (landowner royalties and lease payments) could be minimized by conducting the project on state-owned lands. If a well were productive, then grant
expenses could be recouped from production profits. Such a project could provide a unique opportunity for determining the technical feasibility of using ACVs
as placement equipment, conducting an in-depth economic analysis of production costs associated with the ACV use, and determining the degree to which
impacts on habitat are avoided or mitigated.

Management of Wastewater and Storm Water

The management of wastewater and storm water, especially in coastal urban
areas, is a large and complex problem. Essentially, estuaries and coastal ocean
areas are, in effect wastewater and storm water disposal areas. Although consid-

58   RESTORING AND PROTECTING MARINE HABITAT

erable efforts have been undertaken to control and treat wastewater including the
use of freshwater wetlands for natural treatment of wastewater in some locations
(EPA, 1985; Gearheart and Finney, 1982; Gearheart et al., 1982; Reddy and
Smith, 1987), these remain major sources of nutrients and sedimentation which
affect water quality, and ultimately, the fate or quality of marine habitats. The
need for integrated coastal management to systematically and effectively address
wastewater and storm water issues was examined by the NRC (1993). Coastal
engineering capabilities are resources that could potentially be applied to con-
trolling wastewater and storm water, and thus to improve water quality. Because
this report addresses engineering capabilities to restore and protect marine habitat, the use of marine wetlands and engineering capabilities for other purposes,
such as treatment of wastewater and storm water, were not assessed. Although
there might be potential applications in select locations, perhaps using marine
wetlands as a final stage of treatment, there are significant concerns that any
pathogens and pollutants that were introduced into an ecosystem could threaten
the health of wildlife, fish, and nearby human populations. There are also significant concerns that water quality could be degraded. Therefore, in order for such
applications to be environmentally acceptable, they would have to be seriously
examined with respect to policy, legal, human and environmental health, scientific, and technical considerations.

IMPLEMENTATION FACTORS AFFECTING
USE OF TECHNOLOGY

The foregoing discussion centered on the present use of technology in marine habitat management as seen by practicing experts (Yozzo, 1991; Appendix
D). Several important factors have restricted the use of protection and restoration
technology. They include:

- limited predictive capabilities for shoreline change;
- poor performance of some projects, including lack of project monitoring,
that undermines the credibility of protection and restoration technology, particularly for mitigation projects;
- lack of evaluation procedures and criteria to determine success of restoration projects, particularly in regard to inherent values of environmental (including ecological) benefits;
- lack of national policy and commitment to protect and restore marine
habitats;
- uncertain professional qualifications of individuals or organizations engaged in protection and restoration work resulting in a range of technical expertise that affects project performance;
- a relatively young and rigid regulatory framework in which adaptive management is basically nonexistent;

THE STATE OF ENGINEERING PRACTICE   59

• lack of technical qualifications needed for decisionmaking about and oversight of restoration technology applications among regulatory personnel (discussed in Chapter 5);
• limited information transfer and training for practitioners (discussed in Chapter 5); and
• cost.

Shoreline Change Predictive Capabilities

The capability for predicting shoreline change relative to temporal (time) and spatial process scales is limited, and confidence levels tend to be low. Research that enabled even those accuracies that are attainable is are only about a decade old. Limited prediction capabilities are directly related to limitations in the knowledge of coastal processes, discussed in Chapter 2.

Time Scale Predictions

Storm-related dune erosion can occur in a single day. Localized beach erosion may take a month to a year. Effects of sea level change can take on the order of 10–100 years or longer. The predictive capability (and confidence in the result) decreases as the time scale increases. In coastal engineering, 30–50 years is generally used as the project life span. Predictions of project performance beyond this time scale have little utility within the present state of knowledge of coastal processes. The traditional coastal engineering time scale is unrealistic for marine habitat projects because of their dynamic nature. The understanding of their natural functioning relative to coastal processes is even less well developed. Although near-term predictions are possible for some marine habitat protection and restoration, their appearance and performance much beyond the near term cannot be estimated with reasonable confidence.

Spatial Scale Predictions

Predicting spatial scales is problematic. Coastal engineers deal with orders of magnitude ranging from 10 meters to 10 kilometers. Generally, predictions with moderate confidence levels relative to coastal processes can be made on the 1-kilometer scale relative to specific structures, such as a groin. Broad predictions on any scale have relatively low confidence levels and are particularly difficult on the 10-meter scale. For example, it is difficult to determine if, when, or where a barrier island will move over the long term. With the exception of beach habitat that coexists with traditional coastal engineering work, the coastal engineering profession has not focused much attention on spatial relationships between coastal processes and marine habitat or ecosystem dependencies.

Spatial scale relationships are being vigorously developed within an emerging discipline referred to as landscape ecology (Turner, 1989). Ecologists have achieved moderate confidence levels in predicting habitat change in the near term on a small scale. Spatial relationship predictions for areas over the 1-meter scale are less reliable. Mathematical models and simulations are just beginning to be developed.

Performance of Habitat Protection and Restoration Projects

In the absence of reliable predictive capabilities for all time and spatial scales, project performance, from an applied technology perspective, is the single most important factor in determining the appropriateness and effectiveness of protection and restoration technology. Failure of a project to achieve its objectives does not establish the track record or credibility needed to advance the state of practice, although lessons can be learned through careful documentation and analysis. Inadequate performance of mitigation projects, in particular, has resulted in challenges to mitigation as an environmentally acceptable approach to destruction of habitat in return for a promise of full restoration of a degraded habitat elsewhere (NRC, 1992a). Views on mitigation range from stopping all wetland impact permitting and the associated required mitigation to requiring full execution of all permitted marine wetland restoration (for mitigation) projects *prior* to authorizing the activity for which mitigation was the tradeoff. Because success in marine habitat protection and restoration is critical to advancing the state of practice, an approach to attaining project goals and objectives is described in Chapter 6.

Professional Qualifications of Practitioners

The qualifications of individuals and organizations performing habitat protection and restoration work directly influence the effective application of scientific knowledge and engineering capabilities and, ultimately, project performance. Application by less than fully qualified individuals compounds problems associated with limitations in knowledge and capabilities. Identification of individuals and organizations qualified to perform marine habitat management work can be difficult. Although all states have license requirements for professional engineers, only about one third of practicing engineers are licensed (Anderson, 1992). Few licensing requirements pertain to environmental work; those that do have been enacted by local jurisdictions often lacking the professional expertise necessary to operate a credible specialty licensing program (Anderson, 1992; Eisenberg, 1992). A recent explosion in the number of voluntary registration and certification programs, including some with no professional credibility, has undermined the perception of certification as a means of identifying qualified practitioners (Eisenberg, 1992). These issues are discussed in Chapter 5.

THE STATE OF ENGINEERING PRACTICE

Regulation of Restoration Projects

Based on practical experience, regulatory programs have not been particularly successful in ensuring project performance to design objectives. This situation is attributed in part to the cost of conducting monitoring to determine project performance, the cost of enforcement, the relatively young status of regulatory programs directed toward habitat protection and restoration, and turnovers in federal and state regulatory enforcement personnel. These factors make it difficult to maintain a cadre of qualified regulators.

General Status of Restoration Regulation

The U.S. Fish and Wildlife Service, Forest Service, Soil Conservation Service, and Army Corps of Engineers have been conducting nonregulated habitat restoration for more than 70 years. Regulations governing the type of habitat restoration permissible and its design are less than two decades old. As with most new regulations, permitting issues have dominated the concerns of regulators, regulated industries, and third-party interests (such as environmental groups).

Recently several ad hoc and regulatory agency-sponsored wetland mitigation permit compliance reviews in Florida, Oregon, Louisiana, and New England, received wide notice and third-party comments. All these compliance reviews involved a nonrandom selection process based on projects that could be easily identified and located. Because the criteria used were not part of the original project goals and objectives, a percent failure figure or percent success is meaningless. It is generally accepted that problems exist in most permitted marine wetland habitat restoration projects. No other habitat types were reviewed.

SUMMARY

A broad range of technology has been applied over a wide variety of habitat projects. Although there are some gaps in technical capabilities, they are not limiting factors for most projects. The more constraining factors in technology application relate to an incomplete understanding of the ecological functions of marine habitats relative to habitat enhancement, restoration, and creation. A substantial body of literature is available describing marine habitat management projects, technologies, and monitoring regimes. Valuable lessons can be learned from both successful and unsuccessful projects when comprehensive monitoring is planned and executed. These lessons can be applied in subsequent project planning, design, and implementation. The major gaps in scientific knowledge and engineering practice and predictive capabilities are known. Research can be conducted to establish the informed basis needed to overcome scientific and technological impediments to marine habitat management projects. In the absence of suitable predictive capabilities, project performance is the principal technical factor in determining the appropriateness of restoration technology. This does not provide a suitable basis for resolving uncertainties. Application of the technology is impeded by inadequate professional qualifications of some practitioners and regulators and by the regulatory process itself.

4

The Application of Protection and Restoration Technology in Marine Habitat Management

Whether a particular marine habitat protection or restoration project should be undertaken depends heavily on whether there is reasonable probability that the desired habitat can be successfully established and maintained. Many projects have been completed; some achieved stated objectives, others have not. Each has site-specific features and responses, and experience sometimes suggests broader application. Descriptions and case studies are available, and the body of literature about specific technologies is growing (Appendix C). These materials are an essential resource for learning about technology and project performance. Coastal engineering projects that did not adequately address marine habitat in planning, design, and construction are also a valuable resource. Individually or collectively, projects offer opportunities for the adaptation and use of protection and restoration technologies in other settings.

The site-specific case studies summarized in Appendix B are representative of the best and the worst of several hundred marine habitat management projects for which documentation is available. Their successes and failures relate to planning and implementation and to potential applications of technology. Site-specific case studies include:

- habitat assessments using species life histories (including shrimp habitat loss from port development in Tampa Bay);
- waterway development impacts in the Savannah River, Georgia estuary;
- Chesapeake Bay protection and restoration initiatives;
- Tampa Bay wetland restorations;
- San Francisco Bay wetland restorations;

64   RESTORING AND PROTECTING MARINE HABITAT

- environmentally sensitive development of Kiawah Island, South Carolina;
- Seabrook Island, South Carolina inlet engineering;
- marsh restoration and creation using dredged materials;
- creation of waterbird nesting islands in North Carolina; and
- underwater feeder and stable berms.

Additionally, three case studies examine specific technologies:

- artificial reef technology and applications;
- bioengineering applications for coastal restoration in the United States and Germany; and
- GIS applications in marine habitat management.

Locations of the cases studied are shown in Figure 4-1.

CASE STUDY FINDINGS

The findings presented in this section are drawn from the committee's assessment of the case studies provided in Appendix B and the case study and project literature identified in Appendix C.

Setting clear, reasonable goals in the planning stages is critical to project performance.

Project performance hinges on effective goal setting because the goals are the primary basis for planning and design. Thus, managers must decide at the outset on a project's end product. Among the factors to be considered in the goal-setting process are:

- factors specific to the region, habitat, and species involved;
- possible institutional constraints, such as funding and regulatory limitations;
- ecological concerns;
- project specific performance criteria as a basis for gauging success; and
- a time frame for evaluating project performance.

When project managers clearly defined how a certain measure or structure will serve the project site, there was a basis for determining whether and to what degree project objectives were satisfied. Although a project may achieve its goals and objectives, benefits to the natural environment depend heavily on how well ecological considerations were incorporated in goal setting and design.

The Dauphin Island, Alabama, national demonstration project for underwa-

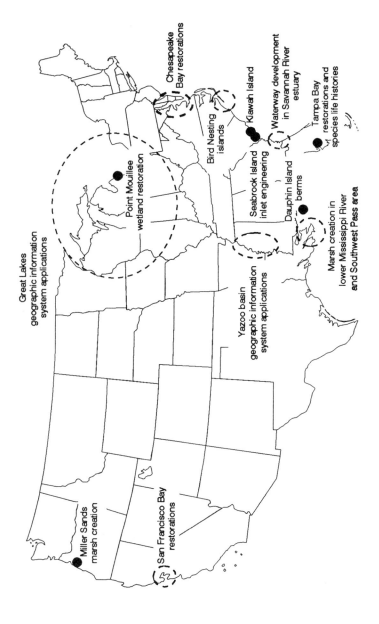

FIGURE 4-1 General locations of habitat protection and restoration projects and applications of technology examined in Chapter 4.

66   RESTORING AND PROTECTING MARINE HABITAT

ter berms illustrates the use of traditional coastal engineering technology in shoreline protection and habitat restoration. The project protects not only areas of both commercial and residential interest through attenuation of wave energy and erosion but coastal habitat as well. Project proponents foresaw positive impacts on marine habitat because the berms would replace deep water habitat with habitat that is essentially an artificial reef. During project coordination, U.S. Army Corps of Engineers (USACE) project managers determined that the underwater feeder and stable berms would complement beach nourishment measures rather than replace them in shore stabilization efforts. Performance could then be compared with what could be reasonable using traditional shore stabilization measures. Because of uncertainty about effects on the marine habitat, standby measures for relocating dredged material to traditional disposal sites were included. A long-term monitoring program was established to provide data for assessing project performance. Data and analysis indicate that the berms are performing as designed for shore stabilization and also as effective fisheries habitat, particularly the stable berm (Clarke and Pullen, 1992). Careful planning in this case contributed to a successful demonstration project; it has served as a model for similar shoreline protection efforts in New York, North Carolina, Texas, and California.

A multidisciplinary approach to project planning and implementation, involving a stable, multidisciplinary team, increases the chances for success.

Marine habitat protection and enhancement planning and implementation necessarily require the expertise of both coastal scientists and engineers. Multidisciplinary studies ensure that all elements of coastal processes and functions are taken into account. The key to the Kiawah Island, South Carolina, development project's success was an independent multidisciplinary professional team that performed a comprehensive environmental assessment of the area (Mark Permar, personal communication, December 4, 1992). The development corporation's engineering team met frequently with the independent assessment group to exchange information and concerns. Their reflections were incorporated in design and construction. Project objectives for development and habitat management are being met. Because practitioners cite the lack of communication between engineers and scientists and a lack of knowledge of basic ecosystem processes as barriers to beneficial applications of technology, the multidisciplinary approach at Kiawah Island is a useful model for future projects. Pointe Mouillee, Michigan, Miller Sands, Oregon, and several other projects that incorporated multidisciplinary teamwork for planning, implementation, monitoring, and open communication with the affected publics have achieved and continue to achieve performance objectives. It is noteworthy that restoration underway in coastal Louisiana pursuant to the Coastal Wetlands Planning, Protection and Restoration Act (P.L. 101-646) involves an interagency task force for planning and develop-

PROTECTION AND RESTORATION TECHNOLOGY 67

ing restoration projects. In contrast, the U.S. Army Corps of Engineers' Savannah River estuary project did not achieve design objectives; technology was applied without adequately taking ecosystem and hydraulic processes into account. Waterway improvement objectives were not achieved and fisheries habitat was severely impacted (design flaws have since been corrected, although not before adverse impacts occurred in the ecosystem). These projects are detailed in Appendix B.

A long-term management strategy involving preproject, concurrent, and postproject monitoring can provide valuable information from both successful and unsuccessful projects that can be incorporated into planning and design of subsequent projects.

For valuable insight on performance of design relative to field conditions, a comprehensive monitoring regime is required. Well-planned preproject, concurrent, and postproject monitoring allows a team of coastal scientists and engineers to learn from past successes and failures. At Windmill Point, Virginia, primary project objectives for the first marsh creation project designed by the Army Corps of Engineers were not met. A temporary protective sand dike serving as a breakwater in an area that was often exposed to high wave energy eroded before the marsh had stabilized. Although most of the marsh washed out, two remnant islands and a protected shallow water habitat remained and proved useful as fish and wildlife habitat. These conditions were ascertained through extensive monitoring of the project area for more than 20 years, from planning through evaluation. The important information gained was incorporated into the planning and design of subsequent projects. Other projects that demonstrate the value of long-term monitoring include the Dauphin Island's underwater berms in Alabama, Salt Pond Three restoration in San Francisco Bay, and Miller Sands marsh in Oregon (see Appendix B).

Pilot projects with rigorous performance monitoring regimes are one effective way to study the application and effectiveness of engineering technologies and to promote future project success (NRC, 1990c).

Pilot projects with rigorous monitoring regimes are important to the success of future projects. A pilot study on the construction of offshore underwater stable berms off Norfolk, Virginia, preceded the Dauphin Island national demonstration project. The study involved berm construction and a long-term monitoring program to determine project performance. Analysis of the data that were collected confirmed the effectiveness of stable berms to prevent shoreline erosion, even in the event of large, episodic storms. Just as the Norfolk study was used in planning the Dauphin Island project, results from the Dauphin Island national demonstration project were used for other projects along the Atlantic,

68 RESTORING AND PROTECTING MARINE HABITAT

Gulf, and Pacific coasts. Continued monitoring of these projects is providing further information on their performance relative to episodic storms.

It is sometimes necessary to implement pilot studies slowly. Experience shows that they must be carefully planned and executed so that data obtained are adequate for scientific and engineering analysis. Rushing a project to implementation may be at odds with the time frame needed to effectively collect a full range of scientific information about the site and project performance. Thus, projects that are urgently needed would not appear to be optimal candidates for pilot studies. Yet, even where a project is not optimal for supporting scientific research, it may nevertheless provide a unique opportunity to gain insights not feasible using laboratory experiments. Although the potential value of demonstration and pilot projects can be high if lessons from them can be broadly applied, they nevertheless tend to be expensive relative to the information gained, primarily because of both near- and long-term monitoring needs and associated costs.

Available technology can potentially be applied to a greater extent to benefit marine habitat through the use of alternative, non-tradition, and innovative solutions.

Alternative applications of available technology have sometimes resulted in the unplanned creation of valuable habitat and demonstrated that there may be a potential for broader, planned application of the technology. For example, the unplanned creation of waterbird nesting islands along the Gulf, Atlantic, Great Lakes, and Pacific coasts demonstrated the potential use of dredged material as a resource rather than as a waste (spoil). For example, artificially created nesting islands in North Carolina estuaries were originally mounds of material dredged for the purpose of maintaining navigation channels (Appendix B; Landin, 1992a). The islands then developed naturally, ultimately providing habitat suitable for a range of waterbirds and other nesting birds, including habitat for some threatened and endangered species. The successful colonization of these sites by waterbirds, although unplanned, demonstrated that the concept could be more broadly applied. In general, the subsequent creation of islands with dredged material in other locations, some done accidentally and some intentionally, has also provided waterbird nesting habitat. At the islands' present state of development, only a trained eye can distinguish these from natural islands. The general success of nesting islands suggest that other alternative, nontraditional, and innovative applications of technology may also be feasible, particularly as it relates to the use of dredged material in habitat protection and restoration work.

Habitat restoration (and sometimes creation) replaces one habitat type with another.

PROTECTION AND RESTORATION TECHNOLOGY

Restoration projects reestablish degraded habitats, albeit replacing one that is judged to be of inferior quality but that may be supporting or complementing habitat for a single species. Created habitats may or may not establish habitat at the expense of another, depending on prior use of a project site. For example, the creation of nesting islands for sea and wading birds discussed earlier and in Appendix B replaced deep water fish habitat with island and intertidal water habitat. The fact that habitat is converted from supporting some species to supporting others often creates competition between the missions and habitat interests of the various federal and state agencies responsible for habitat management. Similarly, even environmental groups may find themselves in conflict when favored species are threatened by or are not covered to their satisfaction in restoration and creation plans.

To prevent unintended and potentially devastating losses of critical habitat, a holistic ecosystem approach to management of marine habitat is required. Seagrass beds associated with coastal wetlands offer a safe haven for many juvenile fishes. A salt marsh restoration or creation can provide a source of nutrients to these juvenile fishes, but the marsh will be virtually useless if seagrass beds are lost during construction or thereafter through changes in water quality and hydrology. By working together, ecologists and engineers can identify critical habitat and plan measures to prevent habitat degradation and loss.

Flexibility in the planning and design of marine habitat protection and restoration projects to accommodate local conditions can improve the potential for successful outcomes.

What works in protection or restoration projects at one site may not work at another due to differences in local conditions. Examination of projects in different regions indicate that different approaches can be used effectively to restore vegetation as an element of marine habitat projects. Two successful habitat creation and restoration projects (Mississippi River delta and Pointe Mouillee, Michigan) allowed natural vegetation to colonize and without plantings. The Miller Sands, Oregon, project, on the other hand, required use of eight intertidal plant species to recolonize the site. These projects achieved revegetation objectives because the approach used was purposefully matched to local conditions.

When there are gaps in scientific data needed for decisionmaking, expert local knowledge can be solicited. For example, incomplete planning during port development resulted in filling one shallow water area of Tampa Bay. Although the environmental sampling required under the permitting process was conducted, sampling for possible overwintering shrimp populations at the proposed fill site was not performed. Placement of fill to create industrial land resulted in the loss of some of the most important muddy bottom habitat for overwintering shrimp; 25 percent (1,200 of 4,800 acres) of the habitat for over wintering shrimp was destroyed. This loss could have been avoided had project managers identified the presence of an existing commercial fishery and obtained local information (Appendix B).

Federal, state, and local policies geared toward marine habitat management influence project performance.

Federal, state, and local policies are generally seen both as a stimulus for coastal restoration and as impediments to habitat protection and restoration (Chapter 5). Without regulatory programs, there would be little impetus for mitigation and restoration aside from environmental advocacy. Policies having a positive influence include Florida's 1987 Surface Water Improvement and Management Act (SWIM) from which recent wetlands restoration projects in Tampa Bay benefited. The act established a dedicated restoration (and creation) program. SWIM efforts in Tampa Bay focused on the physical creation of lost habitats, such as wetlands and seagrass beds. Recognizing that their staff were not sufficiently experienced to design and supervise restoration projects, SWIM programs managers contracted with a multidisciplinary team. The ensuing comprehensive planning, design, and implementation resulted in all nine Tampa Bay projects' achieving project objectives.

SUMMARY

Successes in marine habitat protection and restoration have often involved multidisciplinary collaboration; careful planning, design, and implementation; and long-term management strategies, including performance monitoring. Where project success has not been achieved, these same features were typically absent. Valuable lessons learned from both successful and unsuccessful projects can be applied in subsequent project planning, design, and implementation.

5

Institutional Issues Affecting
Marine Habitat Management

The wealth of information and practical capabilities that are available for applying engineering technologies to protect, enhance, restore, and create marine habitats are discussed in Chapter 3. Yet much of this potential remains unused or underused in day-to-day marine habitat protection and management activities. This situation reflects the staying power of the status quo at all levels of government and industry; it also reflects society's institutional framework for approaching stewardship of marine habitat resources. Although protection or restoration of marine habitat is implied in *no net loss of wetlands* (a goal espoused by the 1988 National Wetlands Policy Forum), a sustained, universal commitment has not been demonstrated. Other than wetlands, marine habitat is not well-addressed in national policy. General, albeit poorly defined, goals have been developed to achieve *no net loss* (National Wetlands Policy Forum, 1988). But there are no universal guidelines or standards for even the most basic restoration work, and those guidelines that are available are not enforced consistently. Nor are there national or state licensing requirements for practitioners, although local license requirements are beginning to appear (Eisenberg, 1992). The information exchange network is evolving, but many practitioners are still groping for information on restoration techniques, experience, and guidelines. Important information about the biological and physical structure of specific habitats and life history patterns of aquatic plants and animals is often not available. What is disseminated often focuses exclusively, or nearly so, on projects involving emergent wetlands. In addition, there are major disincentives and few incentives for either public or private initiative. Coastal engineering as a discipline faces a great challenge and opportunity to advance the state of practice as it relates to these institutional weaknesses. Engineers, scientists, and policymakers could improve professional development, establish universally accepted performance standards, improve technology transfer, and remedy institutional constraints in many ways, as discussed in this report.

INSTITUTIONAL ISSUES

The Absence of National Direction

There is no national commitment to protect, enhance, restore, and create marine habitats. Current programs and policies lack a clear focus on managing whole ecosystems and area marked by fragmented and uncoordinated action (NRC, 1992a).

The commitment most like a national policy is found in the Coastal Zone Management Act (CZMA)[16 U.S.C. 14-51 et. seq.]: to "preserve, protect, develop with proper environmental safeguards, and where possible, restore and enhance the resources of the nation's coastal zone." Its inherent ambiguity is reflected in the history of conflict over development permits under state programs that implement the act and in rounds of litigation wherein the federal government opposes state safeguards for marine resources (for example, *Secretary of Interior* v. *California*, 52 LW 4064 [Sup. Ct. 1984]; *Norfolk Southern Corp.* v. *Oberly*, 24 ERC 1586 [D.C. Del. 1985]). The most powerful legal authority for the protection and restoration of marine resources is found not in the CZMA but in Sections 404 and 1313 of the Clean Water Act (CWA). The regulatory program that implements the acts' provisions is jointly administered by the EPA and the USACE. Section 404 regulates dredge and fill activities and wetlands including coastal waters and estuaries. Section 1313 establishes requirements for development and approval of coastal water quality standards. Additional legal authority has been conferred on EPA and the NOAA under the 1990 amendments to the CZMA to set both coastal water quality criteria and technical standards for agriculture.

Except for protection and despite the aforementioned legal authorities, no single federal agency has primary responsibility to protect, enhance, restore, or create marine habitat. This has resulted in a lack of coordination among the programs of the various agencies, although present agency responsibilities do provide some checks and balances. Recognizing that marine habitat is only one of the many important environmental responsibilities of federal agencies, reorganizing agency structure and responsibilities for marine habitat management purposes alone is not supportable. Nevertheless, it would be desirable to improve coordination requirements and processes while also retaining the beneficial aspects of the existing checks and balances.

More than a dozen federal construction, regulatory, management, and construction agencies, including EPA, USACE, the NMFS, USFWS, the Federal

INSTITUTIONAL ISSUES   73

Emergency Management Agency (FEMA), the Soil Conservation Service (SCS), and the Bureau of Reclamation have responsibilities for marine habitat management. The location of the field offices are based on considerations other than marine habitat and one agency's field office locations bear no relation to those of another. This complicates coordination of marine habitat management responsibilities and projects. Responsibility is also distributed to regional bodies, such as regional fishery management councils. At the federal level alone, a project in Louisiana, for example, may concern the Army Corps of Engineers offices in New Orleans and offices and laboratories in Vicksburg, Mississippi; the EPA in Dallas; the NMFS in Baton Rouge; the USFWS in Lafayette, Louisiana; the SCS in Alexandria, Virginia; and the Gulf Coast Fishery Management Council in St. Petersburg, Florida. The situation is similar on every seaboard. Coordinating a single marine project among these federal agencies, to say nothing of coordinating a plan, can be a demanding challenge.

Agencies with significant responsibilities for protecting and restoring marine habitat, such as NMFS and USFWS, regularly find their environmental interests in conflict with those of other federal and state development agencies; their environmental interests may also be subordinated to or competing with interests of other programs within their agencies. Competition for stewardship versus exploitation of resources can result (NRC, 1992a).

The authority of some agencies with responsibilities for marine habitat management is limited mainly to commenting on development proposals. A consequence of this limited authority is the agencies' inability to insist on the full use of avoidance and restoration technology to maintain marine habitats. Both the NMFS and USFWS have equal authority under the Fish and Wildlife Coordination Act of 1958 to request that a permit be denied for a development project subject to the Section 404 process. The internal policies of these agencies on when to elevate decisionmaking to a higher level are different and are also affected by the number of permits, which vary by the numbers of species and geographic areas for which each agency is responsible and staff resources that are available. For these reasons, the NMFS, which manages fisheries but not fish habitats (national marine sanctuaries are managed by NOAA's National Ocean Service), elevates its concerns about marine habitat restoration projects and requests denial of permits less frequently and more selectively than the USFS. Further, both agencies are inconsistent in submitting comments on proposed development activities; often they fail to evaluate fully the adverse effects on wildlife (Bean, 1983).

The Army Corps of Engineers and the USFWS entered into a funding agreement (Fish and Wildlife Funding Agreement) whereby the Corps transfers funds to the USFWS to support USFWS obligations under the Fish and Wildlife Coordination Act. The NMFS has no such agreement. With the additional funds, the USFWS can devote more effort evaluating and commenting on activities that impact marine habitat than it otherwise could. Because both the USFWS and

NMFS are vested with similar responsibilities under the Fish and Wildlife Coordination Act, it is reasonable to expect that both would benefit from such agreements. Then both would have more opportunities to produce balanced reviews of impacts on marine habitats.

Marine resource protection and enhancement projects are further limited by the vast difference in federal funding provided to ports, highways, canals, and coastal development projects, as opposed to restoration and regulatory functions. In 1990, Congress partially addressed this imbalance in the Coastal Wetland Planning, Protection, and Restoration Act (P.L. 101-646), known as the Breaux–Johnson Bill, which authorized appropriations generated from a gas tax on small engines for the restoration of coastal resources; these monies are presently directed almost exclusively to Louisiana. In sum, the federal establishment is operating in the marine environment through a various separate agencies, under conflicting and limited authorities, and under severe funding restraints.

Without a strong national priority within each agency to improve the status and acreage of marine habitats, these resources will continue to deteriorate or be lost, notwithstanding the availability of coastal engineering technology that could be used. Goals could be developed for the many pieces that comprise the coastal picture. The Army Corps of Engineers, for example, could adopt a national goal concerning wider use of dredged material as a resource for marine habitat management and establish milestones for each of its districts. Similar goals could be developed for mitigating coastal habitat losses and, for that matter, their avoidance. EPA goals to relieve waters of excess nutrient loads and other marine pollutants could be specifically targeted to marine habitats. Another approach is acquisition of marine habitat from the private or commercial sectors to protect it from development. The purchase of acreage for use as habitat preserve could be a USFWS goal. Such acquisitions would be visible and measurable signs of progress. Another option is to designate marine habitat under federal jurisdiction for special protection, such as is done in NOAA's Marine Sanctuaries Program.

Federal, state, and local agencies operate coastal projects that have been in place for decades. In most cases, these projects were initially designed for a single purpose. A systematic review of such projects to determine the feasibility of modifications to benefit marine habitat is desirable; in fact, the Army Corps of Engineers has specific authority (Section 306, Water Resources Development Act of 1990) to review its projects. Other agencies that need similar authority could request it, but have not done so.

Conflicting Guidance

Although coastal habitat restoration projects are more common in recent years under the impetus of Section 404 and CZMA regulatory programs, state, federal, and regional agencies have not agreed on guidelines for addressing the basic issues involved in marine habitat restoration and other resource improvements. Policies and objectives compete not only among the agencies with marine habitat responsibilities but also among habitat-related programs within the agencies. The differences in agency responsibilities greatly affect agency support for projects and often result in conflicting guidance. The conflicting guidance plus the absence of a process that at least maximizes cooperation, threatens project success. Each agency's authority and program objectives could be reviewed to identify the conflicts that are relevant to marine habitat management as well as those that are beneficial.

Government agencies, coastal developers, biologists, and engineers do not necessarily agree on what a successful restoration project entails. The lack of agreement on criteria to evaluate results becomes especially acute when a project is proposed as an offset to or in "mitigation for" known losses from a proposed activity that converts natural habitat. Evaluation of the project's purposes, its location, the natural functions to be restored, their quantity, quality and value, and their similarity or dissimilarity to the resources lost is the subject of ad hoc negotiations producing widely different requirements. They vary not only from region to region but also among permittees for developing identical resources at nearly identical times within the same geographic area.

These disparities erode the credibility of marine restoration for developers and environmentalists alike. For developers, the process is an exercise in developing the least-cost option, an additional price to be negotiated. For environmental groups, it is a form of roulette, with the likely incremental loss of some if not all the marine resources at stake.

One existing mechanism that could be used to remedy the fragmented organizational authority is regional fishery management councils. The United States has eight regional councils with responsibility mandated under the Magnuson Fishery Conservation and Management Act (16 U.S.C. 1801 et. seq.) to maintain fishery stocks at levels that can be harvested and not depleted. They do so by developing a fishery management plan for each fishery they are managing. As specified in the Magnuson Act and in the policies and procedures of each council, habitat must be considered as part of plan development and of regulations for management under the plan. Each council has a habitat committee responsible for examining plans. The committee may develop rules and regulations for the habitat of fishes that are managed, even when the habitat is landward of the council's usual area of responsibility. The council also reviews permit requests submitted to other agencies, and the agencies must address their questions and reservations. Council authority for habitat conservation is rarely used except in the permitting of artificial reefs and the creation of special management zones for habitat enhancement of fishery resources (Robert Mahood, personal communication, March 8, 1994). Most activities that directly impact marine habitat are regulated in some manner, although the operation of recreational boats is with few exceptions not regulated to protect marine habitat (such regulation would be very difficult due to political considerations, the vast areas in which recreational boating activity occurs, and limited enforcement resources). Although there has been considerable variability in the performance of the FMCs, the infrastructure is in place. Potentially, the FMCs could be used to promote improvements in the stewardship of the nation's valuable marine habitat resources and an ecosystem approach to fisheries management, although measures to ensure stewardship at appropriate levels would need to accompany increases in responsibility.

FMC actions involving marine habitats could benefit greatly from some type of general criteria and integration of specific goals. These could involve national, regional, and local habitat management plans that are coordinated among the agencies and interested parties. Although hard economic values of particular species and their population levels would probably remain difficult to quantify, the relative importance of the general elements and the desired scale of habitat needs could be discerned to assist decisionmakers in resource allocations. Where measurable project goals have not been established (and in some cases where they have), the project site is compared with an adjacent control or natural area, particularly for determining faunal similarities such as fish populations (Lewis, 1992). For example, Landin et al. (1989c) compared 11 sites to 29 similar reference sites over 19 years in the fortieth of a series of studies. These comparative studies can be used to set performance standards for individual projects. It is hoped that relative economic values can be translated into specific projects and costs. This information, in turn, would be useful in identifying project objectives and priorities. The potential for opportunistic habitat creation as an alternative to current responsive mitigation techniques could then be realized. Habitat project coordination, although challenging (NRC, 1985d), is highly desirable for directing and encouraging future development of technological systems and innovative methods in support of marine habitat work.

Limited Compliance, Monitoring, and Enforcement

The unavailability of accepted standards and criteria for marine habitat restoration is exacerbated by the frequent absence of requirements for follow-up monitoring to determine the effectiveness of the effort and even by the absence of enforcement necessary to ensure basic compliance. Although the Army Corps of Engineers and other agencies do require monitoring, it needs to be carefully structured to provide effective measures of performance. Determinations are frequently performed in a cursory manner; because the habitat looks as it should, it is considered a success. But restoration work may overlook fundamental ecosystem functions. Tidal creeks and channels associated with marshes, for example, offer a haven for juvenile fishes and exhibit high biological productivity. When these areas are not incorporated in restoration, the site's ecological value is diminished. Restoration as a mitigation effort often pays too little attention to ecosystem functioning to be effective, then monitoring must be both technically and scientifically sound to be effective.

INSTITUTIONAL ISSUES

A recent survey by the Army Corps of Engineers and the state of Florida determined that, of all coastal mitigation projects analyzed over a recent 3-year period, more than one half were not completed and nearly one third had not even begun (Roberts, 1991). One consequence, among others, of this failure to ensure compliance is to make it less costly for a developer simply to go through the motions to construct something that looks right than to provide an ecologically viable product, albeit at a potentially higher cost. Practitioners employing sound marine habitat restoration practices and technology are then at a competitive disadvantage when the efficacy of project construction techniques and habitat performance is not validated.

The lack of monitoring perpetuates the lack of knowledge about what works and what does not. Monitoring of coastal restoration projects varies widely with the nature of the habitat in question, the restoration technology, the capabilities of the project sponsor and contractors, and the funds available. Success rates among ecosystems vary from 10 to 80 percent. Expenditures for the design, engineering, construction, and monitoring of a successful restoration project may well exceed $1 million, depending on its scope. Whether it would be far more cost effective not to alter or destroy marine habitat than to restore or replace it would depend on site-specific circumstances. It is important to recognize that the time frame that is required for the return of all natural functions is not known; it may be on the order of decades. Therefore, a project is not necessarily a failure if all functions have not returned within a couple of years. This is a particularly important consideration with respect to restoration or creation projects offered in mitigation of habitat conversions and to the mitigation banking concept, particularly in those instances where an existing habitat is converted before the replacement habitat has been fully established and is performing to whatever criteria are accepted for the replacement project.

Despite the risk of failure in restoration projects and the potentially high costs of true success, government agencies and private developers are turning to the promise of restoration and creation as a means of complying with regulatory requirements and the announced federal goal of *no net loss*. One problem is that developers want to move ahead without waiting for a determination of whether a restoration or creation effort is successful, a process that may take more than 10 years. The alternatives of advanced mitigation and mitigation banking are experimental. The real issues in mitigation are that it lacks standards and certainty in performance, although improvements in each area can increase costs due to monitoring and corrective action that may be indicated (thus affecting the project cost-benefit ratio). Applied indiscriminately and without strict guidance, monitoring, and analysis, restoration used as mitigation trades resource losses for promises. This can jeopardize both the technology and the philosophy behind mitigation and restoration. To the extent that restoration and creation technology succeeds, it will be believed and supported. To the extent that it is viewed as a pretext to destroy marine resources, it will fail (Kusler and Kentula, 1990; Landin, 1992a; National Wetlands Policy Forum, 1988; Thayer, 1992).

Regulatory Programs and Constraints

Although regulatory programs for the protection of marine resources are a major impetus for restoration, they are also major impediments to effective habitat protection and management. Section 404 of the CWA and coastal management program requirements (stating that harm to marine resources should be avoided where possible or minimized and mitigated where impacts cannot be avoided) has stimulated development of new technology to restore and create marine habitats. Without these requirements, developers were seldom motivated to invest in marine habitat projects. To a considerable extent, therefore, advances in enhancement, restoration, and creation technology will be made in close proportion to the rigor with which the regulatory programs are implemented. Experience with the CWA and other pollution control laws shows that new technologies appear for all kinds of processes, from bleaching paper to treating sewage, once regulations require them.

The benefits of strong regulatory programs notwithstanding, a real danger is their being too rigid for innovative applications of restoration and creation technology. Practitioners report that the conflicts arising from state and federal agency regulations and regulatory programs constrain successful restoration (Yozzo, 1991). Regulators need to look beyond simple opposition to any proposed change. Specifically, large-scale restoration and creation projects are needed for important resource areas. They could be funded in part by the parties responsible for loss of the areas planned for human development. In addition, partnerships may need to be developed to mobilize resources and to spread funding responsibilities. Such arrangements are appropriate for mitigation banking, an approach for which the federal government could provide leadership and guidance.

Disincentives

Federal and state agencies continue to operate under policies that have not kept pace with environmental protection generally or the restoration and creation of marine habitat specifically. Despite recent federal legislation incorporating an ecosystem approach to management, powerful constraints remain.

The most obvious disincentive is the lack of funding for both restoration and the regulatory programs whose authorities facilitate some but not all private restoration. Practitioners cite funding as the most important constraint (Yozzo, 1991); funds are simply not available. Given this situation, hard choices need to be made. The general lack of funding is exacerbated by funding imbalances that reflect the continuing bias for projects for which economic benefits can be quantified. The imbalances also reflect the common property nature of marine re-

INSTITUTIONAL ISSUES

sources that, because they belong to no one, fail to garner the strength of the constituency generated by shippers, real estate developers, and other private concerns. The WRDAs of 1986, 1990 and 1992, attempted to redress this imbalance, at least within the Army Corps of Engineers, by directing that further development projects incorporate the benefits from environmental enhancement of marine systems. To ensure adequate consideration of enhancement of marine systems during project evaluation, ways to make habitat protection, enhancement, restoration, and creation economically competitive and desirable as project components need to be further developed (Landin, 1991). Ways to provide innovative private funding and sharing of environmental costs are now encouraged under Section 103 of WRDA 1992.

Cost is also a factor in precluding or at least slowing the development and application of technology to micromanage habitats. For example, control of water levels in small habitats may require maintenance of an infrastructure that responsible agencies often cannot afford. In turn, they are not motivated to develop innovative techniques that could lower the costs. A case in point is the possible development of comparatively small mechanical systems to modify the transport patterns of sand near tidal inlets, both to improve navigation and to prevent erosion in localized areas. Such systems (Clausner et al., 1990; Jenkins and Bailard, 1989) and analogous ones for transporting sediment out of reservoirs into downstream water courses, debated more than two decades ago, have not yet been implemented. Field testing is generally inadequate for determining their applicability in the coastal zone.

Funding constraints are felt throughout federal agencies, to the level of personnel responsible for providing specific results (for example, so many miles of channel maintained) on a fixed budget. The system lacks the flexibility to add environmental costs, even for greater environmental benefits.

Strict cost standards are still imposed internally on projects critical to coastal restoration, such as the use of dredged material for marine habitat creation. The total volume of dredged material in coastal Louisiana, for example, estimated at 90 million tons per year, is about the amount needed to balance the current rate of natural subsidence and subsidence of human origin such as that resulting from hydrocarbon and groundwater extraction. Levee systems prevent about 10 million tons of material from naturally entering and replenishing the marsh (Davis, 1992; Kesel, 1988), except where water control structures have been built and levees breached. However, the material is not always dredged near where it is most needed to support environmental work. Even with the massive amounts of material available and despite its importance for feeding existing marshes, the Army Corps of Engineers continues to apply a self-imposed least-cost environmentally acceptable disposal standard. In practice, this equals *least cost*, requiring local project sponsors to assume the additional cost of using dredged materials to achieve environmental objectives. Sediments that could benefit marine habitat management are often dumped offshore, or more often, into confined disposal facilities where the sediments are lost to the ecosystem.

In addition to funding disincentives, the most fundamental institutional constraints on adopting new and beneficial technology are the power of the status quo and the added cost of conducting business. Port authorities, construction firms, federal agencies, landowners, and others prefer the predictability of the status quo unless it is clearly in their interest to change processes and practices. They resist changes that increase costs unless they perceive a tangible benefit. Resistance to change is apparent in the slow adoption of existing technology that would prevent harm to marine systems altogether, such as the increased use of directional drilling and the use of overmarsh vehicles to access oil and gas locations, as well as in simple restoration technology, such as backfilling dredged canals on their abandonment. None of these technologies is a panacea to avoid harm to marine habitat, but each can potentially reduce significant adverse effects. Resistance (in the form of maintaining the status quo) lies at the heart of the problem and reinforces all the difficulties noted in institutional change. A further complicating factor is that conflicts often arise when reconversions are attempted; for example, fishermen often object to backfilling access canals.

The Lack of Incentives

Because threats to the coastal zone are varied, a broad understanding of the range of problems is needed so that incentives to protect coastal resources can be developed. An explosive coastal population, degraded water quality, and large-scale sea level rise and erosion are just some of the threats. The totality of existing programs offers some incentives and some disincentives to remedy the trend of habitat degradation and loss, but many programs fall short of desired objectives. The Coastal Barrier Resources Act, for example, restricts the use of federal funds for development in designated coastal areas in an attempt to discourage development of vital areas. Although the program has deterred some development, more areas need to be designated under the act for it to have any large-scale impact. The National Flood Insurance Program was similarly designed to minimize losses from development in flood prone areas, including the coastal zone. There is anecdotal evidence that success in minimizing losses also has the effect of attracting coastal development, creating further pressure on marine habitat. Other programs, such as those under Section 404 of the CWA and the Swampbuster program of the Food Security Act of 1990 (which authorizes the SCS Wetland Reserve Program with a goal of 1 million acres by the year 2000), do not specifically address marine habitat management, although these authorities can be applied in conjunction with management programs. Only those activities involving the deposition of dredge or fill material are regulated under Section 404; much litigation is associated with determining what constitutes a deposition. Further, the Section 404 permit process does not deter coastal development projects. Nevertheless, CWA provisions constitute powerful legal authority if used creatively and effectively by federal authorities with marine habitat management responsibilities.

On the private side, few economic incentives appear to be available to landowners, developers, engineering firms, and others interested in solving marine resource problems. Creative use of large-scale and carefully controlled mitigation banking is one possibility. Several states are experimenting with relief from taxation, and reduced tax assessments as financial rewards for individual environmental initiatives.

Many new types of incentives are feasible. One possible incentive to prevent wetlands loss is a property tax break for landowners who preserve their wetlands. The establishment of nonprofit wetland preservation trusts, providing donors with tax benefits and financial assistance, is another. Fishery habitat protection could be funded by Fishing Stamps in the same way that Duck Stamps are used to protect waterfowl habitat. These are just a few ways to develop incentives under or modeled after the current system. There is a long way to go, however; using market incentives to preserve coastal areas is means to improve the incentive base. With the Clean Air Act Amendments of 1990 as a model, government at all levels could use economic principles to motivate polluters and developers to preserve habitat. Transfers of development rights may be possible through a bank established to buy, sell, and guarantee loans for the private transfer of development rights from preservation and agricultural areas to designated growth areas or through land exchanges. For example, the Chesapeake Bay Critical Area Commission used transfers of development rights to preserve vital marine areas within the bay area.

One incentive that has met with considerable success in minimizing the adverse environmental impacts of industrial development is identification of the best available technology for industrial categories under the Clean Water and Clean Air Acts. This concept has not been applied to the dredging or restoration industries, whose activities both heavily impact the coastal zone and hold the promise for considerable restoration benefits. Whether advanced by incentives or rigid technology standards, advancement in the technologies of damage avoidance and restoration at reasonable costs is overdue. Although some incentives can be established within the current institutional boundaries, it is unlikely that the full potential of incentives will be realized broadly until national priorities for marine habitat protection and restoration are set and implemented.

Decisionmaking

Most activities that directly impact marine habitat are regulated in some manner, although the operation of recreational boats is with few exceptions not regulated to protect marine habitat (such regulation would be very difficult due to political considerations, the vast areas in which recreational boating activity occurs, and limited enforcement resources). The decisionmaking process associated with regulation involves numerous agencies, is generally time consuming, and suffers to some extent from a lack of mutual understanding and communication among the parties involved. Technical aspects of engineering activities are generally not understood by some of those involved, in some instances the regulators. On the other hand, engineers need to recognize that those with whom they must communicate are mostly nonengineers such as regulators, scientists, elected and appointed officials, and members of the interested public. Although the process is cumbersome because of the multiple interests involved, it nevertheless works. A single agency cannot be expected to develop the necessary expertise to evaluate activities without information and advice from outside sources. Establishment of a "superagency" for centralized management is unrealistic and contrary to the need for a balance of interests in the decisionmaking process (NRC, 1985d). Absent establishment of time constraints associated with decisionmaking, it is difficult to expect significant improvements in the time required to evaluate regulated activities.

Professional Development

Historically, the engineering profession has responded well to emergent societal demands and concerns (NRC, 1985a,c). With heightened public environmental consciousness, the profession faces a great challenge and opportunity to contribute to conservation endeavors. Unfortunately, the pace of technological changes and societal pressures may exceed the engineering profession's ability to respond effectively (NRC, 1985c), but engineers and scientists concerned with marine habitat protection and management need not wait for institutional or technological advances to improve the state of practice. As practitioners become more involved in innovative projects, they will place greater demands on the system for better educational, regulatory, and technological advances, and more opportunities to effect change in the system will emerge (Blackburn, 1993).

The technical competence of regulatory personnel as an institutional factor is of particular concern, and the turnover rate is high in many regulatory offices at both national and regional levels. This situation can result in a loss of institutional memory within an office and, for the regulators, little experience in regulatory matters, a limited understanding of the technology that is applied, and poor understanding of scientific and engineering criteria for assessing project performance. As is true of engineering and environmental professionals engaged in marine habitat management, most regulators are not specifically licensed or certified to work in environmental disciplines. If, as is frequently the case, neither builders nor permitting personnel have formal training or lengthy experience in marine habitat protection and restoration, then regulators with uncertain qualifications (but considerable position-related influence) are overseeing practitioners with equally uncertain qualifications and performance records. It is then

INSTITUTIONAL ISSUES

difficult to differentiate between the successful, experienced regulator and the one who lacks the knowledge, skills, and experience to perform effectively. Although professional training courses are available, especially for federal regulators, the opportunity to participate in such training is often limited by workloads, training opportunities, and travel costs, among other factors. The ultimate result is that the ineffective or incorrect application of technology that might result from defective regulation can inadvertently discredit habitat protection and restoration.

Education

Ecology Training for Engineers

Coastal engineering is the composite of relevant engineering disciplines applied in the coastal zone. It is usually taught at the graduate level. Even so, engineering programs that incorporate ecological principles in their perspectives, attitudes, and philosophy are rare at both the undergraduate and graduate levels. An awareness of the need to incorporate interdisciplinary studies is growing (NRC, 1985a). Nevertheless, additional interdisciplinary training and practical experience under the supervision of qualified professionals is usually needed for engineers wishing to enter the coastal engineering field.

Academic institutions could require engineering courses relating to ecological studies. Students whose career goals are in the coastal engineering profession, for example, could be exposed to courses on marine habitat types, functions, environmental monitoring, and evaluation criteria. Although it is difficult to stretch the demands of an ever expanding engineering curriculum, the demand for multidisciplinary planning in all aspects of engineering practice require that academic institutions instill in the students an appreciation of how other disciplines affect the success of the engineering profession. On the job training and continuing education are important to maintaining, building, and refreshing skills in any profession, but they cannot substitute for the essential base knowledge provided through engineering curricula. A challenge for academic institutions in this regard is acceptance by the faculty that multidisciplinary programs are essential to the success of the practicing engineer (Blackburn, 1993).

Engineering Training for Scientists

Unlike engineering training, ecology training often includes courses on science and society or environmental science and public policy. These courses are generally offered at the graduate level and are not required. It is usually in these courses that engineering issues are raised. Awareness of the value of the relationship between the ecological sciences and engineering in determining the success of projects with environmental components is growing; courses dedicated to this relationship could be developed to provide a more substantial and practical basis for scientists entering related fields.

Curriculum Needs

Engineering curricula are fixed and limited by tradition, accreditation criteria, and faculty interests. Examination of course descriptions indicates the absence of a strong movement to include ecological principles in the engineering curriculum, even in institutions with coastal environmental and public policy programs. The majority of engineering curricula are professional-task oriented. Curricula requirements provide little opportunity for courses beyond the primary disciplines, and in most programs, such courses as science and society are electives. With only a few exceptions, truly interdisciplinary curricular efforts are found in graduate programs, and they are modest. Even when an undergraduate curriculum is truly interdisciplinary, students usually complete a double major to achieve this objective. Concurrently, if departments do acknowledge the need for an aquatic ecology course and it is available in another academic unit, under current academic philosophy it is offered only as an elective. Educational institutions could recognize the importance of meeting important multidisciplinary needs including the introduction of engineering principles to environmental science and ecology students. A corresponding goal for engineering students, particularly those planning to work on environmental projects, is exposure to ecological principles that are now essential to successful engineering practices.

Continuing Professional Education

Significant changes in the traditional engineering curriculum are not expected. The demands on student time to pursue pure engineering requirements continue to grow. Institutions cannot expand the engineering curriculum to equip the graduating engineer fully to address ecological components of engineering projects. But academic institutions can instill in the students a recognition that successful professional development includes more than continued engineering education. To some extent of more immediate importance, it also includes educational and professional development relating to environmental considerations that are inherent in engineering practice. Engineers who practice in specific branches of engineering for many years become specialists, but often at the expense of losing touch with engineering fundamentals and the new issues and problems that engage the profession. The need for training across disciplines is acute. All groups involved must become aware of these needs before significant positive changes in the system can occur.

In-house training programs and workshops are one mechanism to keep practitioners up to date on the principles and tools of the profession. The content of training programs and criteria for standards of performance could be determined

INSTITUTIONAL ISSUES

by the professionals in the academic community, government, and private sector. Special sessions that address these issues could be developed and presented at regional and national meetings. Sessions on wetland ecology could be presented at the annual meetings of professional and trade organizations. The latter does occur, but the emphasis could be placed on the practicing coastal ecologists' use of information from these workshops.

Ecologists also need continuing education programs to understand the limitations, questions, and opportunities in engineering practices in the marine environment. There have been fewer training programs directed at the ecological than at the engineering audience. Generally, ecologists tend to be more broadly trained, a fact that may account for their adaptability to problem solving when they work with engineers on specific projects. Practitioners report that planning and implementation by individuals with ecological training and an understanding of the constraints of coastal engineering practices resulted in more successful marine habitat restoration projects, depending on what criteria were used to determine success.

Professional Regulation

Few agencies and institutions involved in marine habitat protection and management require third party accreditation for their employees, although some engineering firms require professional engineer licenses for attaining senior status (Yozzo, 1991) (see Box 5-1 for regulation and certification terms). However, professional licenses are rarely required for work in marine habitat management, nor are market forces or custom sufficiently developed to motivate voluntary

---

BOX 5-1
Professional Regulation and Certification Terms

Licensing An authorization in the form of a license granted by a government or an entity to perform or provide a function or service. Licensing is rooted in a government's police powers and is applied for the purpose of protecting public health, safety, and welfare.

Registration A listing of an individual or entity with and by a government or nongovernment body. A listing does not grant authority or address qualifications.

Certification A voluntary act by an individual and a certifying entity that, in some organized fashion, measures an individual's qualifications to perform a specialized function. No authority or privilege is conveyed, although custom or market forces may require or necessitate an individual's obtaining certification.

Accreditation A voluntary act similar to certification, except that it is applied to institutions and programs, not individuals.

SOURCE: Anderson (1992)

certification of individuals or accreditation of organizations engaged in marine habitat management beyond that noted above.

Existing Licensing Requirements   Professional licensing statutes for engineers exist in all states. Because of exemptions in the laws, however, only about one third of all practicing engineers hold professional engineer (PE) licenses (Anderson, 1992). Professional engineer licenses by themselves do not ensure that an individual is trained or current in environmental or coastal engineering practices or in the application of protection and restoration technology. But licensing provides at least one way to define competency.

Voluntary Registration and Certification Programs   Another approach to professional regulation is voluntary registration or certification (Box 5-1). The latter is sometimes an intermediate step toward formal regulation through professional licensing. The first voluntary certification for environmental engineers was introduced in 1955 by the American Academy of Environmental Engineers (AAEE) (Anderson, 1992). Currently more than 60 professional organizations that operate voluntary registration or certification programs for individuals in various environmental disciplines. Some certification programs have substantial expertise, experience, and peer review requirements and are considered credible by environmental and engineering professionals. However, a number of registration and certification programs are nothing more than a listing or issuance of a certificate upon payment of a fee. Some registration and certification organizations publish directories that are simply listings or that include brief professional profiles of certified experts (Anderson, 1992). The sheer number of registration and certification programs works against the credibility of all of them (Eisenberg, 1992).

None of the organizations operating credible programs has the constituency or interdisciplinary breadth necessary to encompass all environmental and engineering professionals working in habitat protection and restoration (Eisenberg, 1992). Although several professional organizations with credible voluntary certification programs are working on a national standard and organization for professional certification, the effort has just begun (Anderson, 1992).

Project proponents as well as individuals offering coastal engineering services for marine habitat management may be unaware of certification programs for ecologists, environmental professionals, and environmental engineers. They may also not be aware that marine habitat project managers do not use certification as a criterion for selection of individuals for work on a project.

Some Pros and Cons of Certification and Accreditation   Voluntary certification and accreditation are not panaceas; they do not guarantee professional qualifications or competency. However, the fact that an individual or organization has invested time, effort, and resources in obtaining a specialty certification or accreditation from a credible organization and is willing to ascribe to a professional code of ethics is another filter or test of professional qualifications. Certification does not eliminate the project sponsor's implied responsibility to verify an individual's credentials, background, project history, and references. The same screening applies to noncertified individuals as well.

Certification can be used to build personal confidence and professional credibility within peer groups. It can also help build the professional standing of individuals who serve as expert witnesses. If credible accreditation were developed within the marine habitat management field, it too could serve as one screening measure in determining an organization's capabilities and reliability. Yet not all individuals in the engineering disciplines support specialty certification and accreditation. Some see little return on the investment of time and resources. Others do not perceive personal improvement in individual credentials, professional recognition, or an organization's professional reputation.

Professional Regulation as an Institutional Constraint   Under the present circumstances, it is difficult to determine which practitioners can effectively apply habitat protection and restoration technology. In the absence of accepted professional credentials, some local jurisdictions are establishing their own licensing requirements for environmental work. If this trend continues, many licensing requirements with widely varying criteria will likely result (Eisenberg, 1992). Multijurisdictional licensing could easily result in a jumble of time-consuming and costly overhead requirements. Such a development would be a substantial institutional constraint for an emerging discipline, particularly because many respected practitioners in both small and large companies work nationwide.

Public Education

Educating the public and the policy officials is very important for the preservation of marine habitats because history shows that a well-informed public provides the impetus for policy and sociological change (Water Quality 2000, 1992). Public support requires public understanding of what is involved in marine habitat destruction and how it can affect the structure of the coastline, protection of the mainland from storms, habitats of migratory birds, nursery grounds for fish and shellfish, and the public at large. Public education on marine habitats is a primary mission and objective of the National Sea Grant College Program of NOAA. Extensive information on curricular development and implementation and public education is available from Sea Grant Colleges and their associated extension programs. It is also important that the public in districts directly or indirectly affected by marine habitat losses understands the implications for themselves and the ecological system. Public expectations must be guided by accurate information about reconstructed habitats and what they can be expected to accomplish. To achieve these information objectives, the public education

88   RESTORING AND PROTECTING MARINE HABITAT

process would need to cross all affected and interested public sectors. It could then help the public focus on the issues and would further needed change in public policy and administration.

Limited Information Transfer

Considerable national attention is focused within the scientific community on emergent wetlands and by the Army Corps of Engineers on use of dredged material as a resource. Each year, the Society of Wetlands Scientists holds national forums at which information on progress is shared and published. A wetlands restoration workshop (with published proceedings) has been held annually since 1974. Similarly, the USACE hosts an annual forum in which developments in beneficial uses of dredged material are discussed and published. Other conferences and meetings also occur on related topics such as wetlands, fisheries, water quality, and wildlife. Environmental journals and magazines periodically feature articles and papers on habitat restoration. *Restoration & Management Notes*, a quarterly, serves as an information exchange forum that features restoration activity in coastal communities. A growing number of publications that provide technical insight and case histories. The National Sea Grant Program and the six USACE national dredging and wetlands research programs are particularly rich sources of restoration materials. Considerable regional restoration information is also available, for example, for the San Francisco Bay area, coastal Louisiana, Chesapeake Bay, and Florida. There is also a substantial body of literature that includes project-specific documents, but no information is available on the degree to which this literature is reaching a broad cross section of practitioners. Available information tends to be compartmented within subdisciplines and is not always readily useful or adaptable. Many of the documents acquired for this report are project-specific reports with limited circulation. Substantially more could be done to track marine habitat projects to develop a broader understanding of planning and approval, application of technology, performance, and monitoring regimes.

SUMMARY

National policy in marine habitat management lacks specific, well-developed goals and a sustained, universal commitment to action. A clear focus on managing entire ecosystems is also absent. There is no well-defined national commitment to protect or restore natural resources in the coastal zone. Although powerful legal authority for the protection and restoration of marine resources exists, it is found in the CWA rather than in enabling legislation directed specifically at the coastal zone. No federal agency has primary responsibility for balancing marine habitat protection and restoration needs with other natural resource interests. There are few common boundaries in agency jurisdiction,

INSTITUTIONAL ISSUES

location of field offices, and interests in marine resources. Marine habitat management is a responsibility of each Fisheries Management Council but, except for artificial reefs, is not well developed. There is an imbalance in federal funding provided for infrastructure development in the coastal zone relative to stewardship of coastal resources, including limited funding of some agency staffs with regulatory responsibilities in marine habitat management. Few guidelines or standards are available, and where available, they are neither consistently applied nor enforced. No formal agreements exist on criteria for measuring among parties interested in restoration work. Follow-up performance monitoring of restoration projects and enforcement of related permitted activities is often incomplete, cursory, or not done at all, leaving performance to chance and denying acquisition of data for development of valuable experience. There are few incentives and many disincentives to invest in marine habitat restoration projects; their net effect is to discourage public and private initiative. Valuation of marine habitat in benefit-cost analyses is difficult and highly subjective. National policy concerning placement of dredged material biases decisionmaking toward least-cost disposal regardless of possible environmental benefits from (more costly) placement at alternate sites. Incentives to motivate more private protection and restoration investment individually or through partnerships would require substantial policy and procedural changes at federal and state levels.

Undergraduate engineering curricula generally do not provide the multidisciplinary exposure needed for coastal engineering work. Graduate studies and training and experience beyond academic courses are required. Similarly, graduates with science backgrounds generally have limited exposure to engineering disciplines. Multidisciplinary collaboration could be advanced at the field level through continuing professional education designed to enhance cross-discipline exposure. Because there are no state licensing requirements for restoration practitioners and no universally recognized voluntary professional certification programs for individuals or accreditation programs for companies, the professional qualifications of engineers, ecologists, and environmental professionals are difficult to assess. A substantial body of relevant literature exists, albeit with a heavy focus on emergent wetlands. An information exchange network has not evolved, and widespread dissemination cannot be assumed.

Institutional weaknesses could potentially be overcome by improving professional development, establishing universally accepted performance standards, improving technology transfer, establishing universally accepted certification programs and, perhaps in the future, professional licensing requirements comparable to PE licenses, and remedying institutional constraints.

6

Improving Project Performance

Project success can be defined from various perspectives, but there are no universally accepted measures for gauging project performance or guiding evolving practices (Chapter 2). Regardless, a successful project must be sound with regard to scientific and engineering principles, and these need to be reflected in projects from conceptual stages through construction, performance monitoring, and any corrective action that may be needed.

PROJECT PERFORMANCE

Marine habitat protection and restoration are not exact science or engineering. A definitive, quantifiable outcome may not be attainable in the near or even long term. Further, project performance needs to be determined on a case-by-case basis to allow for site-specific conditions (Fonseca, 1992; USACE, 1992). Nevertheless, a means is needed to gauge performance. Whenever possible, performance criteria need to be quantitative and measurable (Berger, 1991; Canter, 1993; Westman, 1991). Use of functional performance criteria such as dissolved oxygen profiles in aquatic systems is an option, however, the methodology is less well developed than those for measuring ecosystem structure (Cairns and Niederlehner, 1993).

Restoration Project Failure

The considerable discussion of defining success stems in part from concern over significant gaps in basic knowledge about ecosystem functions and how to

IMPROVING PROJECT PERFORMANCE

replicate them. The fact that ill-planned or poorly implemented protection and restoration projects can cause more harm than good argues for a cautious approach to restoration. At the same time, the urgency imposed by continued marine habitat losses demands informed action even if scientific knowledge about ecosystems is incomplete. Recognizing that the state of practice is imperfect, project planning must reflect a general understanding of why projects fail so the basic causal factors can be considered in project goals, objectives, design, and implementation and monitoring.

Failed projects often exhibit one or more of the following characteristics (Landin, 1992c, 1993a):

- incomplete understanding of natural processes;
- poor sites or location;
- poor design;
- incorrect, sloppy, or poorly timed construction or implementation;
- lack of commitment by the permit applicant or contractor;
- inadequate monitoring and corrective action; and
- lack of expertise.

Any of these characteristics can cause failure in one or more of the following technical factors required for successful restoration work (Landin, 1992c):

- correct hydrology or elevation (stable water supply);
- suitable soil/substrate for biotic success;
- protection from wind, wave, current, and wake energies or designed resistance to these forces; and
- correct plant species and propagule selection and installation.

The Decision Model

Because the ultimate outcome of each project is performance that satisfies goals and objectives, a practical decision model is needed to guide the formation of goals and objectives, project construction and maintenance, and performance assessment (Landin, in press-a). Such a model would be

- holistic in application;
- multidisciplinary in character;
- highly disciplined (for credibility with the scientific, engineering, and regulatory sectors); and
- flexible (to accommodate the dynamic nature of habitat protection and restoration work over a suitable time scale).

The major components of a decision model for marine habitat protection

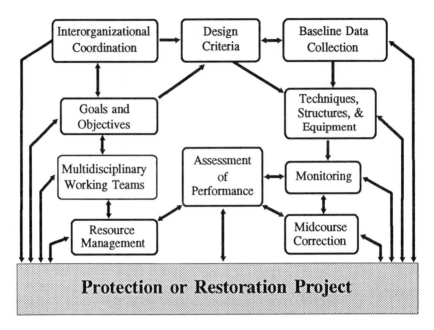

FIGURE 6-1 Decision model for achieving success in marine habitat protection and restoration projects.

and restoration (Figure 6-1) reflect an interactive and iterative approach. The model can be adjusted to fit specific circumstances.

THE DECISION PROCESS

Goals and Objectives

Setting achievable project goals (expected results) and objectives (major project elements for attainment of expected results) requires both a comprehensive understanding of the ecosystem of which the project site is a part and a thorough understanding of the social setting. Only then are all interests addressed in the planning and implementation. Project objectives will depend on whether the site will permit or support protection, enhancement, restoration, creation, or a combination of the above. Both near- and long-term objectives are essential because construction or implementation is only an interim step in project development and ultimate performance.

Both ecological and social factors may need to be considered at the outset. They may influence not only the form of the protection or restoration work but also who approves and funds it. For example, a site may be targeted for both natural and human uses, such as recreation. Sometimes the reasons for undertak-

IMPROVING PROJECT PERFORMANCE

ing a restoration project are secondary, as is typically the case in navigation projects, which are the funding or material sources for restoration. The primary project objective is then likely to be channel improvement rather than restoration. The dredged sediments cannot be used unless the first objective is met (Landin, 1992c).

An important but often inadequately addressed component of project decisionmaking is involving all the diverse parties so that their interests and concerns are accommodated and they accept ownership in project goals and objectives (Kagan, 1990; NRC, 1992b). Planners and decisionmakers are often reluctant to expose their plans prematurely, but interagency and public coordination late in a project can severely constrain its implementation and approval (Hamons, 1988; Kagan, 1990). Thus opening the planning process soon after project needs are identified is generally preferable. An open process is a principal way to ensure that all pertinent interests and concerns are identified and accommodated by decisionmakers, insofar as practical.

Project Design

Project design follows establishment of goals. Experience shows that design and implementation flexibility is key to project success. The design phase includes establishment of project-specific objectives and interorganizational coordination. Design is site specific, although there are general guidelines for all habitat types (Landin, 1992c). For example, criteria for design and construction of intertidal wetland restoration and sea bird nesting islands are clear and well tested. Most seagrass restoration and other aquatic and marine restoration are still being tested.

Baseline Conditions

Once the need for a marine habitat protection or restoration project has been identified, conditions that existed prior to disturbance or alteration need to be identified, insofar as practical, as do the nature, extent, and impact of present onsite ecological and physical conditions. This information provides a frame of reference for determining what improvements can be made and for developing improvement-specific goals and objectives. For example, a site may be able to support partial restoration to provide a habitat attractive to specific target species, such as clapper rail (an endangered species in California) and the salt marsh harvest mouse at Muzzi Marsh in the San Francisco Bay area (Berger, 1990a). Performance criteria could include establishment of vegetation of sufficient form, quality, and quantity to support target populations. Ultimate success is recolonization (natural or transplanted) of the site at planned levels. Effective application of both scientific knowledge and engineering capabilities is required. For example, when environmental factors are not adequately addressed in design, engineering components may satisfy design parameters but natural functioning of the site at design levels is not achieved. It will likely be necessary to collect at least some baseline data before specific design can be completed. Additional baseline data may be necessary if vital information such as current or wave data prove inadequate (Landin, 1992c).

Design Protocols

Permissibility and success of a project also depend on selected design protocols. Conditions and parameters that define the required physical domain must be established. The degree of complexity of the design depends on the type of habitat desired. The physical characteristics of the physical domain in turn determine management options, including operation and maintenance protocols, through application of engineering principles and technology.

Performance Criteria

Specific criteria for measuring success and a monitoring and assessment program need to be established and agreed to prior to project implementation so that all interested and affected parties' expectations are clear (Berger, 1991; Canter, 1993; Westman, 1991). Whenever possible, performance criteria need to be quantitative and measurable, although functional assessments may be an alternative in some cases.

Depending on the goals, objectives, and reasons for their establishment, different sets of criteria are needed to measure performance. For example, a project offered in mitigation for development might be held to strict ecological standards for natural functions because marine habitat is disturbed or converted elsewhere. A project providing habitat for a few client species might not require restoration of all natural functions to satisfy the species' habitat requirements in a prescribed time frame. Benefits to other species would be ancillary to principal project objectives. Of course, it is desirable to achieve multiple species benefits whenever possible. Given the gaps in scientific and engineering knowledge of ecological interdependencies, the restoration of all natural functions and diversity would improve the long-term prospects for performing to design objectives.

Technology Transfer

Design would greatly benefit from incorporation of the latest technical information. This may not always be the best tested information nor information that has been published in the scientific and engineering literature. Most information on local restoration is unpublished or can be found in federal and state agency reports and documents; there are two reasons:

IMPROVING PROJECT PERFORMANCE

- Most on-the-ground managers of restoration projects have neither the time nor the job incentives to write and publish their techniques.
- Most scientific journals exclude how-to manuscripts as applied rather than basic research or as not scientific enough for their subscribers.

Nevertheless, considerable information is available that could be used to guide restoration work if it were identified and acquired (see Appendix C).

Multidisciplinary Teamwork

Planning, design, and implementation are improved by a multidisciplinary technical team consisting of engineers, wet soils experts, environmental specialists, hydrologists, and other specialists, depending on the project's environmental and social setting. For example, the assistance of cultural resource and real estate experts may be necessary.

Planning also requires that the team meet regularly to coordinate design components and to coordinate with nonteam partners and interested parties such as cost-sharing partners and resource agency personnel. The potential for success is enhanced when the multidisciplinary team is established for the life of a project, thereby maintaining continuity. An example of the importance placed on interdisciplinary planning is the U.S. Army Corps of Engineers use of specially trained Life Cycle Project Managers in many of its districts to initiate and follow through on all phases of specific projects (or groups of related projects); the Corps also forms restoration and mitigation teams as part of the overall project (Landin, 1992c). The Soil Conservation Service, other agencies, and several large consulting firms use similar strategies for their contracted work.

Cost Effectiveness and Economies of Scale

Project cost is an important factor in determining overall success. With limited financial resources on almost all possible marine habitat restoration projects, low-cost, low-maintenance, stable structures and flexible designs are essential. A lack of funds is not the only reason for low-maintenance goals; the lack of long-term commitments of the agencies that would be responsible for maintenance and management is an important factor. Sites requiring perpetual maintenance may be lost in a matter of years from unintentional neglect, limited budgets, and a limited workforce (Landin, 1992c).

Habitat restoration requiring extensive construction, by definition, cost more than using natural forces, although the latter may take longer. Natural factors can sometimes be used not only to reduce initial construction costs but also to create conditions favorable to natural maintenance of a site, thereby lowering maintenance costs.

Whether the cost effectiveness of some marine habitat projects can be improved by taking advantage of economies of scale is uncertain. Although it may be possible to lower the cost per acre for some large-scale projects, it is not clear, relative to biological productivity or use by fish and wildlife, whether large-scale restorations offer greater potential as habitat than do small projects of 0.5–2 acres. For example, some small-scale restoration projects that are well-balanced within their ecosystems have been productive. The fact that federal agencies engaged in nonregulatory restoration work seldom attempt a restoration project of less than 10 acres (most encompass hundreds and sometimes thousands of acres) does not necessarily mean that larger is better. Only federal agencies have the mission, resources, and workforce to follow through on extremely large-scale projects (Landin, 1992c).

Evaluation of cost effectiveness is a highly challenging task. Conventional formulas for benefit-cost analysis do not always account for the full value of a habitat (Chapter 5). Further, the functional life of a particular technology is not always known, especially when the technology is new and has not been tested over the long term. Yet when at least some useful information is available with respect to the technology and the habitat, some economies of scale may be possible

Implementation and Construction

Many well-conceived and executed projects fail owing to a lack of appropriate operating protocols, particularly for maintenance of required hydrologic conditions. Although shortcomings generally result from undetected design flaws, numerous marine habitat restoration projects, both regulatory and nonregulatory, that had adequate designs were poorly implemented or constructed (Landin, 1992c).

Good construction techniques are known and practiced. Descriptions of successful engineering and environmental techniques are available from the Army Corps of Engineers, SCS, and EPA primarily, with site-specific information available from the USFWS and NMFS (Allen and Klimas, 1986; WES, 1978, 1986; Kusler and Kentula, 1990; Landin, 1992c; Landin and Smith, 1982; Landin et al., 1990a; SCS, 1992; Soots and Landin, 1978; USACE, 1986, 1989a,b). Good construction techniques include:

• use of correct equipment (such as: light-foot-pressure tracked vehicles for work on a soft substrate; and suitable dredged material placement equipment, for example, correct pipe sizes, dispersive pipe heads, and diffuser pipes, to achieve elevation without prominent mounding);
• use of suitable site preparation and planting gear, which may range from standard farm equipment to bulldozers and from hand planting to use of adapted mechanical planters;

IMPROVING PROJECT PERFORMANCE

- erection of appropriate temporary or permanent protective structures (such as breakwaters); and
- use of predictive tools (such as GIS, and assessment aids including physical and numeric models).

This generic list is only partial; good practice would expand and adapt it to site-specific restoration projects.

When the project location and design are acceptable, then restoration or enhancement success depends on

- use of the correct construction methodology and equipment, and
- the training, expertise, and attention given to detail and specifications by the project implementors (such as contractors, dredging inspectors, and site managers).

Good plans, designs, and specifications will not compensate for a poorly implemented or constructed project (Landin, 1992c).

Performance Monitoring, Measurement and Analysis

Determination of how well a project is performing once implemented requires a scientifically and technically sound, well-planned and well-executed monitoring program. Further, a monitoring regime is only useful if the data that are collected are sufficiently analyzed and applied in a timely manner in determining corrective action regimes for projects that are not performing to design and performance criteria and in the planning and implementation of future projects.

Establishing the period during which performance will be monitored is important (Risser, 1988; Westman, 1991). For seagrass bed restoration or creation, cursory postproject monitoring (simply to see whether the grasses are growing) does not indicate growth patterns or the overall present or possible future health of the ecosystem. Frequent monitoring may be required if the time for vegetation to become established at the site is uncertain (Fonseca, 1992). In general, 0–5 years is considered short-term monitoring for coastal wetlands. Monitoring beyond 5 years is considered long-term (Landin, 1992c).

Marine habitat protection and restoration projects are successful in the absence of monitoring, but the failure to monitor is not sound engineering, scientific, or management practice. Environmental and engineering monitoring is essential for the following reasons (Canter, 1993; Landin, 1992a):

- Provision of baseline data and other essential technical information.
- Documentation of techniques, on-site changes, and chronological events, such as colonization for both the project and subsequent applications.

- Documentation of performance and evaluation of the viability of restoration work.
- Warnings of impacts or impact trends that are approaching critical levels that would necessitate corrective action.
- Assessment of predictive methodologies.

Monitoring Regimes

Monitoring needs vary according to habitat type, site-specific conditions, and ultimately, available resources. With regard to environmental and engineering concerns, general monitoring guidelines can be applied. The NRC (1990b) identified a conceptual approach to designing monitoring programs and defined and examined the specific elements of designing and implementing a monitoring program. The approach that follows may be useful to habitat managers in forming a monitoring program for coastal marshes, wildlife islands, mud flats, and other submerged aquatic habitats.

Goals and Performance Criteria Initially, it is important to establish both goals for project performance and specific criteria for determining success (NRC, 1990c). These criteria determine which environmental and engineering sampling methodologies are appropriate (Berger, 1991; Cairns and Niederlehner, 1993; Landin, 1992c; Westman, 1991). It is also important to validate all monitoring methods and equipment used in order to determine variations among sampling stations. Only then can any changes recorded be correctly evaluated.

Preproject Monitoring Determination of goals and performance criteria are aided by preproject monitoring. Preproject baseline data, at the minimum, need seasonal data for no less than 1 full year. They are necessary for addressing year-round, migratory, and temporary habitat use as well as essential functional dynamics of the ecosystem. Some data may be available for some sites, but preproject monitoring will likely be necessary. Data for nearby natural habitats are also useful in determining how well and how long it may take a restoration project to achieve a reasonable level of equality. During project implementation, regular monitoring is needed to document water quality, sedimentation, and immediate and visible effects as to whether or not organisms are inhabiting the area.

The Time Frame for Postproject Monitoring Postproject monitoring begins immediately on completion of construction to establish continuity with preproject monitoring and to document conditions at the site. For the first year, it is generally appropriate to visit the site and collect data (including data from on-site monitoring systems) not less often than monthly. Weekly or biweekly monitoring may be necessary if rapid changes at or in use of the site are indicated. After

IMPROVING PROJECT PERFORMANCE 99

the first year, monitoring can generally be relaxed to monthly, perhaps seasonally. After 2 years, seasonal monitoring (at least four times per year) generally suffices. From 3 to 5 years, which is still considered short term, monitoring ranges from seasonal to annual, depending on the stability of the habitat and other site-specific factors. From 5 to 10 years, annual or biennial lower-level (and lower-cost) monitoring usually suffices. Lower-level, lower-cost monitoring can then be conducted at 5-year intervals through the project's twentieth anniversary. Annual or biannual visual inspections or limited sampling at some sites might be prudent to detect any obvious signs of developing problems. For sites with slower-growing wooded vegetation (such as is found in intertidal swamps and maritime forests), periodic site visits are desirable for several decades (Landin, 1992c).

Monitoring Parameters Effective, responsible monitoring and inspection are multidisciplinary. Engineers need data on elevations, consolidation of materials, sedimentation, and topographical changes from preproject through postproject phases. Scientists require baseline data on fish and shellfish, micro- and macro-invertebrates, wildlife, vegetation, soils, water (physical, chemical, and biological parameters), habitat structure, functional dynamics, and other environmental factors during all project phases.

On marshes of all types, seagrasses, mangrove forests, scrub and shrub, and other vegetated sites, all plantings need to be evaluated to determine survival rates, percentage of coverage, reproduction, and other growth indicators (Fonseca, 1992; Landin et al., 1989c). Where plants are allowed to colonize naturally, chronology data documenting colonization of plantings, macro- and microinvertebrate colonization and utilization, and associated functional dynamics are needed. Where plantings are not appropriate owing to the nature and type of habitat, data are needed on the invasion of undesired vegetation and its removal. Experience shows that on restored and created habitat sites, below-ground biomass does not reach natural site levels for more than two decades. Thus root formation and chemical changes in the new soils need to be carefully documented to reflect the natural processes taking place (Landin et al., 1989a,c, 1990a). A useful approach is to compare progress with conditions at a similar habitat site in the area. Although similar habitat would probably be at a mature or climax condition, it can nevertheless serve as a frame of reference for setting objectives.

Monitoring is also feasible for underwater berms, artificial reefs, other deeper water habitats, and seagrass beds. Meriting monitoring are current and wave movements and resulting sediment transport, colonization and habitat utilization by motile and nonmotile organisms, including their abundance and diversity, consolidation, topographic changes, and water quality. For seagrass beds, survival rates, coverage, and other indicators of growth should be included (Landin et al., 1989c; LaSalle et al., 1991).

Establishing permanent observation points (for example, camera stations) prior to project construction and at least three (or more) permanent transects across an out-of-water site (such as marshes or islands) can greatly facilitate data collection and aid in establishing statistical validity of the data that are collected. Random quadrants (up to 10 per transect) can be used regularly for either destructive or nondestructive sampling, depending on the experimental design. Soil borings, collection of data on micro- and macroinvertebrates in the soils and on above- and below-ground biomass, and all vegetation parameters can be taken from the quadrants. The same transects can be used as belts through the establishment of a 10 meter line on either side to record all wildlife. Enclosure cages may also be installed if nutria or waterfowl grazing is expected to cause problems with data collection.

The establishment of sampling points for in-water sites and mud flats can include fish nets, Breder traps, and other fish-sampling apparatuses. However, they may have to be set up after a project is built owing to changes that take place on-site during construction. Apparatuses used for preproject fish and other in-water data may have to be removed if permanently installed because of changes in site condition, such as elevation. Where shorebird feeding pressures are expected, installing enclosure cages on mud flats and sites adjacent to the shore may be feasible (Landin, 1992a; Landin et al., 1989c).

Maintenance and Management

Because fully developing and attaining marine habitat protection and restoration project goals typically requires years, a long-term management strategy is needed. Yet, effective maintenance and management are often overlooked. For example, a permit applicant for a mitigation project is usually required to provide baseline data (monitoring and inspection) for a maximum of only 3, sometimes 5 years. This short time period does not provide for determining long-term performance or entail the need for midcourse corrections. Similarly, federal agencies do not always allow for long-term maintenance and management.

Establishment of a long-term management strategy is desirable as part of the project approval process. An effective management strategy incorporates a commitment and the resources to execute it, monitoring regimes, and responsibility for corrective action that may become necessary during a project's design life.

SUMMARY

Success can be defined from ecological or practical perspectives. Defining success as achieving project goals and objectives is sufficiently flexible to accommodate both ecological and social (including economic) objectives and to provide a means for judging project performance in the absence of complete science and engineering knowledge. Success as determined by predefined measures can be achieved through careful coordination and planning, effective design, implementation, construction protocols and techniques, extensive monitoring and inspection, and maintenance and management. Technology transfer, adequate communication, and networking among restoration practitioners are vital, as is the need for good science and engineering. A multidisciplinary project design and implementation team can generally overcome or accommodate gaps in scientific or technical knowledge affecting design and performance.

7

Research Needs

Applied and basic research has provided considerable technical information to aid in marine habitat protection and restoration—in addition to the wealth of documentation for specific projects and technology applications. Yet, the results of basic and applied research are not always readily available; nor do they appear to be well utilized in marine habitat management.

RESEARCH PROGRAMS RELEVANT TO MARINE HABITAT MANAGEMENT

Federal Programs

Marine habitat research has been driven primarily by related missions of federal and state agencies. The research was sponsored to support these missions by improving the capabilities needed to meet assigned responsibilities. Some of the research was conducted by laboratories and field research facilities maintained by the U.S. Army Corps of Engineers (USACE), the National Marine Fisheries Service (NMFS) and National Oceanic and Atmospheric Administration (NOAA), the U.S. Forest Service (USFS), the Soil Conservation Service, the U.S. Fish and Wildlife Service (USFWS), the Environmental Protection Agency (EPA), and the Department of Energy (DOE). Most federal agencies with responsibilities for coastal zone or marine habitat management and the National Science Foundation also sponsor extensive basic and applied research under contract with colleges, universities, private foundations, businesses, and sister agencies. For example, the Army Corps of Engineers' water resources,

102

navigation, and, more recently, wetlands regulation missions are prime directives and funding sources. Thus, it not only conducted research but also provided research funds for other agencies, academia, and private organizations. Under existing federal and agency policies, most of this research is oriented toward practical application, and is holistic in nature (WES, 1992). Most basic coastal research using federal funds may be sponsored only to the degree that the resulting product can be used for an applied purpose.

State and Private Programs

Some coastal states have active research programs that include cooperative efforts under the Sea Grant Program, marine experimental stations and extension services, and sponsorship of research facilities and consortia with colleges and universities. Some conservation organizations sponsor or conduct research applicable to marine habitat management.

Industry-Sponsored Research

Companies engaged in restoration or dredging sponsor or conduct virtually no basic and little applied marine habitat protection and restoration research although applied research may be a component of projects with which they are involved. Despite its prominence in the coastal engineering profession, the dredging industry follows rather than leads the market for developing and implementing innovative technologies. Some innovation is occurring within the limits of existing technology, but the industry has not invested in research and development of technology intended for use in marine habitat management. Its position is that if a need for new technology is identified and there is an economically viable market for its use, then the industry will either develop the technology or transfer it from international applications. The U.S. marine habitat restoration market, insofar as it pertains to use of dredged material, is viewed as too small to justify investing in specialized dredging or dredged material placement technology.

Basic Research

Colleges and universities with strong coastal identities and research components conduct much of the basic research pertaining to marine habitats. Although their funding is generally from federal and state public agencies, academia has covered a broad range of research needs. The result is that substantial information relevant to habitat protection and restoration is available to the technical community, but not always conveniently or readily.

Considerable basic ecological research is sponsored by NOAA's Sea Grant Program. Results are routinely published and available from state offices of Sea

Grant. There is generally no national distribution although publications are sometimes announced in newsletters and professional journals.

Basic research conducted by federal agencies includes several decades of intertidal research in the Savannah River estuary by the DOE's Savannah River Ecology Laboratory; NMFS work involving seagrass and fisheries species (Thayer, 1992); USFWS basic research on coastal species management; USFS basic research on marine habitats; and USACE work on the long-term fate of dredged material, long-term monitoring (environmental and engineering), contaminated sediments, equipment, structures, engineering technology, wetlands, habitat restoration, and critical processes. Extensive documentation is available covering most Army Corps of Engineers research.

Applied Research

In addition to other federal agencies that conduct basic research of interest to marine habitat management, the EPA and the Federal Highway Administration (FHA) conduct applied research. EPA is administering a 5-year, $10 million Wetlands Research Program. Although the program has a regulatory focus, the EPA is broadening it beyond research relevant to Section 404 of the CWA to correspond with a broadening of the agency's role and interests in marine and other habitats (Mary E. Kentula, EPA Corvallis, Oregon, personal communication, March 16, 1992). In addition, EPA's Superfund responsibility, which includes coastal sites, may provide an opportunity to include coastal habitat research. The FHA administers a major applied research program applicable to land transportation infrastructure in the coastal zone, where wetlands may be impacted (Charles DeJardine, FHA, personal communication, October 3, 1992).

The Army Corps of Engineers has a substantial investment in research capabilities and applied research. In 1973, the Corps established the Dredged Material Research Program, which has been carried forward to five other research programs, each with separate funding: Dredging, Dredging Operations Technical Support, Environmental Effects of Dredging, Long-term Effects of Dredging Operations, and Dredging Research Programs. Each has strong engineering and environmental components requiring multidisciplinary cooperation and teamwork. More than $150 million has been allocated to these programs over the past 20 years. During the late 1970s, in response to the agency's wetland regulation responsibilities, the Corps of Engineers initiated its Wetlands Research Program. Although it is intended to support regulatory actions, since 1990 the program has been expanded to include multidisciplinary and multipurpose applied research; $22 million has been committed to these efforts through 1994. Currently one third is directed to wetland protection, restoration, and creation. About one-half of these research projects are being conducted in the coastal zone. The Corps of Engineer's restoration research overlaps considerably with its research to encourage substantially more frequent use of dredged material as a resource (Landin, 1991).

The NMFS and USFWS are both actively involved in pertinent applied research: the NMFS Coastal Habitat Restoration Program (Thayer, 1992) and the USFWS North American Waterfowl Management Plan (Robert Misso, USFWS, personal communication, March 17, 1992). In addition, the Soil Conservation Service has both Conservation Reserve and Wetland Reserve Programs, while, although not specifically research oriented, are positioned to work with and use research information from other agencies to implement habitat restoration (B. M. Teel, SCS, personal communication, March 19, 1992).

Interagency Coordination

Many federal research programs involve federal and, in some cases, state agencies with interests in marine habitat management. Because of the many agencies involved and their different missions and responsibilities, overlap and redundancy of effort as well as inefficient technology transfer are inevitable. Recently, in the face of budget austerity and national level interest in habitats generally, there have been efforts to improve the efficiency of research programs through interagency coordination. As an example, in 1989, 12 federal agencies with wetland responsibilities established a permanent interagency committee to improve their wetlands research programs. Information on federal-level wetlands research, including funding, was compiled in a public report as part of the committee's findings (WES, 1992). Although these efforts to prevent redundancy and overlap were only partially successful, they made progress in providing a more thoughtful and systematic wetlands research agenda. This approach could be used for research supporting marine habitat management.

New opportunities may develop for interagency coordination under the Coastal America Program. It is an interagency initiative to improve the stewardship of coastal resources by effectively addressing habitat degradation and loss, nonpoint source pollution, and contaminated sediments. A consortium of federal agencies made a substantial investment of resources in formulating the initiative. Its implementation and long-term support are yet to be demonstrated.

Leadership of federally sponsored restoration research is not yet established. The USACE, the NMFS, the USFWS, and the EPA are interested in a central role in setting coordinated research agendas (Thayer, 1992). The agencies are reluctant to relinquish directive authority and discretionary capabilities to other agencies or administrations because of concerns about competing interests, perspectives, and focus as well as about funding. Assessment of agency capabilities to lead or coordinate a national research agenda for marine habitat protection and restoration is beyond the scope of this report.

MULTIDISCIPLINARY RESEARCH

Although completed research covers a wide spectrum of engineering and environmental needs in the coastal zone, including multidisciplinary cooperation in research, not all important areas are well-addressed. Some involve crossover research efforts that require multidisciplinary teams, especially in wetlands restoration. But the research in these areas has been sporadic, limited in funding and sometimes in scope.

Despite the considerable applied research, understanding the basic processes affecting marine and other coastal habitats is the least developed. The gaps in knowledge about baseline habitat requirements and species interactions within coastal ecosystems are substantial. Much is known about some life requirements of some commercially important fish species, but less is known about the organisms on which they feed and other components of their ecosystems that allow survival or stress the species. These gaps not only affect the efficacy of engineering and environmental practices but also influence research on structures, biological techniques, equipment, and technologies for habitat protection and restoration. Existing coastal engineering technologies provide a relatively substantial capability, but they do not meet specialized restoration needs. Engineering gaps include specialized equipment and methodologies for placement and stabilization of construction materials in marshes and intertidal habitats, structural design, use of soft sediments as substrate materials, and the locking of contaminants in sediments to prevent habitat degradation. Advances in each of these areas could advance the state of practice in protecting and restoring marine habitats. Excess sediments and contaminants that adversely affect water quality and marine habitats also need to be addressed at their source within affected watersheds. Otherwise, the full benefits of advances in protection and restoration technologies will likely not be realized in some areas.

ENVIRONMENTAL TECHNOLOGY NEEDS

The four key technical components in marine habitat restoration are soils and substrates, hydrology (for wetlands), vegetation, and energy. When they are adequately satisfied, the aquatic and wetlands habitat conditions will be appropriate for colonization of the particular habitat by vertebrates and invertebrates. The presence of these animals is essential to restoring and sustaining natural functions. The technical components must all be effectively understood, addressed, and accommodated for restoration efforts (and use of marine habitat as shoreline protection) to succeed. Determining how to achieve optimal hydrology, which plant species and propagules to use, what elevations are appropriate, what physical, chemical, and biological soil components that affect habitat productivity are necessary, and how to deal effectively with the physical energies that influence a habitat is not well established for all coastal habitat types. A better understanding of each component and its collective implications would provide a more complete scientific basis for practical application of restoration technologies. Specific areas for research are described below.

Soils and Substrates

Coastal soils may include many variables, including textures ranging from clays, sand, shell, and rock rubble. The physical means of working with these soils to form them into suitable substrates for marine habitat restoration is limited. Needed soil-related research includes:

- conversion of bottom sediments and upland soils to suitable substrates for intertidal habitats;
- transportation and storage of hydric soils;
- care and protection of seed banks;
- consolidation and settling properties;
- characteristics and origins of soils;
- placement technology for all habitat types; and
- suitability of foundation materials.

Vegetation

Applied restoration research on plant materials includes some life-cycle requirements work on dominant intertidal marshes and other intertidal vegetated habitats. However, significant gaps include:

- species hardiness and adaptability;
- ease in propagation and transplanting for restoration purposes;
- long-term stability of substrates and plant communities;
- invasion potential (and eradication techniques, when required);
- the suitability of plant communities to provide attractive habitats for fish and other organisms; and
- use of native versus introduced species.

Fonseca (1990, 1992) identified the following specific research needs for seagrasses:

- Definition and evaluation of functional restoration of seagrass beds.
- Compilation of population growth and coverage patterns in all regions to better define growth patterns.
- Evaluation of the resource role of mixed species plantings.
- Investigation of impacts of substituting pioneer for climax species in transplanting on a compressed successional basis.

108   RESTORING AND PROTECTING MARINE HABITAT

- Refinement of culture techniques for propagule development.
- Optimization of transplant techniques, with emphasis on the use of fertilizers.
- Investigation of the importance of maintaining genetic diversity for restored beds.
- Standardization of site evaluation methodologies.

Physical Energy Systems

The physical energy affecting marine habitats is usually derived from winds (wave and coastal currents), currents (tidal or river), and wakes. All are affected by bathymetry and any energy-dampening features around or near the habitat. Technology is sufficiently advanced to predict performance of some marine habitat restorations under conditions of low physical energy. Some research conducted over the past 30 years has addressed the use of bioengineering in sites exposed to moderate physical energy. However, significant gaps remain. Research on sites exposed to high physical energy is limited, and it remains difficult to restore habitats at these sites without major protective structures. The use of geotextiles has met with some success but is not widely applied except to hold hydraulically placed sediments or for shoreline protection (PIANC, 1992b). Underwater berms are used more extensively. Neither their effectiveness in attenuation of physical energy relative to protecting coastal habitats nor their capacity to create more favorable conditions for restoration has been established, although some are functioning well as artificial reef habitat. In some instances, existing currents may be used to distribute dredged sediments to create coastal wetlands. A better understanding of the effect of energy systems on habitat could expand opportunities for restoration in areas of moderate and high physical energy.

Socioeconomic Factors

Social and economic considerations are often treated as secondary or minor to the more technical disciplines of environmental and coastal engineering. Yet socioeconomic factors are typically critical to the approval, authorization, appropriations, and acceptance of protection and restoration projects. A major gap is the inability to place a value on habitats that can be equated to the value of alternative uses. As a result, the environmental and economic benefits of habitats are typically valued at less than the alternative uses. For example, it is well known that marine habitats are essential for nearshore commercial finfish and shellfish populations. Yet there is no accepted methodology for establishing the value of each acre of habitat relative to fisheries populations, whereas the economic value of an industrial development can be projected and quantified (although not always accurately). An accepted methodology for determining the economic value of habitat and the collection of data to support such analyses are

RESEARCH NEEDS

gaps that could be filled by basic research. This research could draw on previous studies that have attempted to measure the benefits associated with protection of wetlands ecosystems (Anderson and Rockel, 1991; Batie and Mabbs-Zeno, 1985; Batie and Shabman, 1982; Batie and Wilson, 1979; Bell, 1989; Bergstrom et al., 1990; Brown and Pollakowski, 1977; Costanza et al., 1989; Farber, 1987, 1988; Farber and Costanza, 1987; Kellert, 1984; King, 1991; Lynne et al., 1981; Raphael and Jaworski, 1979; Shabman et al., 1979; Shabman and Batie, 1978; Shabman and Bertleson, 1979; Skaggs and McDonald, eds., 1991; Thibodeau and Ostro, 1981; Tschirhart and Crocker, 1987).

ENGINEERING TECHNOLOGY NEEDS

Principal gaps in engineering technology as it pertains to marine habitat management relate to precise placement and stabilization of dredged material, geotextiles, specialized equipment, structural design, contaminated sediments, and multipurpose applications, described below.

Placement and Stabilization of Dredged Material

Methods for using sandy sediments have generally been developed and refined. They are used in beach nourishment, for wildlife islands, and as substrates for wetlands and other habitats, although this latter use is sometimes controversial because of changes caused in local environments. Methods for effective use of clay and silt sediments (or sand, clay, and silt mixtures) have not been adequately researched. These soft substrates are rich in nutrients, and once stabilized, they can provide for abundant growth and productivity of coastal organisms. The key word is stabilization. Coastal engineers already know how to confine soft sediments. Substantial gaps for clays and silts exist in capabilities for:

- environmentally compatible use in habitat restoration;
- consolidation without confinement;
- bringing them out of suspension when needed to stimulate more rapid marsh or mud flat formation;
- formation of artificial reefs and berms;
- prevention of their loss into the vast ocean system; and
- locking in contaminants to reduce biomagnification.

Basic research in these areas would require multidisciplinary collaboration. Considering that about 300 million cubic yards of dredged material are dredged annually in the United States, improved capabilities to use dredged clays and silts in habitat protection and restoration could change much material that is disposed of into a valuable resource.

Geotextiles

A companion technology to improved stabilization techniques is geotextile fabric. The use of geotextiles in water resource management has expanded rapidly. In the past 15 years, the technology has advanced from 10-by-4-foot nylon bags filled with in situ sand to prevent erosion and hold back unconsolidated sandy sediments, to more flexible sand-filled Longard tubing up to 100-by-4-foot lengths laid on the estuary floor, to customized geotextile barriers up to 6 feet in diameter (PIANC, 1992b). These largest geotextiles can contain areas of up to 25 acres using pressurized and packed silt material as filling and have up to a 30-year life. The Army Corps of Engineers is field testing the latest generation of geotextiles, but the use of this technology in restoration is not widespread. There appear to be substantial opportunities for innovative use of geotextiles in protecting marine habitats, particularly with regard to erosion control, shoreline stabilization, and dredged material placement.

Specialized Equipment

Some of the new equipment for dredged material placement has have not been fully tested in a wide variety of field conditions. Equipment must function without causing more harm than good to fragile environments. Innovative placement technologies developed overseas (especially in Germany, the Netherlands, and Australia), could potentially satisfy this need. But there is little impetus for technology transfer. Studies and field tests would establish whether the technology could be adapted for use in marine habitat management.

Structural Design

Coastal engineering structures were traditionally designed to interact with and effect coastal processes to prevent erosion and stabilize shorelines. Such structures are generally not designed, constructed, or systematically evaluated for their effects on marine habitat. Nonetheless, the effects can be profound, particularly for circulation patterns and sediment transport. The engineering of the lower Mississippi River to maintain navigation channels and the construction of levees for flood protection, for example, resulted in sediment starvation of marshes. Installation of water control structures and selective breaches in levees to provide for natural replenishment of marshes have demonstrated that there is room for innovation in traditional engineering structures. Traditional coastal engineering structural applications could be examined to determine whether and to what degree design rules can be modified to minimize impacts on various marine habitats. The potential of coastal engineering structures in habitat protection could also be assessed.

Placement and Handling of Contaminated Sediments

The traditional technology for placement of contaminated sediments is confinement. But removal of sediments can release contaminants into the sediment transport stream and thus into ecosystems. Removal and placement of contaminated sediments, followed by capping with clean sediments, have been attempted in only two U.S. harbors (Landin, 1988a). More extensive work is constrained by uncertainties over the risk associated with the contaminants and their potential effects on ecosystems. Improvements in environmental risk assessment testing capabilities and assessment methodologies are indicated (Cairns and McCormick, 1992; Simmonds et al., 1992; Stout and Streeter, 1992).

Keeping contaminated sediments saturated by keeping them under water has proven best under laboratory and field test conditions to prevent mobility and environmental biomagnification (Lee et al., 1978, 1985; NRC, 1987b; NRC, 1989a; Scott et al., 1987; Simmers et al., 1986). Whether contaminants could be locked into sediments to prevent these adverse environmental effects, whether they could be decontaminated, and if they could, whether there are opportunities for beneficial use in marine habitat management have not been established. Research in this area is of interest insofar as environmentally safe dredging and placement could prevent damage to marine habitats in a system where contaminants have been deposited. The primary motivations for research, it should be noted, are not potential uses in protection or restoration, but management of those contaminated sediments that threaten environmental quality or that need to be moved for navigation projects in an environmentally safe way.

Multipurpose Applications

Multipurpose applications are those that are intended to serve ecological as well as social objectives such as shoreline protection, recreation, and public education. These applications generally involve either the use of bioengineering (the coupling of engineering technology with living plant material) or construction of multipurpose habitats using engineering technology. Bioengineering can be applied in habitat creation or restoration and for shoreline protection. When applied to shoreline protection, there may be ancillary benefits in the form of habitat. However, establishment of full natural functioning might not be an element of design, and might not be technically possible at some locations. Bioengineering has been attempted on a limited scale to stabilize shorelines. Maryland, Texas, and some other states technically and financially assist private landowners in using bioengineering as a natural alternative to structures, such as bulkheads. The largest bioengineering applications have been attempted in reservoirs (Allen, 1988, 1990; Allen and Klimas, 1986; Hammer, 1989). Results and several field tests in coastal locations indicate a broader potential for use of this technology to provide natural protection of shorelines in moderate wave energy coastal areas (Allen, 1988, 1990, 1992). Bioengineering use costs about 75 percent less than physical structures. Because habitat is created and costs are reduced, further development of bioengineering could substantially advance the state of practice, particularly private owners' application to some shorelines. Bioengineering applications developed in Europe and Australia but not yet tested in the United States could be assessed.

Creating or restoring diverse habitats using engineering technology is not a new concept. Diverse habitats offer a variety of essential life-requirement opportunities for various species including both fish and wildlife. Diverse habitats are thus preferable to habitats designed to support only a few species, although the latter may be the only option in some locations due to local conditions. Currently research in this area is limited. Emphasis in recent years has been on wetlands. However, declining stocks of important commercial fishes that depend on a range of marine habitats suggest the need for more attention to ecosystem requirements, including wetlands but not excluding other habitat types found in water bodies, adjacent uplands and islands, and river systems and watersheds supplying water and sediments to coastal estuaries.

SUMMARY

Marine habitat management research is multidisciplinary in nature and interagency in scope. There are needs for both basic and applied research regarding scientific knowledge and engineering capabilities. A better understanding of coastal processes and baseline information on coastal biota, soils, vegetation, water quality, and other scientific parameters are essential to advancing restoration practice. Likewise, engineering requirements for shoreline stabilization, erosion control, coastal energy, dredging, and dredged material placement are important and timely. Technology transfer is lagging behind research results and technology application. To advance the state of practice, emphasis could be placed on protection and restoration of marine habitats under existing research programs. An umbrella organization could be established to coordinate the federal research agenda. Alternately, a lead agency could be assigned to guide the national research effort.

8

Conclusions and Recommendations

The nation's marine habitats are precious national assets. Their ecological and economic importance are greatly threatened by both human activity and natural forces. Habitat conversion and degradation resulting from industrial, residential, and recreational activities and pollution are adversely affecting the ecological diversity and balance required to maintain the health of each ecosystem, including important fisheries resources. Unless effectively mitigated, the degradation and loss of natural functions and coastal acreage in an ecosystem inevitably and adversely affect the system's physical structure and biological productivity. Even then, near- and midterm loss of natural functions can be substantial because human pressures on remaining natural sites will increase as coastal populations continue to grow.

Marine habitats can be protected, enhanced, restored, or created with current science and engineering capabilities (although restoration of natural functioning can vary significantly). Scientific and engineering knowledge, procedures, and technologies for shoreline protection and for habitat enhancement, restoration, and creation (collectively referred to in this report as restoration technologies) are substantial, although not complete. The knowledge and technology bases nevertheless provide a strong foundation from which to launch a credible coastal engineering program to arrest habitat loss and degradation. The same base could support programs to achieve a net gain in high-quality marine habitat acreage through well-planned and well-executed protection and restoration initiatives. If habitats are restored, steps should be taken to prevent their subsequent degradation and loss, otherwise the effort will be for naught.

Further collaboration of the scientific and engineering communities is essential to advancing the scientific and technical bases for habitat protection and restoration. Multidisciplinary goal setting, planning, teamwork, and synergistic application of scientific and engineering knowledge have shown that specific habitat protection, enhancement, restoration, and creation objectives can be achieved more reliably by improving collaboration among practitioners in the scientific and engineering disciplines.

The principal obstacles to wider use of coastal engineering capabilities in habitat protection, enhancement, restoration and creation are the cost and the institutional, regulatory, and management barriers to using the best available technologies and practices. Existing scientific and engineering capabilities will not achieve their full potential in protecting and restoring marine habitat in the absence of a focused policy to guide their application. Also needed are increased flexibility in decisionmaking to allow consideration of innovative and alternate approaches to achieve goals and objectives; improved communications among practitioners, regulators, and decisionmakers; and better professional preparation for all facets of marine habitat management. Development and use of economic incentives are also needed to stimulate habitat protection and restoration by private parties and the industrial sector.

Among the recurring examples of institutionally constrained applications of restoration technology are use of dredged material for habitat improvement and creative use of marine habitats to provide nonstructural shoreline protection. Institutional constraints foster a general wariness of innovative but unproven applications of technology. Innovative use of technology is also constrained by uncertainties over the ability to replicate natural functions through restoration projects, inadequate transfer of information on technology applications, inadequate preparation for decisionmaking and project implementation, and a paucity of incentives to protect and improve marine habitat.

Protection and preservation of natural habitats are inherently better than waiting for damage or loss to occur, but economic incentives to encourage preservation of marine habitat in a natural state are few. Quantification of economic value and environmental benefits remains extremely difficult and controversial. When assessed for alternative uses, marine habitat acreage has typically been valued for natural functions at less than for industrial, commercial, recreational, or residential uses. The public has limited awareness of the environmental and economic benefits that can be achieved through consistent application of existing knowledge and technology to coastal habitat projects. Realizing these benefits fully will be difficult unless public awareness programs are implemented in support of committing public resources to protection and restoration work on the scale needed to achieve a net gain in acreage.

Applied research based on theoretical principles but conducted project by project has been an important means for advancing the state of practice. Even projects that did not meet design objectives provided important experience for future applications of technology in marine habitat management. The results and

CONCLUSIONS AND RECOMMENDATIONS

lessons learned from applied research in marine habitat protection and restoration have been supported by a variety of sources, including government agencies, academic institutions, and nonprofit groups. Not all the successes and failures are documented; nor are the worthwhile results sufficiently distributed. But much information is available and is in sufficient quantity and quality to justify continuation and expansion of both applied and basic research on habitat protection, enhancement, restoration, and creation.

DO HABITAT PROTECTION, ENHANCEMENT, RESTORATION, AND CREATION TECHNOLOGIES WORK?

Scientific Knowledge and Engineering Capabilities Can Be Effectively Applied

Current scientific knowledge and coastal engineering capabilities, although not complete, can be used effectively to protect, enhance, restore, and create marine habitats. Success in meeting project objectives is most readily achieved when multidisciplinary application of scientific knowledge and coastal engineering capabilities is systematically carried throughout planning, construction, and post project monitoring and evaluation. Knowledge of marine and estuarine systems can be applied effectively and enhanced with well-planned monitoring of the ecosystem's functions before, during, and after restoration activities, including comparisons with similar natural habitats. Traditional coastal engineering technology has considerable potential for providing protective measures for habitat management projects.

Coastal engineering technologies, such as the use of dredged material for establishment of emergent wetlands, beach nourishment and the construction of offshore underwater berms from natural materials for coastal storm protection, have proved effective in enhancing and creating marine habitat. Use of these technologies has been successful at reduced costs because of improved equipment and reductions in the distances over which dredged material is transported for placement. Dredging technology is especially important as a means to move and place bottom sediments. Most dredged material is uncontaminated and is therefore a valuable natural resource; its judicious placement is a fundamental and principal application of technology in marine habitat management. Nevertheless, under the present federal guidelines for cost sharing, use of dredged material primarily to protect marine habitats may be beyond the financial resources available to many prospective project sponsors.

The development of marine habitat for natural protection of shorelines, as in estuarine settings with low to moderate physical energy from waves and currents, is largely unexploited because of institutional constraints, including a lack of economic incentives. The federal and state agencies responsible for marine habitat management have been successful in applying restoration technology to enhance and protect natural shorelines only when it was the least costly alternative. Restricting project funding to only the least-cost alternative has resulted in fewer opportunities to apply restoration technology than could be realized with greater decisionmaking flexibility.

A Multidisciplinary Approach Improves the Potential for Success

The planning and execution of marine habitat projects are best accomplished using an integrated, multidisciplinary approach because no one discipline brings the full body of scientific and engineering knowledge needed. When narrow single-discipline perspectives dominated, successful project development and implementation were hindered. Coastal engineering projects involving marine habitat can be improved through a multidisciplinary, holistic approach to guide project development from goal and objective setting through performance monitoring, measurement, and evaluation.

RECOMMENDATION: Federal and state agencies, project sponsors, and practitioners of marine habitat protection, improvement, and creation should require multidisciplinary project planning, design, implementation, evaluation, and management. The methodology employed should:

- *evaluate and set goals and priorities;*
- *clearly define measures of success;*
- *accommodate institutional factors;*
- *effectively address known ecosystem functions, seasonal variations in habitat use, hydraulics, hydrology, and other engineering and scientific considerations;*
- *establish a rigorous monitoring regime; and*
- *maintain the integrity and continuity of the process.*

Among the agencies that should require multidisciplinary processes are the U.S. Army Corps of Engineers, the U.S. Fish and Wildlife Service, the National Marine Fisheries Service, the Environmental Protection Agency, and state and local authorities with marine habitat management responsibilities.

Determination of Project Success Depends on
Sound Performance Criteria and Monitoring

Successful project performance is the most productive, conclusive, and reliable means of demonstrating the viability of restoration technology and building public and professional confidence in its application. Structural and functional monitoring before, during, and after project implementation are crucial to deter-

CONCLUSIONS AND RECOMMENDATIONS

mining the effectiveness of the engineering methods, technologies, and practices used and their relation to natural functions. But many marine habitat management projects lack well-defined criteria that are necessary to assessing their performance. Many projects that look like they have achieved design objectives do not include monitoring programs to establish or document performance relative to scientific and engineering parameters. Refinement of individual project design during implementation to meet project-specific conditions is not often found in project plans, but it is especially important when innovative approaches and emerging technologies are used. Rigorous, well-structured performance criteria and monitoring regimes are needed. Credible criteria and monitoring regimes are based on a scientifically sound understanding of ecosystem functioning, including stability requirements. Such monitoring over a suitable period and at intervals matched to site-specific conditions provides an adequate and credible means to identify design and implementation problems while also promoting accountability in project planning, implementation, maintenance, and operation.

RECOMMENDATION: Public authorities responsible for approving marine habitat projects and project sponsors should formally establish the criteria by which project performance will be assessed as part of the approval process. These criteria, at the minimum, should be based on sound engineering and scientific principles.

RECOMMENDATION: Public authorities and other entities responsible for approving or permitting habitat projects should require project sponsors to commit to long-term maintenance and monitoring for a time span sufficient to show satisfactory performance, to provide the means for determining whether project objectives are achieved, and what, if any, corrective actions may be needed, and to promote accountability.

RECOMMENDATION: Monitoring and maintenance regimes should include:

• frequent near-term monitoring to ensure project development according to design and performance criteria;
• quarterly or semiannual monitoring for 3–7 years after construction to assess performance and provide a basis for determining what corrective action may be needed; and
• long-term monitoring for 5–20 years to document performance and lessons learned.

RECOMMENDATION: Monitoring regimes should be designed to concurrently contribute to the advancement of scientific and engineering knowledge about the technologies and techniques that were employed.

WHAT INSTITUTIONAL IMPROVEMENTS ARE NEEDED?

A National Policy Is Needed to Guide
Marine Habitat Protection and Restoration

The degradation and loss of marine habitats, although regional, are national in their implications. A national policy should be promulgated to give focus to problem solving and corrective action and to obtain the maximum benefit from the public resources committed to activities affecting marine habitats. The application of scientific and engineering knowledge and capabilities that provide the technical means to protect and restore marine habitats should be guided by a national policy with well-defined goals and objectives. Strong national commitment and leadership should guide reasonable cooperative efforts to balance ecological and economic needs and mount programs to change attitudes toward activities that adversely affect marine ecosystems. National policy, processes, and resource decisionmaking should be based on sound environmental, economic, political, scientific, and technical objectives and principles. Direct government intervention should be used when necessary to arrest and reverse the trend of marine habitat degradation and loss.

The need to establish and focus a national effort is urgent. Sufficient scientific and engineering knowledge is available to underpin immediate policy formation. The committee finds it imperative that the federal government promulgate national policy within the next 2 years to arrest the loss and degradation of marine habitats and establish a long-term objective of achieving a substantial net gain in marine habitat acreage.

RECOMMENDATION: The executive and legislative branches of the federal government should establish a national policy to prevent or, when development is determined to be in the national interest, offset the further degradation, conversion, and loss of marine habitat. The policy should specify goals and establish a period for its implementation.

Implementation Goals and Objectives Are Essential

Goals are needed for the many elements comprising coastal ecosystem management. Agencies with marine habitat management responsibilities should examine their missions, goals, and performance to assess whether they are making full use of their existing authorities and fulfilling the responsibilities defined in their charters. There is an urgent need for review of each agency's authorities and program objectives to identify conflicting responsibilities and policies relevant to coastal ecosystem management and to identify and define new policies that will benefit the marine habitat component.

Enhancement and restoration are more costly than preservation, but considering all the benefits and costs, private and social, direct and indirect, each situa-

CONCLUSIONS AND RECOMMENDATIONS

tion must be weighed individually. When all costs and benefits—including long-term ecological impacts as well as short-term economic ones—cannot be measured and compared with confidence, presumption of the best alternative should fall to the protection of what exists. Current and future capabilities to protect, enhance, restore, and create marine habitats should not be used as an excuse for converting natural habitats to other uses in the coastal zone. The decisionmaking process should provide for balanced treatment and consideration of all legitimate interests. Careful consideration should be given to the effect any conversion might have on the ecosystem and dependent species and on national environmental objectives. Once established, a restored or created coastal habitat should be protected from damage from human activities.

RECOMMENDATION: Each federal and state agency with marine habitat management responsibilities, within the scope of that responsibility, should develop habitat protection and improvement goals and objectives based on overarching national policy guidelines, quantify them to the fullest extent possible, and establish milestones for their attainment. Further, federal agencies should exercise their marine habitat management responsibilities in a holistic, integrated manner. Emphasis should first be placed on protecting and enhancing existing marine habitat, followed by restoration and creation of habitats, as feasible.

Institutional Mechanisms Need to Be Improved

Federal and state regulatory programs can play a vital role in stimulating the use of beneficial technology. Through the elimination of overlapping federal agency and state administrative structures and policies that create communication and program implementation problems, significant improvements can be achieved. Existing institutional policies, regulations, and procedures create a narrowly focused framework that often

- creates disincentives rather than incentives to support policy;
- limits options for more effective use of natural resources;
- limits the opportunity for pilot, demonstration, and experimental programs, including technology transfer and adaptation;
- constrains implementation of changes necessary to advance marine habitat restoration practice; and
- results in limited publication of project results, including evaluation of the technologies used, thereby leading to repetition of approaches without the benefits to be gained from experience.

When project goals and criteria for evaluation are realistically set during project definition and approval, the degree of success is governed largely by institutional constraints and the skill with which technology is implemented. The institutional shortcomings are broadly spread throughout the administrative and management structures of all the federal and state agencies involved. At the federal level, there is a lack of comprehensive planning, programming, and budget coordination for project development, monitoring, and research. New ways need to be found to fund acquisition or purchase of development rights for existing marine habitats and to fund marine habitat protection, enhancement, restoration, and creation projects.

Many federal civil works projects in the coastal zone were constructed prior to recognition of marine habitat as an important environmental consideration in design. The potential to incorporate environmental benefits into existing projects that are near marine habitats should be assessed and an implementation program developed.

Standards requiring use of the best available technology for marine habitat management are insufficient and are not well-regulated. Determination of the best measures, whether for protection or habitat improvement, are often not based on an understanding of how a coastal ecosystem works. There is limited flexibility in decisionmaking to encourage or even permit the application of innovative and emerging technologies. Nor is project-by-project learning encouraged as a primary source for essential insight on project construction and operation.

Effective interagency coordination is required to carry out protection, improvement, and creation policies; guide determinations of preservation and improvement needs; and provide a constructive means to address competing interests. But regional coordination of public agencies with marine habitat management responsibilities and private interests is often more ad hoc than planned. Key pathways or mechanisms encouraging the exchange of information, the stimulation of technology innovation, and expert and public review of individual agency goals and progress within a region should be established. Commercial, scientific, and public interest representatives should be particularly useful and involved in these functions. Better coordination and consensus building mechanisms can lead to a more complete basis for decisionmaking on needs for habitat preservation, improvement, and creation; innovative use of technologies; and allocation of resources to publicly and privately sponsored habitat projects.

The ability to comment effectively in a timely manner on regulatory matters pertaining to marine habitat management varies by agency. The U.S. Army Corps of Engineers/U.S. Fish and Wildlife Service agreement on funding transfers provides a means to improve the latter's meeting its coordination responsibilities under the U.S. Fish and Wildlife Coordination Act. A similar level of support, if provided to the National Marine Fisheries Service (NMFS), would enhance that agency's capability to represent the marine resources for which it is responsible.

Well-established coordination infrastructures among some parties with marine habitat management responsibilities could be better exploited to carry out national marine habitat management policy. For example, the NMFS should examine the marine habitat responsibilities and national coverage of marine re-

CONCLUSIONS AND RECOMMENDATIONS   *121*

gions by regional Fisheries Management Councils ensure that marine habitat management responsibilities receive adequate consideration and treatment. Similarly, cognizant state authorities should examine the role and coordination functions of regional fisheries commissions and other regional and local bodies in marine habitat management.

Project results, analyses, and experience are not widely circulated. As a consequence, marine habitat management initiatives are characterized by repetition nationally. Considerable information is often developed during project planning and implementation, but publication of results is often constrained by limited resources or restrictive publication policies. Because of its evolutionary stage of development, marine habitat management efforts would greatly benefit from broader publication of project results.

The economic values of particular species, their population levels, and of their habitats, although difficult to quantify, are essential in establishing policies, goals, and objectives for marine habitat management generally and in setting project-specific parameters. Advancement of the economic valuation of marine resources is needed to improve the allocation of resources for publicly and privately sponsored projects such as shoreline engineering, directional drilling, and construction of offshore underwater berms, thereby providing alternatives to reactive mitigation techniques.

RECOMMENDATION: *All federal, state, and local agencies with jurisdiction over or responsibilities for marine habitat management should:*

   • *collectively and individually modify policy and administrative procedures to improve opportunities for the application of appropriate technology and implementation of marine habitat projects;*
   • *collaborate in developing administrative approaches and programs that encourage and support the innovative application of available and emerging technologies;*
   • *improve interorganizational coordination for better accommodation of competing interests;*
   • *consider the environmental and economic benefits derived from nonstructural measures including the productive use of dredged material, in the benefit-cost ratios of coastal habitat projects; and*
   • *examine the feasibility of improving economic incentives for marine habitat protection and restoration.*

RECOMMENDATION: *The U.S. Army Corps of Engineers should revise its policies concerning the transportation and placement of suitable dredged material to facilitate its use as a resource rather than as a waste product (spoil). Corps emphasis on disposal of dredged material* *in the least cost, environmentally acceptable manner should be reoriented to emphasize its beneficial uses.*

RECOMMENDATION: *Federal agencies should review existing projects to determine the feasibility of initiating improvements that would benefit marine habitat. If the review is beyond an agency's existing authority, the agency should seek both enabling authority from Congress (similar to that provided to the U.S. Army Corps of Engineers in Section 306 of the Water Resources Development Act [WRDA] of 1990 and Sections 203-204 of WRDA 1992) and implementation resources and should establish an implementation program.*

RECOMMENDATION: *In view of the Fish and Wildlife Funding Agreement between the U.S. Army Corps of Engineers and the U.S. Fish and Wildlife Service which enables interagency transfers of funds to enhance USFWS execution of its obligations under the Fish and Wildlife Coordination Act, the Corps and the National Marine Fisheries Service should establish a parallel arrangement to achieve the same objective.*

RECOMMENDATION: *Agencies with responsibilities for marine habitat management should make a concerted effort to publish and otherwise broadly distribute results and lessons learned from marine habitat protection, enhancement, restoration, and creation initiatives.*

Continuing Professional Development Is Essential

Continued professional development, including postacademic training for coastal engineering, is needed to ensure a credible base of expertise within the restoration industry. Improvement is needed in scientific and engineering knowledge within natural resources agencies, engineering and consulting firms, and special interest groups. The limited number of trained people in the public and private sector, coupled with inadequate technical education, limits the effectiveness of marine habitat protection and enhancement efforts. Cross training in the engineering and scientific disciplines fills gaps in technical education, enhances the cooperative effort between the engineering and scientific disciplines, and minimizes the occurrence of irregular and conflicting outcomes in project planning and implementation. Specifically, multidisciplinary training for coastal engineers should prepare them for effective response to the wide-range engineering, ecological, and social issues that influence planning, design, implementation, and operation of marine habitat projects. It also needs to prepare them to work on multidisciplinary project teams. The committee believes that incorporating basic environmental principles in the beginning courses of engineering and sci-

CONCLUSIONS AND RECOMMENDATIONS

entific disciplines would contribute significantly to improved environmental literacy and would lay the foundation for multidisciplinary teamwork and continuing professional development that is essential to advancing marine habitat management practices. Changes in academic curricula to advance environmental literacy are encouraged.

Professional certification programs pertinent to marine habitat management projects, although providing for a minimum of technical education and field experience and sometimes the execution of an ethics statement, do not guarantee that certified professionals can succeed on a given project. Nevertheless, the committee believes that these practitioners are in a better position to meet protection, enhancement, restoration, or creation goals and objectives.

RECOMMENDATION: Continuing professional education of resource agency personnel and practitioners should be required to improve the decisionmaking, planning and design, and implementation of marine habitat management projects.

RECOMMENDATION: Federal, state, and local agency personnel and restoration practitioners involved in planning, approving, and carrying out marine habitat management projects should be encouraged to seek professional certification within their respective disciplines and where appropriate, environmental professionals or other relevant professional designation.

RECOMMENDATION: The Environmental Protection Agency should encourage and support development of nationally recognized standards and meaningful privately operate programs for certification of individuals and accreditation of organizations performing environmental work.

WHAT RESEARCH IS NEEDED TO ADVANCE
THE STATE OF PRACTICE?

In view of increased human dependence on the coastal zone and the increasing pressure on natural resources, marine habitat research should be elevated in priority. A systematic research program would provide a firmer scientific basis for guiding projects and filling technology gaps. For example, technology is needed for placement of dredged material at suitable elevations and in large-scale settings. Research should explicitly consider regional differences in natural processes.

Basic research is needed to overcome technical shortcomings in the scientific aspects of understanding marine habitat needs, functions, and processes. Basic research is also needed to develop a reliable means to predict the result of the application of engineering technology relative to scientific principles on a site-

124   RESTORING AND PROTECTING MARINE HABITAT

specific basis. In particular, research should be directed to providing a capability for predicting the effects of hydrologic and other physical processes on marine habitat. The importance of fully functional habitats in maintaining the dynamics of local and regional coastal ecosystems is widely acknowledged. However, the economic value of maintaining ecosystem dynamics is difficult to quantify and evaluate.

Federal agencies with responsibilities for marine habitat management are engaged in coastal habitat research, and their efforts, although useful, have not been guided by a nationally focused research agenda. But in view of the limited resources available, a centrally coordinated or directed research program is needed; it will ensure the broadest possible reach and provide decisionmakers and practitioners with the information essential to determining the best application of scientific principles and available restoration technologies.

RECOMMENDATION: The nation should undertake a systematic program of fundamental and applied research designed to put habitat protection, enhancement, restoration, and creation technology on firmer scientific footing and to guide technology's use. The research program should address gaps in existing knowledge and technologies through experimental, pilot, and demonstration programs. Dedicated research is needed in the following areas:

- *natural functions in reconstructed habitats;*
- *hydrology and hydraulics of marine ecosystems;*
- *sediment properties influencing the physical and biological performance of habitat enhancement, restoration, and creation projects;*
- *sediment transport by natural energy to support mathematical predictive modeling;*
- *use of dredged material for marine habitat restoration;*
- *habitat utilization by biota in marine ecosystems;*
- *mechanisms of recruitment for marine intertidal biota;*
- *structures and functions of artificial reefs; and*
- *methodologies for economic evaluation of coastal habitats.*

RECOMMENDATION: The executive branch of the federal government should designate an appropriate federal agency to convene an interagency committee to develop and coordinate a national research program for marine habitat management. The research program should establish implementation responsibilities and milestones. The committee should include in its membership representatives of the Departments of the Army, Commerce, and Interior and the Environmental Protection Agency. Means should also be provided to obtain the advice of experts from the scientific and engineering communities.

APPENDIX
A

Biographical Sketches

THOMAS A. SANDS, Chairman, is a partner with Adams and Reese, a law firm in New Orleans. He has extensive background in all aspects of the management of engineering and construction services and water resources programs, with particular emphasis on environmental and regulatory compliance. In addition, he has been involved in environmental litigation concerning compliance with the National Environmental Policy Act and the Clean Water Act. Prior experience includes field and staff assignments with the U.S. Army Corps of Engineers. He served as the senior official responsible for Corps activities within the North Atlantic region and Lower Mississippi Valley region, where he also served as president of the Mississippi River Commission. Major General Sands received a B.S. in military engineering from the U.S. Military Academy, an M.S. in Civil Engineering from Texas A&M University, and a J.D. from George Mason University.

DEWITT (WITT) D. BARLOW III is president and chief executive officer of Great Lakes Dredge and Dock Company. Prior positions with the company include chief engineer and vice president, project manager for the International Division, manager for the Middle East Division, and dredging superintendent and field engineer with the North Atlantic Division. Mr. Barlow received a B.A. from Trinity College, a B.S. and M.S. in civil engineering from Columbia University, and an M.B.A. from the University of Chicago.

JOHN MARK DEAN is a professor of marine science and biology and director of the Center for Environmental Policy, Institute of Public Affairs, at the University of South Carolina. Previously he directed the marine science program and served as coordinator for the South Carolina Sea Grant Consortium. He has

125

conducted research in coastal resource management, ecology of coastal ecosystems, fisheries biology, age and growth of fishes, and integration of science into public policy. Dr. Dean served on the South Atlantic Fisheries Management Council, the National Coastal Resources Advisory Committee, the South Carolina Governor's Natural Resources Education Council, the South Carolina Coastal Council, and the Office of Technology Assessment's Advisory Panel on Coastal Effects of Offshore Energy Systems. He was a member and chairman of the NRC National Science Foundation Predoctoral Fellowship Selection Committee. Dr. Dean received a B.A. in biology from Cornell College and an M.S. and Ph.D. in ecology from Purdue University.

OLIVER HOUCK a is professor of law at Tulane Law School. He has more than 20 years' experience as a practicing attorney, researcher, and teacher on environmental, coastal, and water resources law. Previously he served with the National Wildlife Federation as vice president for conservation and education, general counsel, and director of the resources defense division. Earlier he was Assistant United States Attorney for the District of Columbia. He currently serves on the boards of the Defenders of Wildlife and the Environmental Defense Fund and was a founder of the Coalition to Restore Coastal Louisiana. Dr. Houck received a B.A. in English (cum laude) from Harvard University and a J.D. from Georgetown Law Center.

MARY C. LANDIN is a research biologist with the Wetlands Branch, Environmental Laboratory, U.S. Army Engineer Waterways Experiment Station. She has more than 28 years' experience as a biologist and researcher for private industry, The U.S. Department of Agriculture, and the Army Corps of Engineers, including extensive work in habitat restoration criteria and techniques, mitigation, endangered species, and the beneficial use of dredged materials. She was the lead scientist in the design and management of many restoration and habitat development projects, organized seven international conferences addressing beneficial uses of dredged materials, organized three international conferences on wetlands science, and has written more than 250 technical publications. She chaired an environmental study group for the Lower Mississippi River Delta Development Commission and is a member of the Water Quality 2000 Congress. Dr. Landin received a B.S. in horticulture, an M.S. in wildlife ecology, and a Ph.D. in wildlife management from Mississippi State University.

ROBIN (ROY) R. LEWIS III is founder and president of Lewis Environmental Services and senior adjunct scientist with Mote Marine Laboratory. He has more than 15 years' experience in practical creation and restoration of coastal habitats. Previously he was vice president in charge of the environmental division of Proctor and Refern, an engineering consulting firm, and founder and president of Mangrove Systems, an environmental consulting firm. He also served as a professor of biology, chair of the biology department, and scientific advisor at Hillsborough Community College in Tampa. Mr. Lewis served as a member of a scientific advisory committee that advised the U.S. Army Corps of

BIOGRAPHICAL SKETCHES

Engineers on a harbor-deepening project. Mr. Lewis received a B.S. in biology from the University of Florida and an M.A. in zoology from the University of South Florida. He is certified as an Environmental Professional by the National Association of Environmental Professionals and as a Senior Ecologist by the Ecological Society of America.

ASHISH J. MEHTA is a professor of coastal and oceanographic engineering and of civil engineering for the University of Florida. He has more than 20 years' experience in research and teaching on fine sediment transport in estuaries and inlets. Prior positions at the University of Florida include associate and assistant professor and research scientist with the Department of Coastal and Oceanographic Engineering. He was a member of the NRC Committee on Sedimentation Control and is currently serving as a member of the Marine Board. Dr. Mehta received a B.S. in chemistry and physics from the University of Bombay, a B.S. in chemical engineering from the University of California, and an M.S. in chemical engineering and mathematics and a Ph.D. in civil engineering from the University of Florida.

JOHN M. NICHOL is a partner with Moffatt & Nichol, Engineers, where he specializes in coastal, hydraulic, and harbor engineering. Earlier experience includes service as engineer with the U.S. Army Corps of Engineers, job engineer with Guy F. Atkinson Company for construction of wharfs and freeway bridge buildings, and construction engineer with Huntington Harbour Engineering and Construction for a 900-acre waterfront reclamation project. He chaired the American Society of Civil Engineering National Technical Committee for Coastal Engineering and was national director of the American Shore and Beach Preservation Association. Mr. Nichol received a B.S. in civil engineering from Oregon State College and a diploma in hydraulic and coastal engineering from the Technical University in Delft, The Netherlands.

RUTH PATRICK, NAS, is the Francis Boyer Chair of Limnology and Curator of the Limnology Department at the Academy of Natural Sciences. She is a member of the American Philosophical Society and the Academy of Arts and Sciences. Dr. Patrick is an internationally distinguished leader in the field of ecology and limnology with more than 50 years' experience. She has led international expeditions, written extensively, and served on numerous presidential, national, and regional advisory committees. She has also served as chair and member of numerous NAS committees. She has advised Presidents Bush, Reagan, Carter, Nixon, and Johnson on ecological matters pertaining to water. Recently she has been a scientific advisor on the ecological restoration of the Savannah River estuary. Dr. Patrick received a B.S. from Coker College and an M.S. and Ph.D. from the University of Virginia. She has received many awards and honorary degrees for the excellence of her work in botany, ecology, and other scientific disciplines.

ROBERT E. TURNER is a professor of the Department of Coastal Sciences and Coastal Ecology Institute, Louisiana State University. He has more than

128   APPENDIX A

20 years' international experience in research and teaching on coastal ecology, biological oceanography, environment and management, fisheries, and wetlands. Dr. Turner is chairman of the Intecol Working Group on Wetlands and Natural Resources and the Louisiana Governor's Coastal Restoration Technical Committee. He is co-chair of the EPA Gulf of Mexico technical subcommittee on habitat degradation and is editor-in-chief, Wetlands Ecology and Management. Dr. Turner received a B.A. in zoology from Monmouth College, an M.A. in zoology from Drake University, and a Ph.D. in zoology from the University of Georgia.

APPENDIX

B

Case Studies

The case studies presented here illustrate successes and failures in marine habitat management. The examination begins with several cases of substantial damage of human origin within and to marine ecosystems. Incomplete environmental assessments led to destruction of valuable overwintering habitat for shrimp in Tampa Bay. Faulty waterway design for the Savannah River estuary led to alteration of hydraulics (since corrected) that was detrimental to navigation and estuarine ecology with adverse impacts to vegetation and certain fish species that required landscape scale restoration. These two case studies point up the need for multidisciplinary, holistic planning and implementation of engineering projects in the coastal zone insofar as they might impact marine (and other) habitats. The examination then shifts to initiatives with primarily positive results: enhancement, restoration, and creation projects for the Chesapeake Bay region, Tampa Bay, San Francisco Bay region, and Kiawah and Seabrook islands in South Carolina. The need for a multidisciplinary approach again stands out. Additionally, these case studies demonstrate the fact that protection and restoration work, when properly designed and implemented, can lead to physical and biological performance that meets project objectives. Indicated in some of these studies is the need for public involvement in order to build public understanding and support for marine habitat protection and restoration. It can also build support for economically essential but environmentally sensitive industrial and commercial development within the marine environment. Use of dredged material was fundamental in several cases as well. Its use for creation and restoration of marsh, creation of sea bird and wading bird nesting islands, and creation of underwater berms is examined in three additional case studies. The

130   *APPENDIX B*

discussion of nesting islands identifies the competing habitat interests of agencies responsible for habitat management because of differing client species. Then follows a case study on bioengineering applications for habitat restoration. Artificial reef technology is presented in a separate case study. Many artificial reefs have been constructed in U.S. waters and on the continental shelf. Although artificial reef design is quite advanced, most applications in the United States are low-technology projects that are not designed to support specific fish species. The appendix concludes with consideration of the application of Geographic Information Systems GIS to marine habitat management, for example, in wetlands delineation.

HABITAT ASSESSMENTS USING SPECIES LIFE HISTORIES

The complex life history of many marine species often depends on multiple habitats whose use may vary by life cycle phases and seasons. The loss or degradation of critical habitat, because it may not be recognized as important to the life cycle, can devastate a species or a local population. The life history requirements of the commercially harvested white, brown, and pink shrimp (penaeids) illustrate several valuable points for managing coastal resources:

• Habitat requirements vary throughout the life cycle, even among similar species.
• Production varies by habitat.
• Local knowledge is an important management tool.

The range of salinities, temperatures, substrates, and vegetation that shrimp pass through in one year is prodigious. Penaeid shrimp cycles generally begin in the open sea (35 parts per thousand [ppt]) as eggs that mature through naupliar, protozoeal, and zoeal stages. Following the pelagic larval drift, the postlarvae enter estuarine areas on flood tides and seek substrates until the next tide change, when they successively penetrate deeper into the estuary (down to 0 ppt). Eventually they live a benthic existence while they grow in the estuary, an environment that offers food and refuge from predators. After several weeks or months, they move back into the ocean, generally in shallow zones (<50 meters). Fishermen harvest them from the estuaries as postlarvae (for stocking ponds) and as subadults and adults in coastal waters. Most commercially important penaeid shrimp are considered estuarine dependent. Students of shrimp life cycles generally agree that recruitment of larvae into estuaries from the spawning sites offshore is high, so high that postlarval growth and survival in the estuary are probably the most important factors affecting the harvestable adult population size. Mortality in penaeid shrimp stocks is most severe in the larval stages and declines with age. Recruitment success depends on climate, predation levels,

CASE STUDIES   131

food supply, and habitat quality. Of these, what constitute high quality habitat are not precisely known.

Although estuarine salinity and temperature changes affect the annual potential for postlarval survival, the long-term yields are strongly related to both the quantity and quality of intertidal habitat. There are several known examples of this relationship throughout the world. A species may use both emergent wetlands and submerged grassbeds in the same estuary. The commercial harvest of penaeid shrimp per area of estuarine vegetation peaks at the equator and falls to nearly zero north of North Carolina (presumably because of a temperature limitation).

The anatomical differences between brown and white shrimp are almost indistinguishable; even the color differences are not strong soon after harvest. But their habitat requirements are quite different. Compared to white shrimp, brown shrimp are generally more numerous in brackish waters and they prefer higher salinities (10–20 ppt). Most brown shrimp spawn in offshore marine water in the spring and early summer, but some also spawn in the fall; white shrimp spawn from spring to fall. Brown shrimp move into estuaries from offshore sooner than white shrimp (spring and summer) (Turner and Brody, 1983). White shrimp may overwinter in the estuary, whereas brown shrimp do not. Several investigators have observed that the two species use different parts of the marsh during flood cycles, that fish predation varies by species, and that substrate preferences vary. Both species use the edge of the wetland extensively as a food-rich refuge from predators. The elimination of this habitat (through construction of a bulkhead, for example) drastically reduces population densities. Even with apparently similar habitat quality, seasonal use may vary because of differences in migration and emigration patterns. This is not to say that the interior marshes are unimportant to the survival of transient estuarine-dependent organisms. The importance of emergent marshes as a source of detritus for shrimp is well documented. The small resident fishes and grass shrimp that utilize the interior marshes are an important food source for larger estuarine-transient carnivores (such as spotted seatrout and red drum), especially in the fall and winter, when cold fronts cause extremely low tides, forcing these forage species into open waters.

The broad patterns of the pink shrimp life history and habitat use are documented fairly well, but important specific information is often missing. Knowledge of pink shrimp seasonal distributions and habitat use within specific estuaries is often not known, but it can be acquired from local experts and additional sampling. The consequences of not doing so are illustrated by the inadvertently validated construction of two 600-acre diked areas for dredged material disposal in Tampa Bay (Figure B-1). The new placement sites destroyed some of the most important deep overwintering mud bottoms for pink shrimp. The overwintering population had not been previously identified through scientific sampling during normal fisheries surveys. However, a small commercial fishery did ex-

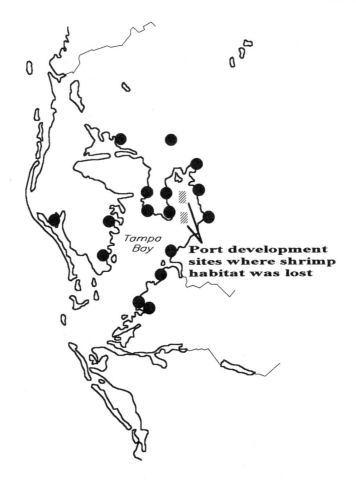

FIGURE B-1 Site of shrimp habitat destruction and completed and active Surface Water Improvement and Management Act restoration sites in Tampa Bay.

ploit that over wintering population for profit. These fishermen did not divulge the pink shrimp habitat use because of financial competition. Fishing vessels were occasionally observed working the proposed permit area, but apparently no one investigated. Thus serious gaps in knowledge of the species' life history were not detected and tidal waters were converted to industrial use under an erroneous assumption. The lesson here is that more complete knowledge of species' life histories can be obtained through site-specific and seasonally varying sampling as well as from local experts' knowledge (Turner and Boesch, 1988).

CASE STUDIES   *133*

WATERWAY DEVELOPMENT IMPACTS IN
THE SAVANNAH RIVER ESTUARY

Two strongly conflicting demands have been made on the Savannah River estuary: to develop it as an industrial center and to preserve its natural resources. Historically, the estuary supported commercial fisheries and navigation, provided valuable wetland habitat for small mammals, and served as breeding, feeding, and resting grounds for indigenous and migratory birds.

Over the years, the Savannah waterfront was developed as an industrial center, deep seaport, and tourist attraction, and maintaining the port complex in view of its important economic contributions to the region is of continuing interest. When the channel was deepened for large oceangoing ships, most shallow water areas where aquatic organisms fed and many lived and bred were eliminated. The estuary's potential to support a well-balanced aquatic ecosystem with the fisheries was substantially reduced.

The upper estuary is divided by a series of islands creating two waterways: the Front and Back channels. The industrially developed Front Channel borders Savannah. The tidal prism is mostly broad and shallow. Intertidal flats and shallow water habitats are found on either side except in areas of industrial development. The cross section is about 10 feet deep across the middle except in the navigation channel. The river flow comprises the rest of the water entering the estuary. The less saline upper estuary formerly supported striped bass, sturgeon, and shad migration and spawning. It was a nursery for larvae development; the Back Channel was especially important as a striped bass and shad nursery.

Over time, runoff and point and nonpoint source pollution from industrial and shipping developments in and above Savannah led to increased organic loading within the estuary. Flushing time increased and sloughing of the banks occurred, increasing navigation maintenance requirements. The U.S. Army Corps of Engineers (USACE) determined that physical modifications were necessary to improve system hydraulics. A tidal curtain was placed in the Back Channel to increase the flow through the Front Channel and lessen sloughing and sediment deposition. Canals were cut through the islands to increase high tide water flushing in the Back Channel. These measures achieved results opposite to those intended.

The cross sectional area of volume of the estuary was increased by deepening and widening without an equal increase in the volume of water entering the estuary. This situation slowed rather than increased flushing times within the estuary. Sloughing of the banks increased and the scouring effect decreased. Sedimentation increased as well, creating greater oxygen demand, particularly at greater depths. Below the tidal curtain, oxygen demand increased, and above the curtain, salinity increased, killing the larvae and freshwater grasses there.

Project design did not adequately accommodate the effect of physical modifications on the tidal prism and associated hydraulic effects. Changes in salinity

134   *APPENDIX B*

and oxygen demands greatly impaired the estuary's capacity to support valuable commercial fisheries and degraded wildlife habitat. Neither navigation nor environmental objectives were served.

Substantial efforts have been made to restore the natural functioning of the estuary. The tidal curtain was removed to restore a more natural hydraulic regime (Georgia DOT, 1989; Pearlstine et al., 1989). Reciprocal transplanting was used to restore vegetation. Good localized results were expected based on extensive field research. The marsh is recovering on a landscape scale, and a fresh water tidal system has been reestablished (Latham et al., 1991; Pearlstine et al., 1990, 1993a,b). The estuary appears to again have the capability to support stripped bass and the bass have been restocked. The fish are rapidly approaching the age class for spawning. The interested agencies have planned a joint sampling effort to determine and assess the spawning when it occurs, and to further assess the estuaries capability to support the bass (W. Kitchens, personal communication, March 15, 1994).

The lower Savannah River situation represents perhaps both worst and best case scenarios. Physical and biological attributes of the estuary were greatly affected by faulty hydraulic design. The resulting damage to the ecosystem exemplifies the unfortunate results of designers' either not understanding or not adequately accommodating the many factors that interact to preserve the essential ecological attributes of an estuarine system. The result was all the more tragic because the estuary appeared to have the capability of supporting waterway improvements without altering basic estuarine ecology. On the other hand, the restoration program is reported to be working remarkably well with respect to hydraulics, water quality, and vegetation. Stripped bass have been reintroduced to the ecosystem and spawning of missing age classes is anticipated.

CHESAPEAKE BAY PROTECTION AND
RESTORATION INITIATIVES

The Chesapeake Bay has been under extreme environmental stress for many years as a result of human activity, particularly pollution from point and nonpoint sources within the estuary and its watershed. Many multijurisdictional and private efforts are underway to improve water quality throughout the region in order to improve the health of the ecosystem, restore important commercial and recreational fisheries, and mitigate the effects of erosion. Over the past 20 years, numerous restoration and enhancement projects have involved the Army Corps of Engineers, the U.S. Fish and Wildlife Service (USFWS), the National Marine Fisheries Service (NMFS), the Environmental Protection Agency (EPA), state agencies of Maryland and Virginia, including port authorities, and private organizations.

CASE STUDIES 135

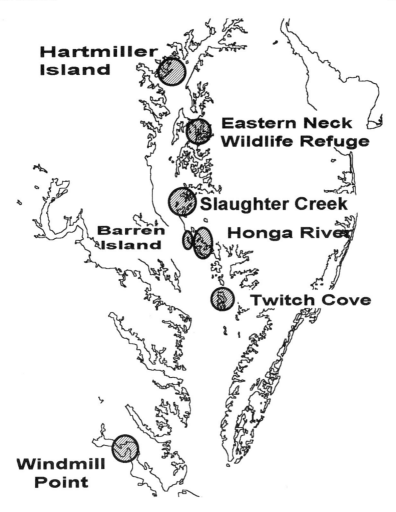

FIGURE B-2 Sites of Chesapeake Bay restoration and protection projects.

Windmill Point, Virginia

The Windmill Point habitat restoration project was the first of its type designed and constructed by the Army Corps of Engineers. Experience with construction techniques and monitoring provided information about physical energies and colonization that were useful in later projects (Boesch et al., 1978; Lunz et al., 1978).

Fifteen acres of fresh intertidal marsh were created with dredged material at Windmill Point in the James River. The site was agreed upon by an interagency state and federal working group. Both dredged sand and silt from maintenance dredging were used in construction. Local physical energy sources included strong river and flood currents, 3-foot tides, and fetches of several miles for westerly winds. A temporary sand dike serving as a breakwater provided site protection. It was breached to allow intertidal exchange. Vegetation planted on the dike enhanced its stability. Natural colonization occurred quickly on the interior protected area of the confinement, but when breaches in the temporary dike washed out, the project failed. The island broke in two in 1983 and most of the marsh washed out. A protected shallow water habitat suitable for fish spawning and a remnant island habitat for wildlife were created in the process. Lessons from this project include:

- Project placement must be suitable for local conditions.
- Strong riverine woody shrubs and trees may be needed to stabilize dikes in similar conditions rather than herbaceous material.
- Dike breaches for intertidal exchanges need to be protected from physical energy that could cause their failure.
- Deliberate dike breaches need to be carefully placed.

Wetlands Restoration

Intertidal wetlands have been restored within the estuary using sandy dredged materials. Examples include 4 acres on the Honga River and 6 acres on Slaughter Creek in 1974 and 55 acres at Barren Island in 1982 and 1985. Periodic monitoring indicates that use of sandy materials in this environment is a viable restoration technique. However, an experimental seagrass planting near Slaughter Creek in 1989 failed because of poor water quality and current action despite efforts to provide protection from physical energies until the site was established in early 1993. Additional wetlands restoration projects were in progress or in planning at Eastern Neck National Wildlife Refuge, Kenilworth Marsh, and Bodkin Island (Maynord et al., 1992).

Oyster Beds

Oyster beds were created using dredged material at Twitch Cove (Smith Island) and Slaughter Creek. The Army Corps of Engineers, in collaboration with the NMFS, used sandy dredged material to raise a deeper area of bay bottom to approximate intertidal conditions that would encourage oyster colonization. The projects achieved design objectives, providing both motivation and justification for similar projects.

At Twitch Cove, 4-foot diameter Longard tubes were used to construct an underwater containment site. The tubes were fabric capsules filled with sediments on-site and placed in predetermined configurations. Dredged material was placed inside the containment area until elevations suitable to oyster production

CASE STUDIES   137

were reached. The dredged material was then capped with substrate that was also suitable for oyster production. The Slaughter Creek project involved construction of a 2.1-acre dredged material mound at an open water placement site. The mound was located near an area that had once been a productive oyster bar but no longer had substrate favorable for colonization of oyster spat (Earhardt et al., 1988).

Maryland Shore Erosion Control

In response to marine habitat losses resulting from extensive shoreline erosion, mostly in Chesapeake Bay, the Maryland General Assembly established the Shore Erosion Control Program (SECP) in 1968. Housed within the Maryland Department of Natural Resources, the SECP set out to protect and improve the quality of Chesapeake Bay and its tributaries through marine habitat protection, enhancement, restoration, and creation. Having gained renewed force in 1985 as part of the state's Chesapeake Bay initiatives, the SECP is an example of a program that, through coordinated, interdisciplinary efforts has consistently and successfully achieved project objectives.

Some of the program's responsibilities include:

- public education;
- periodic assessments of shoreline erosion in Chesapeake Bay;
- provision of technical and other assistance to private and municipal landowners with erosion problems;
- evaluation of new technologies and methods to control shore erosion;
- design and implementation of shore erosion control projects; and
- periodic inspection and monitoring of completed projects in order to recommend preventive and corrective maintenance to property owners.

The program is successful in part because it relies on the participation of citizens, mainly landowners. The state provides matching funds for citizen restoration and protection initiatives. The program also has a revolving loan fund to provide interest-free loans for qualified applicants who wish to undertake restoration/protection projects.

One important feature is the program's emphasis on and encouragement of vegetative nonstructural solutions to shore erosion. To date, more than 10 miles of shoreline in the Chesapeake Bay and its tributaries in Maryland have been protected by the planting of protective vegetation. More than 1.1 million square feet of new wetlands have been created as well.

Recent coordination between Maryland and Virginia and the Norfolk and Baltimore districts of the USACE has given rise to the Chesapeake Bay Shoreline Protection Study. The study will be used to identify critically eroding areas of the bay in an effort to acquire federal funds for important restoration and

138   APPENDIX B

protection projects. The success of the SECP derives from innovative and coordinated planning and implementation practices (Zabawa, 1990).

Multipurpose Sites

Although not a marine habitat project per se, the Hartmiller Island confined disposal facility project near Baltimore provides useful insights into the difficulties of obtaining approval for projects using dredged material, even if environmental objectives are an element of the project.

The Port of Baltimore is a huge economic engine for the state. It is responsible for as many as 150,000 jobs and has an economic value of $4 billion. To maintain and improve navigation channels to the port, extensive dredging is required. Development of a confined disposal facility was proposed in 1960. Extensive planning and assessments were conducted and an 1,100-acre site was selected in 1971. But the general public was not involved until its approval was needed. The port's proposal was to reconnect Hart and Miller islands (formerly Hartmiller Island) with dikes to form a confined disposal facility. The site was evaluated at low biological productivity, its good sheer strength would support the dike's weight, and dike construction materials were available at the site. The port determined that with proper planning and implementation, the site could be established as a wildlife habitat and recreational area (Hamons, 1988).

Substantial opposition developed over environmental and economic concerns. Additionally, under Maryland law, dredged material above a certain point in the channel is considered contaminated without regard to actual chemical composition. Although the port had conducted extensive internal planning, it did not demonstrate its credibility or build public support through public involvement measures. A resulting lawsuit was finally settled in the port's favor by the Supreme Court of the United States. Construction began in 1981, but by the time the facility was completed in 1985, costs had soared from the 1971 estimate of $11.5 million to $58 million. The nonavailability of the confined disposal facility delayed work on other channel improvement projects, substantially increasing costs to the local port owing to federal policy changes that increased the cost-share requirements of local project sponsors (Hamons, 1988).

The project was completed in 1985. Freshwater wetlands are developing rapidly and recreational facilities and upland parkland are available. The freshwater wetlands have attracted large concentrations of waterfowl (Hamons, 1988). Sea birds nest on the dike, and herons, egrets, and other water birds feed inside the facility.

TAMPA BAY WETLAND RESTORATIONS

Tampa Bay is a 400-square mile estuary surrounded by a 2,400-square mile highly urbanized watershed. The cities of Tampa, St. Petersburg, and Bradenton

CASE STUDIES   139

border the bay. Over time, 44 percent of the tidal marshes and mangroves and 75 percent of the submerged aquatic vegetation (seagrasses) were lost (Lewis and Estevez, 1988).

The state recognized the need to arrest losses and restore wetlands through passage of The Surface Water Improvement and Management (SWIM) Act in 1987. Implementation of SWIM Act measures in Tampa Bay has focused on physical restoration of lost habitats, such as wetlands and seagrass beds, to demonstrate the feasibility of such efforts. Research on restored habitat functional equivalency is in progress. Because SWIM program staff were not sufficiently experienced to design and supervise construction of restoration projects, program managers contracted with a multidisciplinary professional team to perform these functions. Its comprehensive planning, design, and implementation resulted in credible restoration work.

The multidisciplinary team included a restoration biologist, engineers, and surveyors. It was responsible for designing projects, obtaining permits, and implementing each project. As of February 1992, nine projects had been completed (Figure B-1). Each required approximately 1 year from design through construction. All nine, totaling 93.1 acres (37.7 hectares) of enhanced or restored habitat, achieved performance objectives. Another 21 projects are planned for 1992 through 1994 (Lewis, 1992; SWFWMD, 1992).

Results of a similar restoration effort by the Florida Department of Environmental Regulation (FDER) in the Tampa Bay area (using pollution fine funds for habitat restoration) are not similar to those of the SWIM initiative. The FDER decided to use its professional staff instead of an experienced multidisciplinary restoration team. Only two projects have been completed in 3 years. Slow progress in using funds for restoration resulted in diversion of accumulated interest to nonrestoration efforts. In the absence of a well-planned restoration program, pressures are building for diversion of additional funds for nonrestoration projects (Garrity, 1992).

SAN FRANCISCO BAY WETLANDS RESTORATION

Land subsidence in the San Francisco Bay system, including the Sacramento–San Joaquin River delta, is a result of extensive diking and pumping to create farmlands over the years. The area's peaty substrate, formed from thousands of years of coastal and riverine wetlands evolution, has largely been farmed. In peat soils, tillage, draining, and fertilization hastened the process of subsidence and degradation. Some bay area lands in the deltas are now as much as 15 feet below the surrounding water levels. As marginal lands (such as subsided farmlands) and other open lands become available, state and federal organizations have joined (within the limit of available resources) to acquire and restore such lands to use as natural habitat. The industrial, commercial, and residential development that has occurred generally precludes full restoration to predisturbed condi-

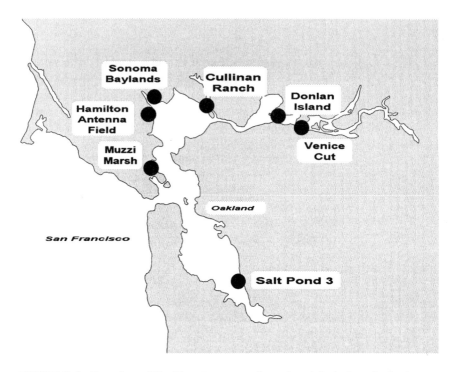

FIGURE B-3 Locations of San Francisco restorations sites visited where dredged material was used or planned.

tions. Thus much of the work consists of partial restoration that focuses on a few indigenous plant species and a few target species that the site may be able to support.

Several wetland restoration projects have used sediments dredged from the bay to restore intertidal elevations (Figure B-3). Four completed projects include Salt Pond Number 3 in south San Francisco Bay (1972), Muzzi Marsh near Tiberon (1978), and Donlan Island and Venice Cut in the San Joaquin River (1983). All have been monitored by the Army Corps of Engineers, the California Coastal Conservancy, and researchers from the University of California at Davis (England and Nakaji, 1990; Landin et al., 1990b). The Salt Pond Number 3 site was compared to three nearby natural salt marshes. All four wetlands achieved goals and objectives established when they were built and are considered successful by project sponsors and monitoring organizations (England and Nakaji, 1990; Landin et al., 1989c, 1990b). All four also continue to be monitored under long-term plans. These projects in turn are being used to guide additional wetland restoration projects that are in planning or already underway in the San

CASE STUDIES   141

Pablo Bay area (north portion of San Francisco Bay) at Hamilton Antenna Field, Sonoma Baylands, and Cullinan Ranch (Landin, 1991).

The conceptual design of the completed and planned projects and those in progress involve leaving the dike or its remnant intact until dredged sediments are placed. In the completed projects, the dike or dike remnants provided the confinement necessary to hold placement materials until intertidal elevations were established under site-specific tidal conditions. Once suitable elevations were attained, the dike was breached to allow intertidal flow. At Salt Pond Number 3 and Muzzi Marsh, tidal channels were also cut into the heart of the marshes to provide better intertidal flow throughout the site. Both sites were planted with two indigenous dominant plant species to provide habitat attractive to the endangered species (in California) clapper rail and the salt marsh harvest mouse.

The two intertidal river sites (Donlan Island and Venice Cut) were allowed to colonize with typical wetland vegetation following placement of dredged material. Because the dikes at these sites had been compromised prior to construction, dredged material was placed at the point farthest away from the dike opening. This measure was necessary to allow as much time as possible for the sediment to drop out of suspension before the effluent could move back into an already highly turbid river.

Sonoma Baylands, which is being restored by the state, includes an intertidal marsh using sediment from the Petaluma River, a marsh managements unit for waterfowl, and open natural land. Hamilton Antenna Field is planned to become a 300-acre intertidal salt marsh. Construction is projected for completion in 1994 using dredged material to restore intertidal elevations. Cullinan Ranch is a 2,200-acre site owned by the U.S. Fish and Wildlife Service which plans to fill cells with dredged material to restore wetlands. All seven projects discussed were expensive compared to similar-scale projects in other areas of the United States. Yet these costs do not appear to be extreme in relation to typical California land values and construction costs.

ENVIRONMENTALLY SENSITIVE DEVELOPMENT OF KIAWAH ISLAND, SOUTH CAROLINA

In the early 1950s, a family purchased Kiawah Island to harvest pine timber. The family subsequently used the island as a modest personal retreat, selling one lot each year to pay property taxes. When the property was reassessed in 1974, its classification was changed from agricultural to residential, and the resulting tax increases made it economically infeasible to maintain the largely undeveloped island as a private retreat. It was sold to the Kiawah Development Corporation, a Kiawah government investment unit for residential development. The corporation established a development strategy that emphasized long-term planning.

Initial project design activities included a comprehensive multidisciplinary

142   *APPENDIX B*

environmental assessment. The assessment was performed through separate development and construction contracts by a carefully composed team that was given wide latitude and status. The study encompassed climatology, archeology, history, shallow water physical oceanography, estuarine and freshwater sediments, benthic fauna within the sediments, fisheries, phytoplankton and zooplankton, birds, mammals, herpetology, forest and dune vegetation, coastal processes, oyster populations, and marine turtle nesting. The final report discussed each component in detail and synthesized the results as a holistic view of the island in its ecological surroundings.

The development corporation used the environmental assessment as a primary basis for project planning. The assessment began before and then ran concurrently with project planning. During this period, the environmental assessment research team met with corporation development and planning staff to answer specific environmental concerns. Thus the planners could work with their engineering staff to develop environmentally acceptable policies and procedures. Coastal processes information, for example, resulted in removal of a highly dynamic terminal sediment deposition site for the island (recurved spit) from residential development plans. Information on wetland processes was used by the civil engineers to design drainage systems that would use natural runoff to collect rainwater and hold it in ponds. These measures were also intended to maintain the freshwater lens and inhibit salt water intrusion. Plans were also made to maintain a native wetland vegetation border on wetlands for filtration and as wildlife habitat. Architects used biologists knowledge of sea turtles in designing lighting systems that would protect hatchlings. Climatology was used to develop structure height limits to protect forest vegetation. Knowledge of the sensitivity of dune vegetation assisted in developing self-imposed setback lines for ocean-front structures. Power transmission lines would be placed underground, and roads would avoid specimen trees and sensitive wetland areas. In the development and subsequent implementation of these plans, numerous meetings were held so that the scientific team understood the engineering issues and needs and the constraints of the permitting agencies, planners, and marketing staff. In turn, the planners and engineers gained practical insight on environmental considerations and could refine designs to accommodate them.

Integration of the scientific components with the engineering considerations at the outset enabled the scientists to collect the data and develop the environmental information that was most useful for project development. Kiawah Island is now recognized as one of the most environmentally sensitive coastal developments. It is also one of the most financially successful. It has weathered extreme episodic storms; for example, during recent hurricanes, no services were lost and no flooding occurred on the island. Eighteen years after project initiation, the management team reported that it is still using the original reports and planning documents, testifying to the quality and soundness of multidisciplinary planning.

CASE STUDIES   143

INLET ENGINEERING SEABROOK ISLAND
AT SOUTH CAROLINA

Tidal inlets play an important role in the evolution of nearby shorelines and backbay areas, particularly in areas with tide ranges of 2–4 meters with relatively low wave energy, where large ebb-tidal deltas occur. Sediment management in these settings is complex and often depends on knowledge of inlet movement, the timing and rate of sand bypassing, and quantitative sediment budgets. But such information is lacking in many areas or cannot be generalized from one place to another. Interactions between humans and nature at Seabrook Island illustrate both the role of an unstable tidal inlet in the management of adjacent shorelines and the incorporation of inlet dynamics into a nonstructural solution to beach erosion. To the degree that beaches are stabilized naturally, associated marine habitat may benefit as well.

Many up-to-date geological, hydrographic, and coastal engineering studies were available, providing details of the area. Seabrook is an accreting beach-ridge island that derives its sediment from Kiawah Island and Stono Inlet to the north. Captain Sams Inlet, at the northern end of Seabrook, undergoes a natural cycle of inlet migration and spit breaching at 40- to 80-year intervals. The result is active erosion of the Seabrook beach. This situation did not impact human interests until the island was developed during the 1960s. Early shore protection measures included sandbag revetments and groins, riprap, and eventually larger rock, but storms continued to destroy the structures and properties. By 1982, an 8,000-foot section of shoreline was armored with a revetment composed of riprap or larger rock. Continued erosion and lowering of the beach in front of the revetments made the structures vulnerable to wave damage, and sustained maintenance was needed to preserve structural integrity.

Coastal geology and engineering studies indicated that inlet relocation was an affordable alternative to existing practices (Kana, 1989). The project was approved and funded by the Seabrook Island Property Owners Association and the Seabrook Island Company. The plan required soft engineering solutions that did not depend on physical structures at the project shoreline. After much review and many appeals before the South Carolina Coastal Council and Army Corps of Engineers, the necessary permitting bodies, the project was approved with specific design features, objectives and a monitoring process. Completed in March 1983, the project cost approximately $350,000. About 175,000 cubic yards of sand were moved. Unit costs were approximately $0.50 per cubic yard, compared with direct nourishment by dredging sand from offshore at a cost of $1.75–5.25 per cubic yard.

The project has resulted in active accretion of the beaches on Seabrook Island. The relocation of Captain Sams Inlet demonstrated that cost-effective management of a migrating tidal inlet is possible under the physical conditions at the site. The project was both environmentally sensitive and cost effective, indicating the benefits of combining fundamental research on coastal processes with coastal engineering practices. Monitoring demonstrated the fact that only short-term adverse environmental impacts resulted from the disturbances caused by project construction. New dune habitat was established within 1 year. Sediment transport rates suggest that the inlet will return to its 1982 position by the turn of the century. The capability to engineer environmentally acceptable modifications to inlets is potentially adaptable to other barrier island locations.

MARSH RESTORATION AND CREATION USING DREDGED MATERIALS

In some restoration projects there are multiple users to be satisfied, and therefore a multiple-use project results.

Pointe Mouillee, Michigan

The 4,600-acre Pointe Mouillee wetland restoration project in western Lake Erie has many goals:

- containment of dredged materials from Lake Erie;
- restoration of an eroded barrier island;
- enhancement and management of the point as habitat and recreational area;
- improvement of water quality;
- removal and isolation of contaminated sediments from Lake Erie;
- establishment of a nature education program and visitor center;
- establishment of biking, hiking, and jogging trails;
- establishment of fishing grounds and hunting areas;
- provision of a boat harbor and marina;
- support for natural resource activities;
- provision of fish spawning areas, nurseries, and habitats; and
- provision of habitat for wildlife, resident and migratory birds, and small mammals.

The Pointe Mouillee confined disposal facility was built by the USACE to protect and stabilize the area's rapidly eroding shoreline and wetlands. Wetland restoration was encouraged through a slowing of the water flow. Dredged material was used to create waterfowl nesting islands, feeding areas for water birds, and nesting areas for sea birds. Natural resource recreation (that is, fishing, hunting, bird watching, boating, and nature trails) was incorporated in the design. The USACE and the Michigan Department of Natural Resources (DNR) developed a cooperative 30-year management strategy. The DNR is responsible for management of the site's natural resources. The Waterways Experiment Station of the USACE monitors (since 1979) the site for the Corps' Detroit District.

CASE STUDIES   145

Sediments dredged from Lake Erie contain contaminants and thus must be carefully place. The dredged materials that were placed at Pointe Mouillee consisted primarily sand and therefore leach rapidly. Earlier deposits at the site with high ambient levels of contaminants were covered under substantial layers of cleaner material that was placed in subsequent years. Rigorous monitoring conducted at the site indicates that contaminants remaining in the sediments have not resulted in environmental problems.

The success in meeting project objectives has stimulated requests to the Detroit district for additional use of disposal sites to provide wetland and shoreline protection in other areas of Lake Erie. Similar projects have been constructed at Monroe Harbor and Sterling State Park, once primarily recreational beach and park areas (Landin 1984, 1993b; Landin et al., 1989b,c).

Miller Sands Island, Oregon

Three habitats were developed at Miller Sands Island: an intertidal freshwater marsh, a grass/legume meadow for waterfowl nesting and Columbia whitetailed deer habitat, and dunegrass plantings to stabilize sandy dredged material and protect intertidal marsh.

The wetland and dune plantings have spread from an initial 300 square meter area to encompass over 5 square kilometers, and is providing water bird nesting and feeding habitat. The wetland has changed and increased in size considerably owing to annual additions of dredged material, but it largely maintains itself. Monitoring was done by the Waterways Experiment Station and the engineering work by the USACE Portland district. When compared to three reference areas nearby, wildlife use was dramatically greater on Miller Sands Island, and aquatic invertebrate and fish use of the wetland was equal to the reference areas. Several endangered species now use Miller Sands for migratory or year-round habitat (Landin, 1993c; Landin et al., 1988). The island has been designated as critical habitat for endangered salmonoid species.

Southwest Pass, Lower Mississippi River, Louisiana

Marsh development in southern Louisiana is a dynamic process that can be viewed as a battle to stave off some of the shoreline erosion, subsidence, and sediment starvation from levee systems and navigation channels that are resulting in the annual conversion of about 30 square miles per year of Louisiana wetlands, depending on the estimates used, into shallow water habitats (see Figures 3-1 and 3-2) (Turner and Cahoon, 1988). The USACE New Orleans district is developing up to 35,000 more acres of intertidal marsh by deepening and widening the lower Mississippi River, including Southwest Pass, the main outlet to the Gulf of Mexico. Southwest Pass and the Atchafalaya Delta in Louisiana are the two largest new wetlands constructed of dredged material in the United

146   APPENDIX B

States. The Atchafalaya Delta is also being reformed from sediments channeled through the Old River Control Structure on the Mississippi River.

Unconfined dredged material disposal was used to nourish, restore, or create (as determined by site conditions) intertidal marsh on the western side of the Southwest Pass. The dredge pipe was generally placed over the river berm in shallow water areas and slurry pumped through until intertidal elevations were reached. The dredge outfall was progressively moved to other shallow water areas to achieve the same result. Natural colonization occurred in 2–5 years.

Wildlife use of project sites is diverse, and wetland response to the placements is mixed. Some created marsh was destroyed when pipes were not moved soon enough. Subsidence in the area is so rapid that some of the marsh created during the 1970s has already subsided back into shallow water (Landin et al., 1989c)

CREATION OF SEA AND WADING BIRD NESTING ISLANDS IN NORTH CAROLINA

Since the 1890s, the Army Corps of Engineers has used dredged material to construct more than 2,000 islands in U.S. waterways; prior to 1970 virtually all were originally intended as disposal sites. Most were built when the Intracoastal Waterway System was established in the late 1940s and most of the islands are coastal.

At the same time that these islands were being built, coastal populations were increasing vastly. Natural habitats used by water birds were converted for urban and suburban development. The dredged material islands were isolated, unused, and similar to natural beaches and sand bars that are attractive as habitat for colonial water birds. As a result, sea and wading bird colonies relocated to these artificial islands in large numbers. More than 1 million water birds nest on the dredged material islands annually.

These islands have been carefully studied by the Waterways Experiment Station in conjunction with university and private contractors since 1975. Their objective is to determine the design and construction criteria that provide the best conditions for nesting colonies. Results of these studies have been published in government reports, scientific engineering journals, and dredging textbooks and are now used worldwide (Buckley and McCaffrey, 1978; Chaney et al., 1978; Landin, 1978, 1992b; Parnell et al., 1978; Peters et al., 1978; Scharf et al., 1978; Schreiber and Schreiber, 1978; Soots and Landin, 1978; USACE, 1986). The primary factors for sea and wading bird colonization are isolation, location within the waterway, size (more than 10 acres is best), configuration, elevation, presence or absence of dikes, slope of dikes, and substrate (Parnell et al., 1988).

The cost of constructing dredged material islands has risen from $0.50 to more than $4.00 per cubic yard. But costs are not the dominant factor in determining whether to repair and restore an existing island or to build a new one.

CASE STUDIES   147

The principal factor is the competing habitat objectives of federal agencies with habitat management responsibilities for different client species. The issue is not technical—but is one of discord over use of water resources and lands.

Intense opposition to fishery habitat interests is often associated with proposals to repair or build new dredged material islands. Further, because the placement of any structure, including islands, in shallow waters affects or replaces other habitats, it stimulates controversy. Thus restoration of dredged material islands has been erratic and is often delayed until water bird nesting has declined markedly, usually owing to loss of or natural changes to nesting habitat. Especially in Louisiana and North Carolina, state and federal agencies responsible for habitat management have improved their flexibility and willingness to consider the needs of diverse coastal species. But the optimal approach to nesting islands is unresolved.

UNDERWATER FEEDER AND STABLE BERMS
DAUPHIN ISLAND, MOBILE

Many feeder and stable berms have been constructed in the coastal zones in the United States, South Africa, the Netherlands, and Australia (Langan, 1988). That dredged material could be used effective for the construction of underwater berms to reduce beach erosion by dissipating wave energy and improve habitat for marine life was a major conclusion of Section II, Subject 3, Engineering on Sandy Coasts of the XXVI International Navigation Congress, held in Brussels, Belgium, June 17–21, 1985.

The two viable approaches to the design and construction of underwater structures apply: the feeder and stable berm concepts. Feeder berms (for beach nourishment) involve the placement of beach-quality sand in relatively shallow water, 16–18 feet deep, by small hopper dredges. The objective is to add suitable sand to the nearshore system in a manner similar to the natural bypassing of material that occurs at tidal inlets (Richardson, 1986). Stable berms involve the placement of dredged material in deeper water areas, up to 40–42 feet, using a variety of dredged material: silt and fine-grained sand and clay particles.

In 1982, the USACE Norfolk district began a pilot study of stable berms in the Dam Neck placement site off Virginia Beach. Construction drew on maintenance dredged material from the Thimble Shoal channel serving the ports of Hampton Roads (Murden, 1989a,b). Monitoring confirmed that the material was undisturbed even though a series of storms and three hurricanes had struck the area. Based on this study, the Corps proceeded with a national demonstration project offshore of Dauphin Island, Mobile, Alabama.

The plans and objectives for the construction of a feeder berm and a stable berm offshore of the badly eroded strand of Dauphin Island were coordinated extensively with members of Congress, the local sponsor of the Mobile harbor navigation project, and several environmental groups to ensure that the concept

148   APPENDIX B

was fully understood prior to construction. Further, an extensive monitoring program was planned in consultation with concerned parties to determine success or failure in meeting project objectives and to determine whether or to what degree marine habitat could be created using underwater berms an artificial reef. If adverse impacts to the marine environment were detected, then the dredged material would be transported to a historical placement area under contingency plans developed for this purpose (Clarke et al., 1988; Murden, 1988).

During February 1987, about 450,000 cubic yards of beach-quality sand were excavated from the entrance channel to the Port of Mobile and placed along the 18- to 20-foot depth contours. The material was placed parallel to the Dauphin Island shoreline about 3.5 miles offshore and 1.5 miles downdrift from the entrance channel.

The long-term monitoring program, initiated in 1987, includes precision bathymetric surveys before, during, and after construction. It is currently in progress. Monitoring includes fathometer and sidescan sonar surveys, wave and current data compilation, and soil sample analyses. It is intended to identify any adverse impacts on the marine habitat from construction of the nearshore feeder berm and any movement of the berm material (Hands, 1991; Poindexter-Rollings, 1990).

The feeder berm began to move slowly, as forecasted by the use of coastal engineering technology. A survey in January 1988 indicated that the material had begun to move to the west and farther downdrift from the entrance. By August 1989, portions of the berm had moved both westerly and to the north toward the Dauphin Island shoreline. Although the feeder is still a definable underwater feature, the berm material is beginning to merge with the ebb-tidal delta. Civic organizations and members of the engineering and scientific communities judged the project a success, based on these favorable data. Similar successful berms have since been constructed offshore of New York State, North Carolina, Texas, and California.

The stable berm element was begun in February 1988 and completed in May 1990. About 17 million cubic yards of silt and soft plastic clay particles were placed along the 40- to 45-foot depth contours parallel to the Dauphin Island shoreline about 2 miles downdrift and about 5 miles offshore. Extensive monitoring includes bathymetric, subbottom profile, and sidescan sonar surveys; sediment analyses; wave, wind, and barometric pressure data collection; benthic microfauna and vertical sediment profiling surveys; and fisheries investigations with trawling surveys, feeding analyses, and hydroacoustic surveys. These studies were done to determine whether the underwater feature would remain stable, whether the berm would contribute to wave energy dissipation, and whether the berm would improve the fisheries habitat. Initial dimensions of the stable berm were: elevation about 20 feet above the seabed, width 1 mile, and length 2.5 miles. It is the largest underwater berm constructed to date. Materials were exca-

CASE STUDIES   149

vated by a clamshell dredge and transported to the placement area in hopper barges.

Based on the following findings, the USACE considers the project successful (Clarke and Pullen, 1992; Langan and Rees, 1991):

• The project was constructed to design specifications with conventional dredging and positioning equipment.
• A relatively stable configuration was achieved, albeit with use for a wide variety of fine-grained materials.
• Energy of long-period storm waves was reduced by as much as 75 percent (McLellan et al., 1990).
• No adverse impacts on biological resources of the area have been indicated.
• The berm is serving as a refuge and feeding location for juvenile red snapper, other fish species of various age classes, and shrimp (Clarke and Pullen, 1992).

Additionally, construction costs were lessened because the distance to placement was less than to the historical placement area offshore. Extensive monitoring is providing the engineering and scientific data needed to conclude that underwater berms offer a wide variety of potential benefits. Further monitoring and evaluation at other sites could be used to improve quantification of the berm's response to waves, currents, and other forces; with this information, the design criteria for future berms can be broadened and the potential benefits better understood (McLellan and Imsand, 1989).

To date the demonstration projects indicate that the technology is well suited for shoreline protection and the creation of marine habitat. Benefits of the feeder berms include the introduction of beach-quality sand into the nearshore profile. Over an extended period, the supplemental materials are expected to contribute to the creation of a more gentle underwater slope and corresponding reduction in beach erosion. Research indicates that the cost of nearshore placement can be about one half the cost of beach placement (Juhnke et al., 1990). The stable berms are also providing benefits; they are reducing wave energy and improving fisheries habitat.

The potential benefits of underwater berm construction are summarized by Hands and Bradley (1990) as follows:

• enhancement of fisheries;
• stockpiling of sand for later use;
• reduction wave impact and run-up damages;
• augmentation of the sand budget on an eroding coast;
• reduction of offshore sand loss through service as an underwater barrier;
• bolstered foundations or formed cores of offshore structures;

150   APPENDIX B

- channelized migration of fluid muds;
- reduced hauling distances and placement costs; and
- improved monitoring of materials behavior.

ARTIFICIAL REEF TECHNOLOGY AND APPLICATIONS

The construction of artificial reefs has evolved from the dumping of trash, construction materials, tires, automobiles and appliances, and worn-out or excess ships to the sophisticated design structures with specific habitat objectives. The state of the art is highly advanced in Japan, where virtually all coastal habitats have been destroyed or substantially altered. No undisturbed estuaries remain; coastal waters have been heavily polluted by runoff from rivers and discharge from municipalities and industries. As a result, the Japanese government and private interests commit large resources to creating artificial habitat. In the United States, artificial reefs have been constructed in domestic waters and on the continental shelf, primarily as artificial fishing reefs for recreation instead of commercial use. Most of the reefs are unsophisticated in terms of design, construction materials, and placement technology (Bell, 1986; McGurrin et al., 1989 a,b; Seaman and Sprague, 1991; Sheehy and Vik, 1992).

Artificial habitats are constructed from a variety of materials that include bamboo and cork rafts, spheres, midwater fish attraction devices, ballasted trees, plastic seaweed, stones and quarry rock, concrete cubes and culverts, ballasted tires, plastic and concrete blocks (including oil ash stabilized in concrete blocks), derelict and scrap vessels, low- and high-profile steel reefs, and obsolete petroleum platforms (McGurrin et al., 1989; McGurrin and Reeff, 1986; Seaman and Sprague, 1991; Sheehy and Vik, 1992; Shieh et al., 1989). Many reefs are formed simply by dumping or sinking materials and then relying on natural colonization. Except for structures such as ships, control over the form and function of the reef is limited. Designed, prefabricated reefs have some advantages over the less sophisticated reefs; the former can accommodate site-specific and species-specific considerations. This capability permits the use of artificial reefs where other restoration technologies, such as those for restoring seagrass beds, might not be suitable. Although prefabricated artificial reef technology is expensive relative to more traditional techniques, it has more flexibility for use under varying water quality and physical energy conditions. Prefabricated reef technology could also be employed as an interim measure to enhance or provide opportunity for natural recolonization of a damaged site (Sheehy and Vik, 1992).

Artificial Reef Technology in Japan

Comprehensive reviews are available on the evolution and status of Japan's exhaustive efforts to construct and maintain artificial reefs in its nearshore waters (Grove and Sonu, 1991a,b; Sheehy and Vik, 1981a,b). In the 1900s local

CASE STUDIES   151

practices evolved beyond individuals making their own reefs by pushing shore rocks into coastal waters, for example. As fishermen organized cooperatives, they built larger, more effective structures. Then in the 1950s, designed and prefabricated concrete modules were used to make artificial reefs. At the same time, the Japanese government made matching funds available to prefectural and municipal governments and fishing cooperatives (Sheehy, 1982).

Japan's national program for the creation of artificial reefs has for years involved long-term planning and the expenditure of hundreds of millions of dollars; the reefs have "altered the nature of coastal fisheries and have contributed to appreciably increasing the incomes of coastal fishermen" (Sheehy, 1982). Grove and Sonu (1991b) reported that the Japanese government spent an average of approximately $100 million to construct 1.4 million cubic meters of habitat annually for the past 12 years. Japan's next 6-year plan (1988–1994) calls for the expenditure of $933 million (1987 conversion rates) to construct 14 million cubic meters of artificial habitat (Grove and Sonu, 1991b).

Artificial Reef Technology in the United States

Artificial reef technology has largely drawn on available construction materials, such as old ships and rubble. Placement basically involves sinking or dumping materials at a designated site (Bell, 1986; Lewis and McKee, 1989; McGurrin et al., 1989a,b; McGurrin and Reeff, 1986). More recently, efforts have been made to apply more sophisticated design and placement techniques. These include important progress in Louisiana and South Carolina, which is emphasizing design and planning. Programs in both states have significant research efforts to support future artificial development. Specially designed and placed artificial reefs have also been used as a form of mitigation for port development (Sheehy and Vik, 1988b). Private investment in artificial reefs for commercial fishing is constrained by the treatment of artificial reefs and the fishes that inhabit or are attracted to them as common property. Without control of the fishery resources by private companies, for example, commercial investment is unattractive.

Louisiana is converting oil and gas production platforms to artificial reefs when they stop producing and regulations call for their removal from the Gulf of Mexico. Using creative legislation and memorandums of understanding with the state and federal governments, the state has cooperated with the petroleum industry to tip the old structures into the water, remove them as navigation hazards, and mark them for use by anglers. Part of the money saved by the industry is dedicated to research and development in support of the Rigs to Reefs project (Sheehy and Vik, 1982).

South Carolina resource authorities recognized that the state's continental shelf lacks structures that support reef communities. The state became an early proponent of creating artificial habitats to support recreational fishing. Its Wildlife and Marine Resources Department has a section that studies, promotes, and

152   APPENDIX B

assists in developing artificial reefs. Section personnel work with fishing clubs and other private groups and use state and federal funds as well as volunteer efforts to create new structures. The legislature has approved a reef management plan. Placement of new artificial reef structures is regulated by the South Atlantic Fishery Management Council.

BIOENGINEERING APPLICATIONS FOR COASTAL RESTORATION

Bioengineering is the use of plants and plant materials for protection and restoration. In Western Europe, resource restoration has applied bioengineering technology for decades, and is so routine that restoration technology, its costs, and monitoring are automatically included in construction designs before they are approved and implemented. Germany routinely uses bioengineering in reservoir, lake, and streambank erosion control, including preventive structure placement prior to water impoundment. Breakwater designs, cribbing, wattling, soil stabilization amendments, and other techniques are available to German engineers (Allen, 1992). On the North Sea coast where 12-foot tides occur, routine application of bioengineering techniques includes grid systems built with light-foot-pressure equipment to trap sediments and create fast land, a remarkably successful technique in the North Sea environment and one that could have direct applications in coastal Louisiana, for example.

In the United States, where resource restoration has used bioengineering technology for the past 20 years, it is still considered an untested technology. Yet there are dozens of examples of success with temporary and permanent breakwaters coupled with plant materials, erosion control fabrics and geotextiles, layering, wattling, bundling, floating islands, and other techniques in the nation's lakes, reservoirs, rivers, and streams and along the coast. Poor technology transfer may be a problem. This technology, although widely used by federal agencies (the USACE and SCS primarily), is not widely known elsewhere; nor is it routinely addressed in academic curricula.

In cost comparisons with traditional engineering structures prepared by the Waterways Experiment Station, these techniques save as much as 90 percent of protection and restoration costs. For example, riprap typically costs approximately $300 per linear foot and erosion control matting (plants included) an estimated $30–40 per linear foot. Bioengineering appears to have little effect on costs in high energy areas. Yet low-to-moderate wave energy sites have been stabilized with little difficulty along the South Atlantic coast and Gulf coast when plant materials were used along with bioengineering technology.

The National Park Service tested bioengineering techniques in restoring Kenilworth Marsh in the Anacostia River in Washington, D.C., and other agencies are considering using these techniques. Technical information is available from the USACE and SCS (Allen, 1990; Allen and Klimas, 1986; Landin, 1991; PIANC, 1992b).

CASE STUDIES   153

GIS APPLICATION IN MARINE HABITAT MANAGEMENT

GIS are tools for delineating wetlands, evaluating natural resources, predicting impacts on these resources, and helping determine where restoration will be
most effective. Several agencies are exploring GIS use in coastal restoration and
enhancement, including applications in the Chesapeake Bay region. For example, Maryland already uses GIS for wetlands delineation purposes. Figures 3-1
and 3-2 in Chapter 3 were derived from GIS maps prepared by the USFWS. GIS
technology has also assisted in resource evaluation in the Yazoo Basin in Mississippi and Lake Michigan, both discussed below.

In the Yazoo Basin, the USACE Vicksburg district, the Dallas EPA office,
the USFWS Vicksburg field office, and the Mississippi SCS office used GIS to
advance wetland identification on 3 million acres. The GIS mapping of land use
and habitat types was used to determine whether landowners owned wetlands
and the implications to the owners. GIS technology has also aided in developing
a comprehensive levee and channel system, and, based on hydrology, elevation,
and soil types, in predicting restoration mitigation effects for major areas of the
Yazoo Basin.

In the Great Lakes, GIS applications are being developed to predict lake
level changes and associated wetland and other habitat losses. The information
will be used in urban planning, identifying continued habitat changes and losses,
identifying potential habitat restoration areas, and predicting achievement of restoration project objectives.

The Army Corps of Engineers funded costs of the Yazoo Basin GIS applications and both the USACE and the EPA funded the Great Lakes GIS applications. Development of the GIS systems used in these two applications cost several hundred thousand dollars; both agencies will bear the GIS maintenance and
updating costs (Landin, 1991).

Although substantial amounts can be spent on computer hardware and GIS
software, moderately priced GIS software (about $5,000) that can run on desktop
computers is available. High-resolution work, depending on the scale and size of
the database, may require a computer workstation with active hard drives and a
substantial memory capacity. Data acquisition can be expensive; their availability, accuracy, and costs are the limiting factors in use of GIS technology, not the
software or hardware, unless a high capacity workstation is needed. Existing
databases with potential marine habitat management potential are available or
are being developed by some local, state, and federal agencies. In particular,
some local taxing authorities have adopted GIS, conducted aerial reconnais-
sance, and digitized the results to assist in tax assessments. When such data are
available, marine habitat management authorities can use them to identify and
track changes in habitat profiles, including conversions and alterations of human
origin that are not permitted.

APPENDIX

C

Source Reference Table

Many references identified during the study provide information on the application of protection and restoration technologies and project results. A representative number of references on technologies, applications, results, and associated issues are presented here to aid in their use. Materials selected introduce marine habitat protection and restoration needs and provide insight for the application of technology. Full citations appear in the References.

| | | Region and Topic[a] (See note[b] for treatment codes within columns) | | | | | | | |
Author (Date)	Title	A	B	C	D	E	F	G	H
Alevison and Gorham (1989)	Effects of artificial reef deployment on nearby resident fishes	SE GC				1			
Amos and Amos (1985)	Atlantic and Gulf Coasts	NE MA SE GC	1	1	1	1	1	1	
Aquatic Habitat Institute et al. (1990)	Status and trends report on dredging and waterway modification in the San Francisco Estuary	P					4 5		
Barnett and Crewz (1991)	An Introduction to Planting and Maintaining Selected Common Coastal Plants in Florida	SE GC	1 2	1 2	1 2			1 2	
Bell (1989)	Application of wetland valuation theory to commercial and recreational fisheries in Florida	SE	3				3		
Bell et al. (1989)	Utilization of manufactured reef structures in South Carolina's marine artificial reef program	SE				2 3			
Berger (1990a)	Ecological Restoration in the San Francisco Bay Area: A Descriptive Directory and Sourcebook	P	2 4 6 7					2 4 7	2 4 7

| | | Region and Topic[a] (See note[b] for treatment codes within columns) | | | | | | | |
Author (Date)	Title	A	B	C	D	E	F	G	H
Berger (1990b)	Environmental Restoration: Science and Strategies for Restoring the Earth	SE P O	2 3 7	2 3	2 3				4 9
Boesch, et al. (1983)	Subsidence in coastal Louisiana: causes, rates and effects on wetlands	GC	1 3						
Bonnickson (1988)	Restoration ecology: philosophy, goals, and ethics	O							3 9
Broussard (1987)	Report on current marsh management engineering practices	O	2 3						
Cahill (1994)	Federal, state and local public agency management of coastal wetland mitigation projects: The Batiquitos Lagoon Enhancement Project	P	4 5 7				4 5 7		
Cahoon and Cowen (1988)	Environmental impacts and regulatory policy implications of spray disposal of dredged material in Louisiana wetlands	GC	3 2 6						
California State Coastal Conservancy (1988)	Tijuana River Estuary Tidal Flow Enhancement and Wetland Restoration Program	P	3				2		
Chiappone (1994)	Conservation monitoring of benthic communities in the Florida Keys: Ecological methodology	GC							1 4 7

157

Author (Date)	Title	Region and Topic[a] (See note[b] for treatment codes within columns)							
		A	B	C	D	E	F	G	H
Clarke et al. (1988)	Creation of offshore topographic features with dredged material	SE GC							5 6
Cobb (1987)	Mitigation evaluation study for the South Texas Coast, 1975–1986	GC	4 7	4 7					
Crewz and Lewis (1991)	An Evaluation of Historical Attempts to Establish Emergent Vegetation in the Marine Wetlands in Florida	SE GC	9						
Davis et al. (1990)	Environmental Considerations for Port and Harbor Developments	O							3
Engler et al. (1991a)	The nature of dredged material	N							1 5 6
Engler et al. (1991b)	Environmental effects of aquatic disposal of dredged material	N							1 5 6
EPA (1989)	Estuarine Wetland Restoration Monitoring Protocol	P	4						
Florsheim et al. (1990)	Hydrologic and Geomorphic Analysis of the Tijuana Estuary: Technical Appendix	P					9		
Fonseca et al. (1990)	Comparisons of fauna among natural and transplanted eelgrass Zostera marina meadows: criteria for mitigation	N		1					

Author (Date)	Title	Region and Topic[a] (See note[b] for treatment codes within columns)							
		A	B	C	D	E	F	G	H
Foster and Schiel (1985)	The Ecology of Giant Kelp Forests in California: A Community Profile	P			1				
Gannon (1990)	International position statement and evaluation guidelines for artificial reefs in the Great Lakes	GL				3			
GAO (1991)	Coastal Pollution: Environmental Impacts of Federal Activities Can Be Better Managed	N	3			3			
Garrell et al. (1992)	The Long Island Sound Study: Long range management of a critical estuary	MA NE					1 4		
Gorham and Alevizon (1989)	Habitat complexity and the abundance of juvenile fishes residing on small scale artificial reefs	O				1			
Hamilton et al. (1989)	Mangrove forests: An undervalued resource of the land and of the sea	GC			1 3				
Herbich (1992b)	Handbook of Dredging Engineering	SE O						2	2 4 5 6
Hine et al. (1987)	Effect of Hurricane Elena on Florida's marsh-dominated coast: Pasco, Hernando, and Citrus Counties	SE	8						
Hooks et al. (1988)	The Ecology and Management of Wetlands	N	1						

Author (Date)	Title	Region and Topic[a] (See note[b] for treatment codes within columns)							
		A	B	C	D	E	F	G	H
Josselyn (1988)	Effectiveness of coastal wetland restoration: California	P	1						
Josselyn and Bucholz (1984)	Marsh Restoration in San Francisco Bay: A Guide to Design and Planning	P	2						
Josselyn et al. (1987)	An evaluation of habitat use in natural and restored tidal marshes in San Francisco Bay, Calif.	P	1						
Josselyn et al. (1989)	Public Access and Wetlands: Impacts of Recreational Use	P	3						
King (1991)	Economics: Costing out restoration	N							3
Kusler and Kentula (1990)	Wetland Creation and Restoration: The Status of the Science	N	1 2						
Lethbridge (1988)	Environmental considerations for port and harbour developments	O							3 5
Ludwig et al. (1994)	Regulated development in coastal wetlands: An analysis of trends in the Setion 10/404 permit program in portions of the United States	N							3
Macdonald et al. (1990a)	South San Diego Bay Enhancement Plan. Vol. One/Resources Atlas: Marine Ecological Characterization, Bay History, and Physical Environment	P	1 5						

| | | Region and Topic [a] | | | | | | | |
| Author (Date) | Title | (See note [b] for treatment codes within columns) | | | | | | | |
		A	B	C	D	E	F	G	H
Macdonald et al. (1990b)	South San Diego Bay Enhancement Plan. Vol. 3. Enhancement Goals and Concepts	P	1 3						
Mager (1990)	National Marine Fisheries Service habitat conservation efforts related to federal regulatory programs in the southeastern United States	SE	3						
Marine Research Laboratory (1987)	Proceedings of the Symposium on Subtropical-Tropical Seagrasses of the Southeastern United States	SE GC		1 2 3					
Matthiessen (1989)	Planning for sea level rise in southern New England	NE							
Maynord et al. (1992)	Design of Habitat Restoration Using Dredged Material at Bodkin Island, Chesapeak Bay, Maryland	MA	2 5				5	5	
McConnaughey and McConnaughey (1985)	Pacific Coast	P	1	1	1	1	1	1	
McGurrin and ASMFC (1988)	A Profile of Atlantic Artificial Reef Development	MA SE				7			
McGurrin and ASMFC (1989a)	An assessment of Atlantic artificial reef development	SE				2 3			
McGurrin and Reeff	Artificial reef development and deployment	N				2			

Region and Topic

(See note[b] for treatment codes within columns)

Author (Date)	Title	A	B	C	D	E	F	G	H
McGurrin et al. (1989b)	Profiling United States Artificial Reef Deployment	N				2 3			
McKenzie et al. (1990)	Analysis of Marsh Transplant Experiments at Jetty Island, Everett, Washington	P	1 2					2 6	
McClellan and Imsand (1989)	Berm construction utilizing dredged material	GC						5 6 7	
Mendelssohn (1982)	Sand dune vegetation and stabilization in Louisiana	GC						1 2 5	
Mendelssohn et al. (1983)	Dune building and vegetative stabilization in a sand deficient barrier island environment	GC						1 2	
Mendelssohn and Hester (1988)	Texaco USA coastal vegetation project, Timbalier Island	GC						1 2	
Mendelssohn et al. (1991)	Experimental dune building and vegetative stabilization in a sand-deficient barrier island setting on the Louisiana coast	GC						1 2	
Merkel and Hoffman (1990)	Proceedings of the California Eelgrass Symposium	P		1 2 7					
Murden (1989a)	Construction of Underwater Berms	N					2 5 6	2 5 6	

Author (Date)	Title	Region and Topic[a] (See note[b] for treatment codes within columns)							
		A	B	C	D	E	F	G	H
NAEP (1991)	The Environmental Professional, Special Issue: Restoration of Ecosystems	O							1 2 3 4
Nailon and Seidensticker (1994)	Wetland creation efforts in Galveston Bay, Texas	GC	4 5 7					1 4	
Nelson (1985)	Physical and Biological Guidelines for Beach Restoration Projects: Part I	SE						4 5	
New York Sea Grant Institute (1990)	Identification and assessment of technical information requirements for developing coastal erosion management strategies	MA							
NMFS and USACE (1990)	Pilot Study to Determine the Feasibility of Establishing a Nationwide Program of Fisheries Habitat Restoration and Creation	N					1		1
NOAA (1990a)	Biennial Report to the Congress on Coastal Zone Management: Fiscal Years 1988 and 1989	N				1 3 4 7 9			
NOAA (1990b)	Estuarine Habitat Program Implementation Plan: FY 1991	N					3		
NOAA (1990c)	Estuarine Habitat Program Progress Report:	N					3		

Region and Topic[a]
(See note[b] for treatment codes within columns)

Author (Date)	Title	A	B	C	D	E	F	G	H
NRC (1983b)	Fundamental Research on Estuaries: The Importance of an Interdisciplinary Approach	O					1, 9		
NRC (1985d)	Dredging Coastal Ports: An Assessment of the Issues	N					2, 3, 5		
NRC (1987a)	Responding to Changes in Sea Level: Engineering Implications	O					2, 5	2, 5	2, 5
NRC (1989b)	Measuring and Understanding Coastal Processes for Engineering Purposes	O					4, 5	4, 5	4, 5
NRC (1990a)	Managing Coastal Erosion	N						3, 2, 5	5
NRC (1990c)	Studies in Geophysics: Sea Level Change	O					9	9	
NRC (1991)	Opportunities in the Hydrologic Sciences	O							2, 9
NRC (1992a)	Restoration of Aquatic Ecosystems: Science, Technology, and Public Policy	N	1, 2, 3, 4				1, 2, 3, 4		
Payne (1992)	Techniques for Wildlife Habitat Management of Wetlands	N	1, 2, 6, 7						

Author (Date)	Title	Region and Topic[a] (See note[b] for treatment codes within columns)							
		A	B	C	D	E	F	G	H
PERL (1990)	A Manual for Assessing Restored and Natural Coastal Wetlands with Examples from Southern California	P	1 4						
PIANC (1992a)	Beneficial Uses of Dredged Material: A Practical Guide	O	2 6				2 6		2 5
PIANC (1992b)	Guidelines for the Design and Construction of Flexible Revetments Incorporating Geotextiles in Marine Environment	O						2 5	2 5
Reeff et al. (1990)	Atlantic States Marine Fisheries Commission (ASMFC) Recommendations for Atlantic State Artificial Reef Management	MA SE				3			
Restoration Planning Work Group (1990a)	Restoration planning following the Exxon Valdez oil spill	P							8
Restoration Planning Work Group (1990b)	Restoration following the Exxon Valdez oil spill. Proceedings of the Public Symposium held in Anchorage, Alaska, March 26–27, 1990	P							3 8
Sather et al. (1984)	Proceedings of the National Wetland Values Assessment Workshop	N	3						
Schadt et al. (1989)	Biological monitoring at Port of Seattle disposal mitigation sites	P						4 5 6	

Author (Date)	Title	Region and Topic[a] (See note[b] for treatment codes within columns)							
		A	B	C	D	E	F	G	H
SCOR (1991)	The response of beaches to sea-level changes: A review of predictive models	N						4 5	
SCS (1992)	Engineering Field Handbook EFH-1A: Part 650, Chapter 13—Wetland Restoration, Enhancement, or Creation	N	2 5						
Seaman and Spague (1991)	Artificial Habitats for Marine and Freshwater Fisheries	O				1 2			
Sheehy (1982)	The use of designed and prefabricated artificial reefs in the United States	N O				2			
Sheehy and Vik (1981a)	Developments in East Asia	O				2			
Sheehy and Vik (1982)	Artificial reefs—A second life for offshore platforms?	N				2			
Sheehy and Vik (1983)	Recent advances in artificial reef technology	N O				2			
Sheehy and Vik (1988a)	Extending mitigation banking beyond wetlands	O	3						
Sheehy and Vik (1988b)	Mitigation planning for port development	O	3						
Steimle et al. (1990)	A Review of Artificial Reef Research Needs	O				9			

Author (Date)	Title	Region and Topic[a] (See note[b] for treatment codes within columns)							
		A	B	C	D	E	F	G	H
Stone (1985)	NOAA Technical Memorandum NMFS OF-6: National Artificial Reef Plan	N				3			1 2 3
Stroud (1992)	Stemming the Tide of Coastal Fish Habitat Loss: Proceedings of a Symposium on Conservation of Coastal Fish Habitat	N					1 2 3		
Thayer (1992)	Restoring the Nation's Marine Environment	N	2	2	2	2	2		2 3
The Sounds Conservancy (1990)	Intertidal flats: Their value and legal status	NE	3						
Thorhaug (1990)	Restoration of mangroves and seagrasses—economic benefits for fisheries and mariculture	GC	2 3	2 3	2 3				
Titus (1988)	Greenhouse Effect, Sea Level Rise and Coastal Wetlands	N	1 7						
USACE (1984)	Pointe Mouillee: Wetland Establishment in Connection with Disposal of Dredged Material	GL	2 6						
USACE (1989a)	Environmental Engineering for Coastal Protection	N						2 5	2 3 4 5

Author (Date)	Title	Region and Topic[a] (See note[b] for treatment codes within columns)							
		A	B	C	D	E	F	G	H
USACE (1989c)	San Francisco Bay to Stockton navigation project. Monitoring program for created wetlands	P	4						
USACE (1990)	Marsh establishment at Corpus Christi, Texas, 45-foot project mitigation site-wetland development	GC	2 3 6						
Wells and Gratwick (1988)	Canadian Conference on Marine Environmental Quality: Proceedings	CA CP							3 7 9
WES (1988)	Environmental Effects of Dredging	O							1 6
Williams (1990)	Pescadero Marsh Natural Preserve Hydrological Enhancement Plan	P	3						
Williams et al. (1990)	Coasts in Crisis	N							3 7
Zedler (1984)	Salt Marsh Restoration: A Guidebook for Southern California	P	1 2						
Zedler and Langis (1991)	Comparisons of constructed and natural salt marshes of San Diego Bay	P	1 3						
Zedler and Nordby (1986)	The Ecology of Tijuana Estuary, California: An Estuarine Profile	P	1						

Author (Date)	Title	Region and Topic[a] (See note[b] for treatment codes within columns)							
		A	B	C	D	E	F	G	H
Zedler et al. (1992)	The Ecology of Tijuana Estuary, California: A National Estuarine Research Reserve	P					1		

[a]Codes for region and topics

Topic
A   Region
B   Marshes or intertidal
C   Seagrasses
D   Mangrove or kelp forests
E   Reefs
F   Estuaries
G   Beaches or barrier islands
H   Other

Region
NE   New England
MA   Mid Atlantic
SE   Southeast United States
GC   Gulf Coast
P   Pacific/West Coast
M   Midwest
CA   Canadian Atlantic
CP   Canadian Pacific
N   National
O   Other

[b]Codes for treatment:

1   Ecology
2   Technology
3   Policy or economics
4   Monitoring
5   Coastal engineering
6   Use of dredged material
7   Case study or project descriptions
8   Storm or oil spill recovery
9   Other

APPENDIX

D

Summary of Solicited Expert Accounts

More than 75 solicited expert accounts with supporting references were provided by practitioners, resource agencies, and environmental organizations to support preparation of this report. Findings derived from these accountings (Yozzo, 1991) are summarized below. Key references are included in the References. A selective source reference table categorized by habitat type and nature of treatment is included as Appendix C.

Issues related to marine habitat creation, protection, and enhancement were explored in order to assess the diverse concerns of federal and state agencies, academic institutions, public interest groups, and industry. A primary topic was the beneficial application of technology in the marine environment.

Nine geographical regions were represented: Mid-Atlantic, Gulf, Pacific, Southeast, Great Lakes, New England, Midwest, Canadian Pacific, and Canadian Atlantic. Technological applications to habitat projects range from coastal stabilization and artificial reef technology to the use of dredged material and exploitation of natural processes. Although many marine habitats have been restored and created, gaps in the state of practice were reported as shown in Table D-1. It identifies needs that practitioners believe should be the focus of habitat management research in the coming years. The geographical distribution is not a statistically valid sample, but region-specific interests and trends are suggested.

Two topics—(1) dredged material placement and (2) marsh creation, restoration, and management—were priority research needs in seven and eight of the nine regions. Hence these two research areas are deemed high-priority subjects

169

170   APPENDIX D

TABLE D-1   Research Needs Derived on Reported Gaps in the Coastal
Engineering State of Practice

Research Area	Region
Dredged material placement	G, MA, NE, SE, P, GL, M
Marsh creation, restoration, and management	G, MA, NE, SE, P, GL, CA,M
Restoration and management of seagrass beds	G, MA, P, NE, CP
Barrier island/dune restoration and management	G, MA
Shoreline protection and stabilization	G, MA, NE, SE, GL
Shoreline management	G, MA, NE, SE
Artificial reef development	G, MA, NE, SE, P
Restoration of fish spawning and nursery habitat	G, MA, NE, P, GL, M
Coastal landuse planning and public policy	MA, NE, P
Endangered species management	P
Point and nonpoint source pollution	NE, P, M

Abbreviations: CA, Canadian Atlantic; CP, Canadian Pacific; G, Gulf; GL, Great Lakes; M, Midwest; MA, Mid-Atlantic; NE, New England; P, Pacific; SE, Southeast.

in habitat management in all U.S. coastal regions. Restoration and management
of specific habitat types, such as seagrass beds and coastal dune systems, are of
particular significance in the Gulf, Mid-Atlantic, Pacific, New England, and Canadian Pacific regions.

Shoreline stabilization and protection are considered important in the Gulf,
Mid-Atlantic, New England, Southeast, and, particularly, the Great Lakes re-
gion. Artificial reef research is of interest in all coastal regions, except the Great
Lakes, whereas restoration of fish spawning and nursery habitats is of interest in
all littoral regions of the United States. The New England, Mid-Atlantic, and
Gulf regions also stand out with the highest number of research needs identified.

Respondents from all regions provided detailed descriptions of barriers to
successful implementation of technology in habitat management projects. Because some barriers are region specific, they are based on geographic locations,
as summarized in Table D-2.

No entry is shown for the Midwest, Canadian Pacific, and Canadian Atlantic
regions because only one response was received from the Midwest and none
from the other two regions on this particular issue. Lumped under policy constraints are: the requirement for *least-cost* options, lack of agreement among the
different levels of decisionmakers (federal, state and local); and lack of a general

TABLE D-2   Reported Barriers to Successful Implementation of Beneficial Technology in Marine Habitat Projects

Reported Barriers/Constraints	Region					
	MA	G	P	SE	GL	NE
Federal, state, and local policy	◆	◆		◆	◆	
Funding	◆	◆	◆			◆
Inadequate project monitoring	◆		◆	◆		
Perception of a common resource	◆					
Lack of communication		◆				
Antiquated technology		◆				
Reactive management decisions		◆				
Lack of interagency cooperation				◆	◆	
Lack of documented success				◆		
Lack of training, education, and knowledge					◆	
Provincialism						◆

Abbreviations: As in Table D-1.

mitigation policy associated with the NMFS. The perception of resources as common property, especially fisheries, is viewed as a major impediment in the development of artificial reef programs. The use of obsolete dredging technology was cited as another hindrance, although recourse appears available in advanced pump design and plant automation (Herbich, 1992b).

Lack of communication, not only between the engineering and scientific communities but also between engineers and regulatory agencies, was also viewed as a substantial barrier to effective implementation of technology. This deficiency could lead, for example, to a distrust of engineers by biologists, and it hinders promotion of the multidisciplinary approach that appears imperative to bringing projects to fruition. On the other hand, the lack of communication between engineers and regulatory agencies can cause antagonism between the two groups with consequent further alienation, to the apparent detriment of a rational execution of projects. Similarly, a parochial mentality can lead into an unwillingness to apply useful technology developed elsewhere.

Although Table D-2 may indicate that certain barriers are relevant to specific geographical regions, most of these issues are more endemic in nature than the table conveys. This assertion is supported in large measure by the responses on specific issues. Of the 71 respondents involved in habitat creation, restoration, and enhancement projects, only 12 percent used published criteria or guidelines in project design. Although 71.8 percent of the respondents did not respond to this question, the overall implication can still be construed as a reflection of the nascent state of this particular field of engineering in the marine environment. The apparent lack of codification of engineering planning and design standards appears likely to render habitat development or alteration an iterative experiment into the foreseeable future. Similarly, failure to respond to questions relating to employee training programs (81.8 percent), accreditation requirements (83.1 percent), and public education programs (67.5 percent) speaks clearly to an apparent nationwide phenomenon of inadequate training, inadequate education, and inadequate knowledge. It draws into question the capability of many practitioners to perform credibly that might by suggested by a demonstrated commitment to building requisite engineering and scientific knowledge among those entering the field and continuing throughout their professional development programs.

In identifying research needs, respondents were asked what in their view was the single most important technology that merited research and development. Although various topics were listed for future research in habitat protection and enhancement, 77 percent of respondents did not identify the most important technology. A pattern of regional trends is readily discernible from the responses, but certain key issues and research and development areas were cited often enough to render them of global importance. These include:

- creation, restoration, and enhancement of wetland habitats;
- improvements in technology for alternative uses of dredged materials; and
- improvements in public policy and legislation regarding the protection and enhancement of marine environments.

The responses indicate that it is in these three areas that future efforts to improve the application of beneficial technology in the marine environment could be directed.

References

Alevizon, W. S. and J. C. Gorham. 1989. Effects of artificial reef deployment on nearby resident fishes. Bulletin of Marine Science 44(2):646-661.

Allen, H. H. 1988. Wetlands Created for Dredged Material Stabilization and Wildlife Habitat in Moderate to High Wave-Energy Environments. Environmental Effects of Dredging Technical Note EEDP-0702. Vicksburg, Mississippi: U.S. Army Engineer Waterways Experiment Station.

Allen, H. H. 1990. Biotechnical reservoir shoreline stabilization. Wildlife Resource Notes 8(1):1-11.

Allen, H. H. 1992. Bioengineering Techniques Use for Shoreline Erosion Control in Germany. Wetlands Research Program Technical Note No. WRP-VN-EM-3.1. Vicksburg, Mississippi: U.S. Army Waterways Experiment Station.

Allen, H. H., and C. V. Klimas. 1986. Reservoir Shoreline Revegetation Guidelines. Technical Report E-86-13. Vicksburg, Mississippi: U.S. Army Engineer Waterways Experiment Station.

Amos, W. H., and S. H. Amos. 1985. Atlantic and Gulf Coasts. New York: Alfred A. Knopf.

Anderson, S. H. 1980. The role of recreation in the marine environment. Pp. 183-198 in E. M. Borgese and N. Ginsburg, eds., Ocean Yearbook. Chicago, Illinois: the University of Chicago Press.

Anderson, W. C. 1992. Specialty Certification in the Environmental Arena. Presentation to the Metropolitan Washington Environmental Professionals, Washington, D.C., November 19, 1992.

Anderson, R., and M. Rockel. 1991. Economic Valuation of Wetlands. Discussion Paper No. 65. Washington, D.C.: American Petroleum Institute.

Aquatic Habitat Institute and Philip Williams & Associates, Ltd. 1990. Status and trends report on dredging and waterway modification in the San Francisco Estuary. EPA Coop. Agreement CE-009496-01. Oakland, California: San Francisco Estuary Project.

Barnett, M. R., and D. W. Crewz, eds. 1991. An Introduction to Planting and Maintaining Selected Common Coastal Plants in Florida. Florida Sea Grant Report No. 97. Gainesville: University of Florida.

Barnett, T. P. 1990. Recent changes in sea level: A summary. Pp. 37-51 in Sea Level Change. Washington, D.C.: National Academy Press.

173

REFERENCES

Batie, S. S., and C. C. Mabbs-Zeno. 1985. Opportunity costs of preserving coastal wetlands: A case study of a recreational housing development. Land Economics 61(1):1-9.

Batie, S. S., and L. A. Shabman. 1982. Estimating the economic value of wetlands: Principles, methods and limitations. Coastal Zone Management Journal 10(3):255-278.

Batie, S. S., and J. R. Wilson. 1979. Economic Values Attributable to Virginia's Coastal Wetlands as Inputs in Oyster Production. Report No. VPI-SG-77-04. Blacksburg, Virginia: Virginia Polytechnic Institute State University.

Bay Institute of San Francisco. 1987. Citizens' Report on the Diked Historic Baylands of San Francisco Bay. Sausalito, California: Bay Institute of San Francisco.

Bean, M. J. 1983. The Evolution of National Wildlife Law. New York: Praeger Publishers.

Bell, F. W. 1989. Application of wetland valuation theory to commercial and recreational fisheries in Florida. Florida Sea Grant College Report No. 95, Project No. R/C-E-25, Grant No. NA86AA-D-SG068. Tallahassee: Florida State University.

Bell, M. 1986. Needs of marine artificial reef programs in the United States: A state manager's viewpoint. Pp. 552-555 in Proceedings: Ocean 86. Piscataway, New Jersey: Institute of Electrical and Electronic Engineers.

Bell, M., C. J. Moore, and S. W. Murphey. 1989. Utilization of manufactured reef structures in South Carolina's marine artificial reef program. Bulletin of Marine Science 44(2):818-830.

Berger, J. J., ed. 1990a. Ecological Restoration in the San Francisco Bay Area: A Descriptive Directory and Sourcebook. Berkeley, California: Restoring the Earth.

Berger, J. J., ed. 1990b. Environmental Restoration: Science and Strategies for Restoring the Earth. Washington, D.C.: Island Press.

Berger, J. J. 1991. A generic framework for evaluating complex restoration and conservation projects. Environmental Professional 13:254-262.

Bergstrom, J. C., J. R. Soll, J. P. Titre, and V. L. Wright. 1990. Economic Value of Wetland-Based Recreation. Ecological Economics 2(2):129-147.

Blackburn, C., ed. 1993. New Perspectives on Environmental Education and Research. Research Triangle Park, North Carolina: Sigma Xi.

Boesch, D. F., D. Levin, D. Nummedal, and K. Bowles. 1983. Subsidence in coastal Louisiana: Causes, rates and effects on wetlands. FWS/OBS-83/26. Washington, D.C.: Division of Biological Services, U.S. Fish and Wildlife Service.

Bohnsack, J. A. 1989. Are high densities of fishes at artificial reefs the result of habitat limitation or behavioral preference? Bulletin of Marine Science 44(2):631-645.

Bohnsack, J. A., D. L. Johnson, and R. F. Ambrose. 1991. The ecology of artifical reef habitats and fishes. Pp. 61-107 in W. Seaman, Jr., and L. M. Sprague, eds., 1991, Artificial Habitats for Marine and Freshwater Fisheries. San Diego, California: Academic Press.

Bonnickson, T.M. 1988. Restoration ecology: philosophy, goals, and ethics. Environmental Professional 10(1):25-35.

Broome, S. W. 1990. Creation and restoration of tidal wetlands of the southeatern United States. Pp. 37-72 in J. A. Kusler and M. E. Kentula, eds., Wetland Creation and Restoration: The Status of the Science. Washington, D.C.: Island Press.

Broussard, L. J. 1987. Report on current marsh management engineering practices. NOAA Grant NA-87AAH-CZ047 for Louisiana Department of Natural Resources Coastal Management Division. Alexandria, Virginia: Soil Conservation Service.

Brown, L. K., and J. R. Watson. 1988. Facing the crisis: New Orleans District Corps of Engineers environmental projects and plans in port waterways to combat loss of Louisiana's wetlands. Pp. 297-303 in Proceedings of the International Seminar on Environmental Impact Assessment of Port Development. London: International Maritime Organization.

Brown, G. M., Jr., and H. O. Pollakowski. 1977. Economic valuation of shoreline. Review of Economics and Statistics 59(3):272-278.

REFERENCES

Bruun, P. 1962. Sea level rise as a cause of shore erosion. Journal of the Waterways and Harbors Division, American Society of Civil Engineers 88 (WW1):117-130.

Bruun, P. 1981. Port Engineering. Houston, Texas: Gulf Publishing Company.

Bruun, P. 1988. The Bruun Rule of erosion by sea-level rise: A discussion of large-scale two- and three-dimensional usages. Journal of Coastal Research 4:627-648.

Bruun, P. 1989a. Port Engineering, Volume 1: Harbor Planning, Breakwaters and Marine Terminals. Houston, Texas: Gulf Publishing Company.

Bruun, P. 1989b. Port Engineering, Volume 2: Harbor Transportation, Fishing Ports, Sediment Transport, Geomorphology, Inlets and Dredging. Houston, Texas: Gulf Publishing Company.

Buckley, F. G., and C. A. McCaffrey. 1978. Use of Dredged Material Islands by Colonial Seabirds and Wading Birds in New Jersey. Technical Report No. D-78-1. Prepared by Manomet Bird Observatory, Manomet, Massachusetts, for U.S. Army Corps of Engineers Dredged Material Research Program. Springfield, Virginia: National Technical Information Service.

Cahill, J. J. 1994. Federal, state and local public agency management of coastal wetland mitigation projects: The Batiquitos Lagoon Enhancement Project. Pp. 1-11 in M. P. Lynch and B. Crowder, eds., Proceedings of the 13th International Conference of the Coastal Society: Organizing for the Coast. Gloucester, Massachusetts: The Coastal Society.

Cahoon, D. R. and J. H. Cowen, Jr. 1988. Environmental impacts and regulatory policy implications of spray disposal of dredged material in Louisiana wetlands. Coastal Management 16:341-362.

Cairns, J. R., Jr. 1988. Increasing diversity by restoring damaged ecosystems. Pp. 333-343 in E. O. Wilson, ed., Biodiversity. Washington, D.C.: National Academy Press.

Cairns, J. R., Jr., and P. V. McCormick. 1992. Developing an ecosystem-based capability for ecological risk assessment. Environmental Professional 14(3):186-196.

Cairns, J. R., Jr., and B. R. Niederlehner. 1993. Ecological function and resilience: Neglected criteria for environmental impact assessment and ecological risk analysis. Environmental Professional 15(1):116-124.

Caldwell, L. K. 1991. Restoration ecology as public policy. Environmental Professional 13:275-284.

California State Coastal Conservancy. 1988. Tijuana River Estuary Tidal Flow Enhancement and Wetland Restoration Program. Project Summary, File No. 85-026.

Canter, L. W. 1993. The role of environmental monitoring in responsible project management. Environmental Professional 15(1):76-87.

Chaney, A. H., B. R. Chapman, J. P. Karges, D. A. Nelson, R. R. Schmidt, and L. C. Thebeau. 1978. Use of Dredged Material Islands by Colonial Seabirds and Wading Birds in Texas. Technical Report No. D-78-8. Prepared by Texas A&M University for U.S. Army Corps of Engineers Dredged Material Research Program. Springfield, Virginia: National Technical Information Service.

Charlier, R. H., C. De Meyer, and D. Decroo. 1989. "Soft" beach protection and restoration. Pp. 289-328 in E. M. Birgese, N. Ginsburg, and J. R. Morgan, eds., Ocean Yearbook 8. Chicago, Illinois: University of Chicago Press.

Chiappone, M. 1994. Conservation monitoring of benthic communities in the Florida Keys: Ecological methodology. Pp. 305-324 in M. P. Lynch and B. Crowder, eds., Proceedings of the 13th International Conference of the Coastal Society: Organizing for the Coast. Gloucester, Massachusetts: The Coastal Society.

Cintron-Molero, G. 1992. Restoring mangrove systems. Pp. 223-278 in G. W. Thayer, ed. Restoring the Nation's Marine Environment. College Park, Maryland: Maryland Sea Grant.

Clark, D. 1990. Coastal Louisiana Marine Habitat Management Information. Unpublished paper prepared by Louisiana Department of Natural Resources (DNR) for Committee on the Role of Technology in Marine Habitat Protection and Enhancement. Baton Rouge, Louisiana: Louisiana DNR.

Clarke, D., T. J. Fredette, and D. Imsand. 1988. Creation of offshore topographic features with dredged material. Environmental Effects of Dredging D-88-5 (November,990):1-5.

176   REFERENCES

Clarke, D. G., and E. J. Pullen. 1992. Finfish and shellfish use of the U.S. Army Corps of Engineers stable underwater demonstration berm, Dauphin Island, Alabama. Paper presented at the US-ACE/EPA Conference on the Use of Dredged Material for Wetland Restoration, New Orleans, Louisiana, December 1992.

Clausner, J. E., K. R. Melson, J. A. Hughes, and A. T. Rambo. 1990. Jet pump sand bypassing at Indian River Inlet. Proceedings of the 23rd Annual Dredging Seminar. College Station, Texas: Center for Dredging Studies, Texas A & M University.

Cobb, R.A. 1987. Mitigation evaluation study for the South Texas Coast, 1975-1986. Report prepared by Center for Coastal Studies, Corpus Christi State University, for U.S. Fish and Wildlife Service (USFWS). Corpus Christi, Texas: Corpus Christi Field Office, USFWS.

Costanza, R., S. C. Farber, and J. Maxwell. 1989. Valuation and Management of Wetland Ecosystems. Ecological Economics 1(4):335-361.

Costanza, R., and L. Wainger. 1990. No accounting for nature: How conventional economics distorts the real value of things. Washington Post. September 2, 1990, p. B3.

Crewz, D. W., and R. R. Lewis III. 1991. An Evaluation of Historical Attempts to Establish Emergent Vegetation in the Marine Wetlands in Florida. Florida Sea Grant College, Technical Paper No. 60. Gainesville, Florida: University of Florida.

Culliton, T. J., M. A. Warren, T. R. Goodspeed, D. G. Remer, C. M. Blackwell, and J. J. McDonough III. 1990. 50 Years of Population Change Along the Nation's Coasts, 1960-2010. Rockville, Maryland: National Oceanic and Atmospheric Administration.

Daniels, R. C., T. W. White, and K. K. Chapman. 1993. Sea-Level Rise: Destruction of Threatened and Endangered Species Habitat in South Carolina. New York: Springer-Verlag.

D'Avanzo, C. 1990. Long-term evaluation of wetland creation projects. Pp. 487-496 in J. A. Kusler and M. E. Kentula, eds., Wetland Creation and Restoration: The Status of the Science. Washington, D.C.: Island Press.

Davies, T. 1988. The setting of ports in the coastal environment. Pp. 262-263 in Proceedings of the International Seminar on Environmental Impact Assessment of Port Development. London: International Maritime Organization (IMO).

Davis, D. W. 1992. Land reclamation in coastal Louisiana: From 1718 to the present. Pp. 674-680 in M. C. Landin, ed., Proceedings of the Thirteenth Annual Conference, Society of Wetland Scientists. Utica, Mississippi: South Central Chapter, Society of Wetland Scientists.

Davis, J. D., S. MacKnight, IMO Staff, and Others. 1990. Environmental Considerations for Port and Harbor Developments. Washington, D.C.: World Bank.

Davison, A. T. 1991. Hurricane Hugo: "Before and after" observations revealing its impact. Shore and Beach 59(4):28-30.

Davos, C. A. 1988. Harmonizing environmental facts and values: A call for co-determination. Environmental Professional 10(1):46-53.

Dean, R. G. 1991. Impacts of global change: engineering solutions. Pp. 13-17 in Our Changing Planet: Joining Forces for a Better Environment, Proceedings of Symposium in Commemoration of the 20th Anniversary of the Graduate College of Marine Studies. Newark: University of Delaware.

Dean, R. G., and C. Yoo. 1993. Predictability of beach nourishment performance. Pp. 86-102 in D. K. Stauble and N. C. Kraus, eds., Beach Nourishment and Management Considerations, Proceedings of Coastal Zone '93. New York: American Society of Civil Engineers.

Dwivedi, O. P. 1988. Man and nature: An holistic approach to a theory of ecology. Environmental Professional 10(1):8-15.

Dyer, K. R. 1986. Coastal and Estuarine Sediment Dynamics. New York: Wiley.

Earhardt, G., D. Clarke, and J. Shipley. 1988. Beneficial uses of dredged material in shallow coastal waters; Chesapeake Bay demonstrations. Information Exchange Bulletin D-88-6, December 1988. Vicksburg, Mississippi: U.S. Army Engineer Waterways Experiment Station.

REFERENCES

Eisenberg, S. 1992. Presentation to Metropolitan Washington Environmental Professionals, Washington, D.C., November 19, 1992. Subject: National Assocation of Environmental Professionals certification program.

England, A. S., and F. Nakaji. 1990. Reclaiming flooded river islands as wetland and riparian habitat using dredged material. In Proceedings of Beneficial Uses of Dredged Material in the Western United States. Vicksburg, Mississippi: U.S. Army Engineer Waterways Experiment Station.

Engler, R. M. 1988. A review of the mitigative properties of dredged material in relation to the receiving environment. Pp. 215-245 in Proceedings of the International Seminar on Environmental Impact Assessment of Port Development. London: International Maritime Organization.

Engler, R., L. Saunders, and T. Wright. 1991a. The nature of dredged material. Environmental Professional 13(4):313-316.

Engler, R., L. Saunders, T. Wright. 1991b. Environmental effects of aquatic disposal of dredged material. Environmental Professional 13(4):317-325.

EPA. 1985. Freshwater Wetlands for Wastewater Management. Handbook No. 904/9-85-135. Washington, D.C.: Environmental Protection Agency.

EPA. 1989. Estuarine Wetland Restoration Monitoring Protocol. Final draft report prepared by University of Washington Wetland Ecosystem Team, FRI-UM-8918. Seattle, Washington: U.S. Environmental Protection Agency Region 10, Office of Puget Sound.

EPA. 1992. The National Estuary Program After Four Years. Report No. EPA 503/9-92/007. Washington, D.C.: Environmental Protection Agency.

Erwin, K. L. 1990. Wetland evaluation for restoration and creation. Pp. 429-458 in J. A. Kusler and M. E. Kentula, eds., Wetland Creation and Restoration: The Status of the Science. Washington, D.C.: Island Press.

Farber, S. C. 1987. The value of coastal wetlands for the protection of property against hurricane wind damage. Journal of Environmental Economics and Management 14(2):143-151.

Farber, S. C. 1988. The value of coastal wetlands for recreation: An application of the travel cost and contingent valuation methodologies. Journal of Environmental Management 26(4):299-312.

Farber, S. C., and R. Costanza. 1987. The economic value of wetland systems. Journal of Environmental Management 24(1):41-51.

Florsheim, J., P. B. Williams, L. Fishbain, and P. Goodwin. 1990. Hydrologic and Geomorphic Analysis of the Tijuana Estuary: Technical Appendix. San Francisco, California: Phillip Williams and Associates.

Fonseca, M. S. 1990. Regional analysis of the creation and restoration of seagrass system. Pp. 171-194 in J. A. Kusler and M. E. Kentula, eds., Wetland Creation and Restoration: The Status of the Science. Washington D.C.: Island Press.

Fonseca, M. S. 1992. Restoring seagrass systems in the United States. Pp. 79-110 in G. W. Thayer, ed., 1992, Restoring the Nation's Marine Environment. College Park, Maryland: Maryland Sea Grant.

Fonseca, M. S., W. J. Kentworthy, D. R. Colby, K. A. Rittmaster, G. W. Thayer. 1990. Comparisons of fauna among natural and transplanted eelgrass *Zostera marina* meadows: criteria for mitigation. Marine Ecology Progress Series 65:251-264.

Foster, M. S., and D. R. Schiel. 1985. The Ecology of Giant Kelp Forests in California: A Community Profile. Slidell, Louisiana: Division of Biological Services, U.S. Fish and Wildlife Service.

Fritchey, R. 1991. Diversions could save dwindling Louisiana wetlands. National Fisherman (December):28-29.

Gannon, J. E., ed. 1990. International position statement and evaluation guidelines for artificial reefs in the Great Lakes. Great Lakes Fishery Commision Special Publication 90-2. Ann Arbor, Michigan: Great Lakes Fishery Commission.

GAO. 1991. Coastal Pollution: Environmental Impacts of Federal Activities can be Better Managed. Washington, D.C.: U.S. General Accounting Office.

Garbisch, E. W. 1990. Information needs in the planning process for wetland creation and restoration. Pp. 423-427 in J. A. Kusler and M. E. Kentula, eds., Wetland Creation and Restoration: The Status of the Science. Washington, D.C.: Island Press.

Garrell, M. H., M. Beristain, C. L. Arnold, and K. Chytalo. 1992. The Long Island Sound Study: Long range management of a critical estuary. Environmental Professional 14(1):38-49.

Garrity, R. 1992. Pollution Recovery Trust Fund. Mimeographed. Tampa, Florida: Department of Environmental Regulation, Southwest District.

Gearheart, R. A., and B. A. Finney. 1982. Utilization of wetlands for reliable low-cost wastewater treatment. Paper presented at the International Water Resources Association IV World Congress on Water Resources, September 3-11, 1982, Buenos Aires, Argentina.

Gearheart, R. A., S. Wilbur, D. Hull, J. Williams, N. Hoelper, and B. Finney. 1982. City of Arcata Marsh Pilot Project—Second Annual Report. Sacramento, California: California Water Resources Control Board.

Georgia DOT. 1989. Waterways Dredged Material Containment Areas Study: Savannah Harbor. Atlanta, Georgia: Georgia Department of Transportation.

Gooselink, J. P., and R. H. Baumann. 1980. Wetland inventories: Wetland loss along the United States coast. Zeitschrift für Geomorphologie Neue Foldge 43:173-187.

Gorham, J. C., and W. S. Alevizon. 1989. Habitat complexity and the abundance of juvenile fishes residing on small scale artificial reefs. Bulletin of Marine Science 4(2):662-665.

Grant, J. R. H. 1992. Historical Shoreline Response to Inlet Modifications and Sea Level Rise. Masters of Science Thesis. Gainesville: University of Florida.

Grove, F., and C. Wilson, eds. In press. Proceedings of the Fifth International Conference on Habitats for Fisheries. Bulletin of Marine Science, Special Issue.

Grove, R. S., and C. J. Sonu. 1991a. Artificial Habitat Technology in the United States Today and Tomorrow. Unpublished manuscript.

Grove, R. S., and C. J. Sonu. 1991b. Global Trends in Artificial Habitat Technology. Unpublished manuscript.

Guilcher, A. 1987. Coral Reef Geomorphology. New York: Wiley.

Hall, M. J., and O. H. Pilkey. 1991. Effects of hard stabilization on dry beach width for New Jersey. Journal of Coastal Research 7(3):771-785.

Hammer, D. A., ed. 1989. Constructed Wetlands for Wastewater Treatment: Proceedings of the First International Conference. Chelsea, Michigan: Lewis Publishers.

Hamons, F. 1988. Port of Baltimore: Dredged material management master plan. Pp. 112-118 in Proceedings of the International Seminar on Environmental Impact Assessment of Port Development. London: International Maritime Organization.

Hamilton, L. S., J. A. Dixon, and G. O. Miller. 1989. Mangrove forests: An undervalued resource of the land and of the sea. Pp. 254-288 in E. M. Borgese, N. Ginsburg, and J. R. Morgan, eds., Ocean Yearbook 8. Chicago, Illinois: University of Chicago Press.

Hands, E. B. 1991. Wide-area monitoring of Alabama berms. Pp. 98-112 in Proceedings of MTS '91. Washington, D.C.: Marine Technical Society.

Hands, E. B., and K. P. Bradley. 1990. Results of Monitoring the Disposal Berm at Sand Island, Alabama, Report 1: Construction and First Year's Response. Technical Report DRP-90-02. Vicksburg, Mississippi: U.S. Army Engineer Waterways Experiment Station.

Harr, H. R. 1988. The Port of New Orleans. Pp. 290-296 in Proceedings of the International Seminar on Environmental Impact Assessment of Port Development. London, England: International Maritime Organization.

REFERENCES

Heald, E. J. 1969. The Production of Organic Detritus in a South Florida Estuary. Unpublished Ph.D. Dissertation. Miami, Florida: University of Miami.

Herbich, J. B. 1985. Environmental effects of dredging—the United States experience. Dock and Harbour Authority July/August:55-57.

Herbich, J. B. 1990. Handbook of Coastal and Ocean Engineering, Volume 1: Wave Phenomena and Coastal Structures. Houston, Texas: Gulf Publishing Company.

Herbich, J. B. 1991. Handbook of Coastal and Ocean Engineering, Volume 2: Offshore Structures, Marine Foundations, Sediment Processes and Modeling. Houston, Texas: Gulf Publishing Company.

Herbich, J. B., ed. 1992a. Handbook of Coastal and Ocean Engineering, Volume 3: Harbors, Navigation Channels, Estuaries and Environmental Effects. Houston, Texas: Gulf Publishing Company.

Herbich, J. B. 1992b. Handbook of Dredging Engineering. New York: McGraw-Hill.

Hickman, T., and C. Cocklin. 1992. Attitudes toward recreation and tourism development in the coastal zone: A New Zealand study. Coastal Management 20:269-289.

Higgins, S. H., and Fisher, L. E. 1993. The impacts of sea turtle nest relocation in Broward County, Florida. Pp 309-324 in The State of the Art of Beach Nourishment: Proceedings of the 1993 National Conference on Beach Preservation Technology. Tallahassee, Florida: Florida Shore and Beach Preservation Association.

Hine, A. C., M. W. Evans, D. L. Mearns, and D. F. Belknap. 1987. Effect of Hurricane Elena on Florida's marsh-dominated coast: Pasco, Hernando, and Citrus Counties. Florida Sea Grant College Technical Paper 49. St. Petersburg, Florida: University of South Florida.

Hodgin, D. A., C. Truitt, and J. Foote. 1993. Beach compactness regulatory criteria for nesting sea turtles on the southwest Florida shoreline. Pp. 325-339 in The State of the Art of Beach Nourishment: Proceedings of the 1993 National Conference on Beach Preservation Technology. Tallahassee, Florida: Florida Shore and Beach Preservation Association.

Hoffman, R. S. 1990. Recovery of eelgrass beds in Mission Bay, San Diego, California, following beach restoration work. Pp. 21-27 in K. W. Merkel and R. S. Hoffman, eds., Proceedings of the California Eelgrass Symposium. National City, California: Sweetwater River Press.

Hooks, D. D., W. H. McKee, Jr., H. K. Smith, J. Gregory, V. G. Burrell, Jr., M. R. DeVoe, R. E. Sojka, S. Gilbert, R. Banks, L. H. Stolzy, C. Brooks, T. D. Matthews, and T. H. Shear. 1988. The Ecology and Management of Wetlands. Portland, Oregon: Timber Press.

Hummer, C. W. 1988. The Corps' dredging programme and coastal engineering research. Pp. 277-279 in Proceedings of the International Seminar on Environmental Impact Assessment of Port Development. London: International Maritime Organization.

Jenkins, S. A., and J. A. Bailard. 1989. Anti-sedimentation systems for harbors. World Wide Shipping 52(1):70-75.

Johansson, J. O. R., and R. R. Lewis. 1992. Recent improvements of water quality and biological indicators in Hillsborough Bay, a highly impacted subdivision of Tampa Bay, Florida, U.S.A. Pp. 1199-1215 in Science of the Total Environment, Supplement 1992. Amsterdam, The Netherlands: Elsevier Science Publishers.

Josselyn, M. N. 1988. Effectiveness of coastal wetland restoration: California. Pp. 246-251 in J. A. Kusler, M. L. Quammen, and G. Brooks, eds., Proceedings of the National Wetland Symposium: Mitigation of Impacts and Losses. Berne, New York: Association of State Wetland Managers.

Josselyn, M. N., and J. Buchholz. 1984. Marsh Restoration in San Francisco Bay: A Guide to Design and Planning. Technical Report No. 3. Tiburon, California: Tiburon Center for Environmental Studies.

Josselyn, M. N., J. Duffield, and M. Quammen. 1987. An evaluation of habitat use in natural and restored tidal marshes in San Francisco Bay, Calif. Pp. 3085-3094 in Proceedings of Coastal Zone 87. New York: American Society of Civil Engineers.

Josselyn, M. N., M. Martindale, and J.M. Duffield. 1989. Public Access and Wetlands: Impacts of Recreational Use. Technical Report No. 9. Tiburon, California: Romberg Tiburon Centers, Center for Environmental Studies, San Francisco State University.

Josselyn, M. N., J. Zedler, and T. Griswold. 1990. Wetland mitigation along the Pacific coast of the United States. Pp. 3-36 in J. A. Kusler and M. E. Kentula, eds., Wetland Creation and Restoration: The Status of the Science. Washington, D.C.: Island Press.

Juhnke, L., T. Mitchell, and M. J. Piszker. 1990. Construction and Monitoring of Nearshore Disposal of Dredged Material at Silver Strand State Park, San Diego, Calif. CDS Report No. 321. Pp. 203-217 in Proceedings of the Western Dredging Association Conference, Las Vegas, Nevada. Fairfax, Virginia: Western Dredging Association.

Kagan, R. A. 1990. The Dredging Dilemma: How Not to Balance Economic Development and Environmental Protection. Working Paper 90-3, Institute of Government Studies. Berkeley, California: University of California at Berkeley.

Kana, T. 1989. Erosion and beach restoration at Seabrook Island, South Carolina. Shore and Beach 57(3):3-18.

Kellert, S. R. 1984. Assessing wildlife and environmental values in cost-benefit analysis. Journal of Environmental Management 18:355-363.

Kelley, K. 1991. Making the habitat connection. National Fisherman (April):20-23.

Kesel, R. H. 1988. The decline in the suspended load of the lower Mississippi River and its influences on adjacent wetlands. Environmental Geology Water Science 11(3):271-281.

King, D. M. 1991. Economics: Costing out restoration. Restoration & Management Notes 9(1):15-20.

Kirkman, H. 1992. Large-scale restoration of seagrass meadows. Pp. 111-140 in G. W. Thayer, ed., Restoring the Nation's Marine Environment. College Park, Maryland: Maryland Sea Grant.

Kraus, N. 1988. The effects of seawalls on the beach—an extended literature review. Journal of Coastal Research Special Issue 4:1-28.

Kusler, J. A. 1983. Our National Wetland Heritage: A Protection Guidebook. Washington, D.C.: Environmental Law Institute.

Kusler, J. A. and M. E. Kentula, eds. 1990. Wetland Creation and Restoration: The Status of the Science. Washington D.C.: Island Press.

Landin, M. C. 1978. A Selected Bibliography of the Life Requirements of Colonial Nesting Waterbirds and Their Relationship to Dredged Material Islands. Miscellaneous Paper No. D-78-5. Vicksburg, Mississippi: U.S. Army Engineer Waterways Experiment Station.

Landin, M. C. 1980. Building and managing dredged material islands for North American wildlife. Pp. 527-539 in Proceedings of the Ninth World Dredging Conference, Vancouver, Canada, October 29-31, 1980. Long Beach, California: Symcon Publishing.

Landin, M. C. 1984. Wildlife utilization and management of the confined disposal facilities in the Great Lakes. Pp. 73-77 in the Proceedings of the U.S./Canada Great Lakes International Commission Conference, Toronto, Ontario, Canada. Detroit, Michigan: U.S./Canada Joint Commission.

Landin, M. C. 1988a. Beneficial Uses of Dredged Material: Proceedings of the North Atlantic Conference, Baltimore, Maryland. Vicksburg, Mississippi: U.S. Army Engineer Waterways Experiment Station.

Landin, M. C., ed. 1988b. Inland Waterways: A National Workshop on the Beneficial Uses of Dredged Material, St. Paul, Minnesota. Vicksburg, Mississippi: U.S. Army Waterways Experiment Station.

Landin, M. C. 1989. Dredged material: A recognized resource. Permanent International Association of Navigation Congresses (PIANC), Bulletin No. 67:112-120. Brussels, Belgium: PIANC.

Landin, M. C. 1991. Development of the U.S. Army Corps of Engineers Wetlands Research Program. Technical Report WRP-01. Vicksburg, Mississippi: U.S. Army Engineer Waterways Experiment Station.

REFERENCES

Landin, M. C. 1992a. Beneficial uses of dredged material projects: How, when, where, and what to monitor, and why it matters. Pp. 142-148 in Proceedings of Ports 92. New York: American Society of Civil Engineers.

Landin, M. C. 1992b. Need, construction, and management of dredged material islands for wildlife. Pp. 81-100 in J. B. Herbich, ed., Handbook of Dredging Engineering. New York: McGraw-Hill.

Landin, M. C. 1992c. Wetland restoration, protection, and establishment by beneficially using dredged material. Pp. 114-118 in Proceedings of American Society of Civil Engineers (ASCE) Water Forum '92. New York: ASCE.

Landin, M. C. 1993a. History, concept, and examples of beneficial uses of dredged material. In Proceedings of the EPA/U.S. Army Corps of Engineers Workshop on the Uses of Dredged Material for Wetland Restoration. Vicksburg, Mississippi: U.S. Army Engineer Waterways Experiment Station.

Landin, M. C. 1993b. Pointe Mouillee: A 4600-acre multiple purposed habitat constructed and restored in western Lake Erie, Michigan. Pp. 2705-2714 in the Proceedings of the Eighth American Society of Civil Engineers (ASCE) Symposium on Coastal and Ocean Management, New Orleans, Louisiana. New York: ASCE.

Landin, M. C. 1993c. Wetland creation and restoration on the U.S. Pacific Coast. Pp. 2128-2146 in the Proceedings of the Eighth American Society of Civil Engineers (ASCE) Symposium on Coastal and Ocean Management, New Orleans, Lousiana. New York: ASCE.

Landin, M. C. (In press-a). Achieving Success in Wetland Restoration, Protection, and Creation Projects. In Proceedings of the Fourth International Wetlands Conference (INTERCOL IV), September 1992. Scheduled for publication by the International Wetlands Congress.

Landin, M. C. (In press-b). History, concept, and examples of beneficial uses of dredged material. In Proceedings of Sixth Workshop on the Beneficial Uses of Dredged Material, December 1992, New Orleans, Louisiana. Washington, D.C.: Environmental Protection Agency.

Landin, M. C., C. J. Newling, and E. J. Clairain, Jr. 1988. Miller Sands Island: A dredged material wetland in the Columbia River, Oregon. Pp. 150-155 in K. M. Mutz, ed., Proceedings of the Eigth Annual Meeting of the Society of Wetland Scientists, Seattle, Washington, May 26-29, 1987. Denver, Colorado: Planning Information Corporation.

Landin, M. C., E. J. Clairain, Jr., and C. J. Newling. 1989a. Wetland habitat development and long-term monitoring at Windmill Point, Virginia. Journal of Wetlands 11(2):13-26.

Landin, M. C., T. R. Patin, and H. H. Allen. 1989b. Catch the magic!!: Dredged material beneficial uses in North America. Pp. 821-831 in Proceedings of the Twelfth World Dredging Conference, Orlando, Florida, May 2-5, 1989. Fairfax, Virginia: Western Dredging Association.

Landin, M. C., J. W. Webb, and P. L. Knutson. 1989c. Long-Term Monitoring of Eleven Corps of Engineers Habitat Development Field Sites Built of Dredged Material, 1974-1987. Technical Report D-89-1. Vicksburg, Mississippi: U.S. Army Engineers Waterways Experiment Station.

Landin, M. C., A. E. Dardeau, and M. P. Rollings. 1990a. Guidelines for Wetland Restoration and Establishment for Mitigation. Vicksburg, Mississippi: U.S. Army Engineer Waterways Experiment Station.

Landin, M. C., T. R. Patin, and S. P. Miner. 1990b. Use of dredged material to restore wetland hydrology and intertidal elevations to subsided sites in San Francisco and San Pablo Bays, California. Pp. 189-198 in Proceedings of the Twenty-Fourth Western Dredging Association Conference. Fairfax, Virginia: Western Dredging Association.

Landin, M. C., and Y. Seda-Sanabria, eds. 1992. Workshop Proceedings: Beneficial Uses of Dredged Material in the Western United States. Vicksburg, Mississippi: U.S. Army Engineer Waterways Experiment Station.

Landin, M. C. and H. K. Smith. 1982. Reclamation of Wetlands. Pp. 195-207 in Research on Fish and Wildlife Habitat. Report No. EPA-600/8-82-022. Washington, D.C.: U.S. Environmental Protection Agency.

Landin, M. C., and H. K. Smith, eds. 1987. Beneficial Uses of Dredged Material: Proceedings of the Interagency Workshop, Pensacola, Florida. Technical Report D-87-1. Vicksburg, Mississippi: U.S. Army Engineer Waterways Experiment Station.

Langan, J. P. 1988. Benefits of Underwater Berms. Pp. 183-187 in Proceedings of the North Atlantic Conference, Beneficial Uses of Dredged Material. Vicksburg, Mississippi: U.S. Army Engineer Waterways Experiment Station.

Langan, J. P., and S. I. Rees. 1991. The national U.S. Army Corps of Engineers demonstration project: Mobile Bay nearshore and deepwater berms. In Proceedings of the Fifth Workship on the Beneficial Uses of Dredged Material, San Diego, California, May, 1990. Vicksburg, Mississippi: U.S. Army Engineer Waterways Experiment Station.

LaSalle, M. W., M. C. Landin, and J. G. Sims. 1991. Evaluation of the flora and fauna of *Spartina alterniflora* marsh established on dredged material in Winyah Bay, South Carolina. Journal of Wetlands 11(2):191-208.

Latham, T. J., L. G. Pearlstine, and W. M. Kitchens. 1991. Spatial distributions of the softstem bullrush *Scirpus Validus* across a salinity gradient. Estuaries 14(2):192-198.

Lazor, R. L., and R. Medino, eds. 1990. Beneficial Uses of Dredged Material: Proccedings of the Gulf Coast Workshop. Technical Report D-90-3. Vicksburg, Mississippi: U.S. Army Engineer Waterways Experiment Station.

Lee, C. R., J. G. Skogerboe, K. Eskew, R. A. Price, and N. R. Page. 1985. Restoration of Problem Soil Materials at Corps of Engineers Construction Sites. Instruction Report No. EL-85-2. Vicksburg, Mississippi: U.S. Army Engineer Waterways Experiment Station.

Lee, C. R., R. M. Smart, T. C. Sturgis, R. N. Gordon, and M. C. Landin. 1978. Prediction of Heavy Metal Uptake by Marsh Plants. Technical Report No. D-78-06. Vicksburg, Mississippi: U.S. Army Engineer Waterways Experiment Station.

Lee, G. F., and R. A. Jones. 1992. Water quality aspects of dredging and dredged sediment disposal. Pp. 9.23-9.59 in J. B. Herbich, Handbook of Dredging Engineering. New York: McGraw-Hill.

Lethbridge, J. 1988. Environmental considerations for port and harbour developments. Pp. 88-104 in Proceedings of the International Seminar on Environmental Impact Assessment of Port Development. London: International Maritime Organization.

Lewis, R. R. 1982. Mangrove forests. Pp. 153-172 in R. R. Lewis, ed., Creation and Restoration of Coastal Plant Communities. Boca Raton, Florida: CRC Press.

Lewis, R. R. 1987. The restoration and creation of seagrass meadows in the southeast United States. Pp. 153-173 in Proceedings of the Symposium on Subtropical-Tropical Seagrasses of the Southeastern United States. St. Petersburg, Florida: Marine Research Laboratory, Florida Department of Natural Resources.

Lewis, R. R., III. 1990a. Creation and restoration of coastal plain wetlands in Florida. Pp. 73-101 in J. A. Kusler and M. E. Kentula, eds., Wetland Creation and Restoration: The Status of the Science. Washington, D.C.: Island Press.

Lewis, R. R., III. 1990b. Wetlands restoration/creation/enhancement terminology: Suggestions for standardization. Pp. 417-422 in J. A. Kusler and M. E. Kentula, eds., Wetland Creation and Restoration: The Status of the Science, Washington. D.C.: Island Press.

Lewis, R. R., III. 1992. Coastal habitat restoration as a fishery management tool. Pp. 169-173 in R. H. Stroud, ed., Stemming the Tide of Coastal Fish Habitat Loss: Proceedings of a Symposium on Conservation of Coastal Fish Habitat, Baltimore, Maryland, March 7-9, 1991. Savannah, Georgia: National Coalition for Marine Conservation.

Lewis, R. R., M. J. Durako, M. D. Moffler, and R. C. Phillips. 1985. Seagrass meadows of Tampa Bay: A review. Pp. 210-246 in S. F. Treat, J. L. Simon, R. R. Lewis, and R. L. Whitman, eds., 1982, Proceedings, Tampa Bay Areas Scientific Symposium (May 1982). Minneapolis, Minnesota: Bellwether Press.

REFERENCES

Lewis, R. R., and E. D. Estevez. 1988. The Ecology of Tampa Bay, Florida: An Estuarine Profile. Biological Report 85(7.18). Prepared for U.S. Fish and Wildlife Service (USFWS), Research and Development, National Wetlands Research Center. Washington, D.C.: USFWS.

Lewis, R. R., and K. K. McKee. 1989. A Guide to the Artificial Reefs of Southern California. Sacramento, California: California Department of Fish and Game.

Ludwig, M., S. Mello, and T. Faris. 1994. Regulated development in coastal wetlands: An analysis of trends in the Section 10/404 permit program in portions of the United States. Pp. 13-17 in M. P. Lynch and B. Crowder, eds., Proceedings of the 13th International Conference of the Coastal Society: Organizing for the Coast. Gloucester, Massachusetts: The Coastal Society.

Lunz, J. D., T. W. Ziegler, R. T. Huffman, R. J. Diaz, E. J. Clairain, Jr., and L. J. Hunt. 1978. Habitat Development Field Investigations, Windmill Point Marsh Development Site, Virginia: Summary Report. Technical Report No. D-77-23. Vicksburg, Mississippi: Environmental Laboratory, U.S. Army Engineer Waterways Experiment Station.

Lynne, G. D., P. Conroy, and F. J. Prochaska. 1981. Economic valuation of marsh areas for marine production processes. Journal of Environmental Economics and Management 8(2):175-186.

Macdonald, K. B., R. F. Ford, E. B. Copper, P. Unitt, and J. P. Haltiner. 1990a. South San Diego Bay Enhancement Plan. Volume One/Resources Atlas: Marine Ecological Characterization, Bay History, and Physical Environment. Prepared for San Diego Unified Port District and California State Coastal Conservancy. San Diego, California: San Diego Unified Port District.

Macdonald, K. B., R. F. Ford, E. B. Copper, P. Unitt, and J. P. Haltiner. Prepared for San Diego Unified Port District and California State Coastal Conservancy. 1990b. Volume Three: Enhancement Goals and Concepts. San Diego, California: San Diego Unified Port District.

Mager, A., Jr. 1990. National Marine Fisheries Service Habitat Conservation Efforts Related to Federal Regulatory Programs in the Southeastern United States. NOAA Technical Memorandum NMFS-SEFC-260. Washington, D.C.: National Oceanic and Atmospherioc Administration.

Maragos, J. E. 1992. Restoring coral reefs with emphasis on Pacific reefs. Pp. 141-222 in G. W. Thayer, ed., Restoring the Nation's Marine Environment. College Park, Maryland: Maryland Sea Grant.

Marine Research Laboratory. 1987. Proceedings of the Symposium on Subtropical-Tropical Seagrasses of the Southeastern United States. St. Petersburg, Florida: Marine Research Laboratory, Florida Department of Natural Resources.

Matthiessen, J. 1989. Planning for sea level rise in southern New England. Essex, Connecticut: The Sounds Conservancy.

Maynord, S. T., M. C. Landin, J. W. McCormick, J. E. Davis, R. A. Evans, and D. F. Hayes. 1992. Design of Habitat Restoration Using Dredged Material at Bodkin Island, Chesapeake Bay, Maryland. Wetlands Research Program Technical Report WRP-RE-3. Vicksburg, Mississippi: U.S. Army Corps of Engineers Waterways Experiment Station.

McClellan, T. N., and F. D. Imsand. 1989. Berm construction utilizing dredged material. Pp. 811-820 in the Proceedings of the Twelfth World Dredging Conference, Orlando, Florida, May 2-5, 1989. Fairfax, Virginia: Western Dredging Association.

McClellan, T. N., M. K. Pope, and E. C. Burke. 1990. Benefits of Neashore Placement. Pp. 339-353 in Proceedings of the National Conference on Beach Preservation Technology, St. Petersburg, Florida. Tallahassee, Florida: Florida Shore and Beach Preservation Association.

McConnaughey, B. H., and E. McConnaughey, eds. 1985. Pacific Coast. New York: Alfred A. Knopf.

McCreary, S., R. Twiss, B. Warren, C. White, S. Huse, K. Gardels, and D. Roques. 1992. Land use change and impacts on the San Francisco Estuary: A regional assessment with national policy implications. Coastal Management 20:219-253.

REFERENCES

McGurrin, J. M., and ASMFC Artificial Reef Committee. 1988. A Profile of Atlantic Artificial Reef Development. Special Report No. 14 of the Atlantic States Marine Fisheries Commission. Washington, D.C.: Atlantic States Marine Fisheries Commission.

McGurrin, J. M., and the Atlantic States Marine Fisheries Commission (ASMFC) Artifical Reef Committee. 1989a. An assessment of Atlantic artificial reef development. Fisheries 14(4):21-25.

McGurrin, J. M., R. B. Stone, and R. J. Sousa. 1989b. Profiling United States artificial reef deployment. Bulletin of Marine Science 44:1004-1013.

McGurrin, J. M., and M. J. Reeff. 1986. Artificial reef development and deployment. MTS Journal 20(3):3-9.

McKenzie, T., J. P. Houghton, and R. L Thom. 1990. Analysis of Marsh Transplant Experiments at Jetty Island, Everett, Washington. Final Draft Report. Project No. 00021-001. Everett, Washington: Port of Everett.

Mehta, A. J. 1990. Role of Coastal Sedimentary Processes in Marine Habitat Protection and Enhancement. Unpublished paper prepared for the Committee on the Role of Technology in Marine Habitat Protection and Enhancement. Washington, D.C.: Marine Board, National Research Council.

Mehta, A. J., ed. 1993. Beach/Inlet Processes and Management: A Florida Perspective. Journal of Coastal Research, Special Issue No. 18 (Fall, 1993).

Mendelssohn, I. A. 1982. Sand dune vegetation and stabilization in Louisiana. Pp. 187-207 in: D. Boesch, ed., Proceedings of the Conference on Coastal Erosion and Wetland Modification in Louisiana: Causes, consequences, and options. FWS/OBS-82/59. Washington, D.C.: U.S. Fish and Wildlife Services.

Mendelssohn, I. A., J. W. Jordan, F. Talbot, and C. J. Starkovitch. 1983. Dune building and vegetative stabilization in a sand deficient barrier island environment. Pp. 601-619 in Proceedings of the Third Symposium on Coastal and Ocean Management, San Diego, California, June 1-4, 1983. New York: American Society of Civil Engineers.

Mendelssohn, I. A., and M. W. Hester. 1988. Texaco USA Coastal Vegetation Project, Timbalier Island. New Orleans, Louisiana: Texaco USA.

Mendelssohn, I. A., M. W. Hester, F. J. Monteferrante, and F. Talbot. 1991. Experimental dune building and vegetative stabilization in a sand-deficient barrier island setting on the Louisiana coast. Journal of Coastal Research 7(1):137-150.

Merkel, K. W. 1990a. Eelgrass transplanting in South San Diego Bay, California. Pp. 28-42 in K. W. Merkel and R. S. Hoffman, eds., Proceedings of the California Eelgrass Symposium. National City, California: Sweetwater River Press.

Merkel, K. W. 1990b. Growth and survival of transplanted eelgrass: The importance of planting unit size and spacing. Pp. 70-78 in K. W. Merkel and R. S. Hoffman, eds., Proceedings of the California Eelgrass Symposium. National City, California: Sweetwater River Press.

Merkel, K. W. 1991. The Use of Seagrasses in the Enhancement, Creation, and Restoration of Marine Habitats Along the California Coast: Lessons Learned from Fifteen Years of Transplants. Paper presented to National Research Council, Committee on the Role of Technology in Habitat Protection and Enhancement, March 20, 1991, San Francisco, California.

Merkel, K. W., and R. S. Hoffman, eds. 1990. Proceedings of the California Eelgrass Symposium. National City, California: Sweetwater River Press.

Minello, T. J.., R. J. Zimmerman, and E. F. Klima. 1987. Creation of fishery habitat in estuaries. Pp. 106-121 in Proceedings of the First Interagency Workshop on the Beneficial Uses of Dredged Material. Vicksburg, Mississippi: U.S. Army Engineer Waterways Experiment Station.

Montague, C. L. 1993. Ecological engineering of inlets in souteastern Florida: Design criteria for sea turtle nesting beaches. Journal of Coastal Research, Special Issue No. 18:267-276.

REFERENCES

185

Murden, W. R. 1988. Underwater berms in the coastal zone to reduce shoreline erosion rates. Pp. 304-310 in Proceedings of the International Seminar on Environmental Impact Assessment of Port Development. London: International Maritime Organization.

Murden, W. R. 1989a. Construction of Underwater Berms. Permanent International Association of Navigation Congresses (PIANC), Bulletin No. 67:120-127. Brussels, Belgium: PIANC.

Murden, W. R. 1989b. The meeting of the twain. Pp. 1-14 in Proceedings of the Twelfth World Dredging Conference, Orlando, Florida, May 2-5, 1989. Fairfax, Virginia: Western Dredging Association.

Murray, L. 1989. Research by the sea. Texas Shores 22(1):4-7.

NAEP. 1991. The Environmental Professional, Special Issue: Restoration of Ecosystems, Volume 13(3):185-292. Washington, D.C.: National Association of Environmental Professionals.

Nailon, R. W., and E. Seidensticker. 1994. Wetland creation efforts in Galveston Bay, Texas. Pp. 19-27 in M. P. Lynch and B. Crowder, eds., Proceedings of the 13th International Conference of the Coastal Society: Organizing for the Coast. Gloucester, Massachusetts: The Coastal Society.

National Wetlands Policy Forum. 1988. Protecting America's Wetlands: An Action Agenda. Washington, D.C.: The Conservation Foundation.

Nelson, W. G. 1985. Physical and Biological Guidelines for Beach Restoration Projects. Part 1. Biological Guidelines: Part I. Florida Sea Grant College Report No. 76, Project No. R/C-4, Grant No. NA80AA-D-00038. Melbourne, Florida: Florida Institute of Technology.

Nelson, W. G. 1993. Beach-inlet ecosystems of southeastern Florida: A review of ecological research needs and management issues. Journal of Coastal Research, Special Issue No. 18:257-266.

Nelson, D. A., and D. D. Dickerson. 1988. Effects of beach nourishment on sea turtles. Pp. 285-293 in Proceedings of the Symposium on Beach Preservation Technology, March 23-25, 1988. Gainesville, Florida: Florida Shore and Beach Preservation Association.

New York Sea Grant Institute. 1990. Identification and assessment of technical information requirements for developing coastal erosion management strategies. Proceedings of a workshop held February 24-25, 1989. New York Sea Grant Special Report No. 103. Stony Brook: Sea Grant Institute, State University of New York.

Nitsos, R. 1990. Morro Bay eelgrass transplant. Pp. 43-45 in K. W. Merkel and R. S. Hoffman, eds., Proceedings of the California Eelgrass Symposium. National City, California: Sweetwater River Press.

NMFS and USACE. 1990. Pilot Study to Determine the Feasibility of Establishing a Nationwide Program of Fisheries Habitat Restoration and Creation. Prepared by National Marine Fisheries Service and U.S. Army Corps of Engineers. Silver Spring, Maryland: NMFS.

NOAA. 1990a. Biennial Report to the Congress on Coastal Zone Management: Fiscal Years 1988 and 1989. Washington, D.C.: National Oceanic and Atmospheric Administration.

NOAA. 1990b. Estuarine Habitat Program Implementation Plan. Coastal Ocean Program, FY 1991, Version 2.0. Washington, D.C.: National Oceanic and Atmospheric Administration.

NOAA. 1990c. Estuarine Habitat Program Progress Report. Coastal Ocean Program, FY 1990. Washington, D.C.: National Oceanic and Atmospheric Administration.

NRC. 1983a. Criteria for the Depths of Dredged Navigational Channels. Marine Board, National Research Council. Washington, D.C.: National Research Council.

NRC. 1983b. Fundamental Research on Estuaries: The Importance of an Interdisciplinary Approach. Geophysics Study Committee, National Research Council. Washington, D.C.: National Academy Press.

NRC. 1985a. Continuing Education for Engineers. Commission on Engineering and Technical Systems, National Research Council. Washington, D.C.: National Academy Press.

NRC. 1985b. Engineering Technology Education. Commission on Engineering and Technical Systems, National Research Council. Washington D.C.: National Academy Press.

NRC. 1985c. Engineering in Society. Commission on Engineering and Technical Systems, National Research Council. Washington D.C.: National Academy Press.

NRC. 1985d. Dredging Coastal Ports: An Assessment of the Issues. Marine Board, National Research Council. Washington D.C.: National Academy Press.

NRC. 1987a. Responding to Changes in Sea Level: Engineering Implications. Marine Board, National Research Council. Washington D.C.: National Academy Press.

NRC. 1987b. Sedimentation Control to Reduce Maintenance Dredging of Navigational Facilities and Estuaries. Marine Board, National Research Council. Washington, D.C.: National Academy Press.

NRC. 1988. Marine Environmental Monitoring in Chesapeake Bay. Unpublished case study prepared by the Chesapeake Bay Panel of the Committee on a Systems Assessment of Marine Environmental Monitoring. Washington D.C.: Marine Board, National Research Council.

NRC. 1989a. Contaminated Marine Sediments: Assessment and Remediation. Marine Board, National Research Council. Washington, D.C.: National Academy Press.

NRC. 1989b. Measuring and Understanding Coastal Processes for Engineering Purposes. Marine Board, National Research Council. Washington, D.C.: National Academy Press.

NRC. 1990a. Managing Coastal Erosion. Marine Board and Water Science and Technology Board, National Research Council. Washington D.C.: National Academy Press.

NRC. 1990b. Managing Troubled Waters: The Role of Marine Environmental Monitoring. Marine Board, National Research Council. Washington D.C.: National Academy Press.

NRC. 1990c. Studies in Geophysics: Sea Level Change. Geophysics Study Committee, National Research Council. Washington, D.C.: National Academy Press.

NRC. 1991. Opportunities in the Hydrologic Sciences. Water Science and Technology Board, National Research Council. Washington, D.C.: National Academy Press.

NRC. 1992a. Restoration of Aquatic Ecosystems: Science, Technology, and Public Policy. Water Science and Technology Board, National Research Council. Washington D.C.: National Academy Press.

NRC. 1992b. Shiphandling Simulation: Application to Waterway Design. Marine Board, National Research Council. Washington, D.C.: National Academy Press.

NRC. 1993. Managing Wastewater in Coastal Urban Areas. Water Science and Technology Board, National Research Council. Washington, D.C.: National Academy Press.

O'Brien, M. P. 1985. One man's opinion: None so blind as those who won't see. Shore and Beach 53(3):7-8.

Orth, R. J., and K. A. Moore. 1983. Cheasapeake Bay: An unprecedented decline in submerged aquatic vegetation. Science 222:51-53.

OTA. 1984. Wetlands: Their Use and Regulation. Office of Technology Assessment. Washington, D.C.: U.S. Government Printing Office.

OTA. 1987. Wastes in Marine Environments. Office of Technology Assessment. Washington, D.C.: U.S. Government Printing Office.

Parnell, J. F., D. M. DuMont, and R. N. Needham. 1978. A Comparison of Plant Succession and Bird Utilization on Diked Dredged Material Islands in North Carolina Estuaries. Technical Report No. D-78-9. Prepared by Department of Biology, University of North Carolina at Wilmington, N.C., for U.S. Army Corps of Engineers Dredged Material Research Program. Springfield, Virginia: National Technical Information Service.

Parnell, J. F., D. G. Ainley, H. Blokpoel, B. Cain, T. W. Custer, J. L. Dusi, S. Kress, J. A. Kushan, W. E. Southern, L. E. Stenzel, and B. C. Thompson. 1988. Colonial waterbird management in North America. Colonial Waterbirds 11:129-345.

Payne, N. F. 1992. Techniques for Wildlife Habitat Management of Wetlands. New York: McGraw-Hill.

REFERENCES

Pearlstine, L. G., R. D. Bartleson, W. M. Kitchens, and T. J. Latham. 1989. Lower Savannah River Hydrological Characterization. Technical Report No., 35. Gainesville: Florida Cooperative Fish and Wildlife Research Unit, University of Florida, Gainesville.

Pearlstine, L. G., T. J. Latham, W. M. Kitchens, and R. D. Bartleson. 1990. Development and Application of a Habitat Succession Model for the Wetland Complex of the Savannah National Wildlife Refuge, Vol. 2, Final Report. Gainesville, Florida: Florida Cooperative Fish and Wild Research Unit, University of Florida, Gainesville.

Pearlstine, L. G., W. M. Kitchens, and T. J. Latham. 1993a. Modeling Tidal Marsh Succession in the Coastal Savannah River, Georgia. Pp. 445-449 in M. C. Landin, ed., Proceedings of the Thirteenth Annual Conference, Society of Wetland Scientists. Utica, Mississippi: South Central Chapter, Society of Wetland Scientists.

Pearlstine, L. G., W. M. Kitchens, T. J. Latham, and R. D. Bartleson. 1993b. Tide Gate Influences on a Tidal Marsh. Water Resources Bulletin 29(6):1009-1019.

PERL. 1990. A Manual for Assessing Restored and Natural Coastal Wetlands with Examples from Southern California. California Sea Grant Report No. T-CSGCP-021. San Diego, California: Pacific Estuarine Research Laboratory, San Diego State University.

Perry, B. 1985. A Sierra Club Naturalist's Guide: The Middle Atlantic Coast. San Franciso, California: Sierra Club.

Peters, C. F., K. O. Richter, D. A. Manuwal, and S. G. Herman. 1978. Colonial Nesting Sea and Wading Bird Use of Estuarine Islands in the Pacific Northwest. Technical Report D-78-17. Prepared by John Graham Company for U.S. Army Corps of Engineers Dredged Material Research Program. Springfield, Virginia: National Technical Information Service.

Phillips, R. C. 1990. Keynote address: General ecology of eelgrass with special emphasis on restoration and management. Pp 1-5 in K. W. Merkel and R. S. Hoffman, eds., Proceedings of the California Eelgrass Symposium. National City, California: Sweetwater River Press.

PIANC. 1989. Economic Methods of Channel Maintenance. Supplement to Bulletin No. 67. Report of PIANC Working Group No. 14 of the Permanent Technical Committee II. Brussels, Belgium: Permanent International Association of Navigation Congresses.

PIANC. 1992a. Beneficial Uses of Dredged Material: A Practical Guide. Report of PIANC Working Group No. 19 of Permanent Technical Committee II. Brussels, Belgium: Permanent International Association of Navigation Congresses.

PIANC. 1992b. Guidelines for the Design and Construction of Flexible Revetments Incorporating Geotextiles in Marine Environment. Report of PIANC Working Group No. 21 of Permanent Technical Committee II. Brussels, Belgium: Permanent International Association of Navigation Congresses.

Pilkey, O. H. 1989. Statement by O. H. Pilkey Before the Environment, Energy, and Natural Resources Subcommittee of the House Committee on Government Operations, April 28, 1989.

Pilkey, O. H., and H. Wright. 1988. Seawalls versus beaches. Journal of Coastal Research Special Issue 4:41-64.

Platt, R. H., H. C. Miller, T. Beatley, J. Melville, and B. G. Mathenia. 1992. Coastal Erosion: Has Retreat Sounded. Monograph No. 53. Boulder, Colorado: Natural Hazards Information Center, University of Colorado.

Poindexter-Rollings, M. E. 1990. Methodology for Analysis of Subaquous Sediment Mounds. Technical Report D-90-02. Vicksburg, Mississippi: U.S. Army Engineer Waterways Experiment Station.

PTI Environmental Services. 1988. Sediment Quality Values Refinement: 1988 Update and Evaluation of Puget Sound AET. Final report prepared for Tetra Tech, Inc. and U.S. Environmental Protection Agency. Bellevue, Washington: PTI Environmental Services.

Pulich, W. M., and W. A. White. 1991. Decline of submerged vegetation in the Galveston Bay system: Chronology and relationships to physical processes. Journal of Coastal Research, 7(4):1125-1138.

Raphael, C. N., and E. Jaworski. 1979. Economic value of fish, wildlife, and recreation in Michigan's coastal wetlands. Coastal Zone Management Journal 5(3):181-194.

Reddy, K. R., and W. H. Smith, eds. 1987. Aquatic Plants for Water Treatment and Resource Recovery. Orlando, Florida: Magnolia Publishing.

Redmond, A. 1992. How successful is mitigation. National Wetlands Newsletter 14(1):5-6.

Reeff, M. J., J. Murray, J. McGurrin and the ASMFC Artificial Reef Committee. 1990. Atlantic States Marine Fisheries Commission (ASMFC) Recommendations for Atlantic State Artificial Reef Management. Recreational Fisheries Report No. 6. Washington, D.C.: ASMFC.

Restoration Planning Work Group. 1990a. Restoration following the Exxon Valdez oil spill. Proceedings of the Public Symposium held in Anchorage, Alaska, March 26-27, 1990.

Restoration Planning Work Group. 1990b. Restoration planning following the Exxon Valdez oil spill. August 1990 Progress Report. Washington, D.C.: U.S. Environmental Protection Agency.

Rhodes, N. C. 1988. Where seaports begin and where they end. Pp. 105-109 in Proceedings International seminar on environmental impact assessment of port development. London, England: International Maritime Organization.

Richardson, T. R. 1986. Nearshore placement of dredged sand. Environmental Effects of Dredging Information Exchange Bulletin, Volume D-86-3. Vicksburg, Mississippi: U.S. Army Engineer Waterways Experiment Station.

Risser, P. G. 1988. General concepts for measuring cumulative impacts on wetland ecosystems. Environmental Management 12(5):585-589.

Roberts, T. 1989. Habitat value of man-made coastal marshes in Florida. Pp. 157-179 in F. J. Webb, Jr., ed., Proceedings of the Sixteenth Conference on Wetlands Restoration and Creation. Tampa, Florida: Hillsborough Community College.

Roberts, T. H. 1991. Habitat Value of Manmade Coastal Marshes in Florida. Technical Report WPR-RE-02. Vicksburg, Mississippi: U.S. Army Engineer Waterways Experiment Station.

Robertson, A., and T. P. O'Conner. 1989. National status and trends program for marine environmental quality. Pp. 47-62 in National Research Council, Contaminated Marine Sediments—Assessment and Remediation. Washington, D.C.: National Academy Press.

Rose, T. F., T. T. Price, and H. C. Woolman. 1878. History of the New Jersey Coast. Philadephia, Pennsylvania: Woolman and Rose.

Ross, M. S., J. J. O'Brien, and L. Sternberg. 1994. Sea-level rise and the reduction in pine forests in the Florida Keys. Ecological Applications 4(1):144-156.

Roy, P., and J. Connell. 1991. Climate Change and the future of atoll states. Journal of Coastal Research, 7(4):1057-1076.

Sather, J. H., and P. J. R. Stuber, tech. coords. 1984. Proceedings of the National Wetland Values Assessment Workshop. Report No. FWS/OBS-84/12. Washington, D.C.: Western Energy Land Use Team, U.S. Fish and Wildlife Service.

Saucier, R. T. 1992. Geologic processes and history of wetlands of the Mississippi River system. Pp. 26-30 in M. C. Landing, ed., Proceedings of the Thirteenth Annual Conference, Society of Wetland Scientists. Utica, Mississippi: South Central Chapter, Society of Wetland Scientists.

Schadt, T. H., G. T. Williams, and G. V. Blomberg. 1989. Biological monitoring at Port of Seattle mitigation sites. Pp. 953-991 in Proceedings of the Twelfth World Dredging Conference, Orlando, Florida, May 2-5, 1989. Fairfax, Virginia: Western Dredging Association.

Scaife, W. W., R. E. Turner, and R. Costanza. 1983. Coastal Louisiana recent land loss and canal impacts. Environmental Management 7(5):433-442.

Scharf, W. C., G. W. Shugart, and M. L. Chamberlin. 1978. Colonial Birds Nesting on Man-Made and Natural Sites in the U.S. Great Lakes. Technical Report No. D-78-10. Prepared by Northwestern Michigan College for U.S. Army Corps of Engineers Dredged Material Research Program. Springfield, Virginia: National Technical Information Service.

REFERENCES

Schiel, D. R., and M. S. Foster. 1992. Restoring kelp forests. Pp. 279-342 in G. W. Thayer, ed., 1992. Restoring the Nation's Marine Environment. College Park, Maryland: Maryland Sea Grant.

Schmidt, D. V., and R. Clark. 1993. Impacts of Hurricane Andrew on the beaches of Florida. Pp. 279-308 in The State of the Art of Beach Nourishment: Proceedings of the 1993 National Conference on Beach Preservation Technology. Tallahassee, Florida: Florida Shore and Beach Preservation Association.

Schreiber, R. W., and E. A. Schreiber. 1978. Colonial Bird Use and Plant Succession on Dredged Material Islands in Florida, Volume 1: Sea and Wading Bird Colonies. Technical Report No. D-78-14. Prepared by Seabird Research, Culver City, California. Springfield, Virginia: National Technical Information Service.

SCOR. 1991. The response of beaches to sea-level changes: A review of predictive models. Scientific Committee on Ocean Research (SCOR) Working Group 89. Journal of Coastal Research 7(3):895-921.

Scott, J., D. Rhoads, J. Rosen, S. Pratt, and J. Gentile. 1987. Impact of Open-Water Disposal of Black Rock Harbor Dredged material on Benthic Recolonization. Technical Report D-87-04. Vicksburg, Mississippi: U.S. Army Waterways Experiment Station.

SCS. 1992. SCS Engineering Field Handbook EFH-1A: Part 650, Chapter 13—Wetland restoration, enhancement, or creation. Washington, D.C.: Soil Conservation Service, U.S. Department of Agriculture.

Seaman, W., Jr., and L. M. Sprague, eds. 1991. Artificial Habitats for Marine and Freshwater Fisheries. San Diego, California: Academic Press.

Seneca, E. D., and S. W. Broome. 1992. Restoring tidal marshes in North Carolina and France. Pp. 53-78 in G. W. Thayer, ed. Restoring the Nation's Marine Environment. College Park, Maryland: Maryland Sea Grant.

Shabman, L. A., and S. S. Batie. 1978. Economic value of natural coastal wetlands: A critique. Coastal Zone Management Journal 4(3):231-247.

Shabman, L. A., S. S. Batie, and C. C. Mabbs-Zeno. 1979. The economics of wetland preservation in Virginia. Northeast Journal of Agricultural Economics 8(2):101-115.

Shabman, L. A., and M. K. Bertelson. 1979. The use of development value estimates for coastal wetland permit decisions. Land Economics 55(2):213-222.

Sheehy, D. J. 1982. The use of designed and prefabricated artificial reefs in the United States. Marine Fisheries Review 44(6-7):4-15.

Sheehy, D. J., and S. F. Vik. 1981a. Developments in East Asia. 1981. Water Spectrum (Fall):27-37.

Sheehy, D. J., and S. Vik., eds. 1981b. Japanese Artificial Reef Technology. Aquabio Report No. 80-TT-720. Annapolis, Maryland: Aquabio.

Sheehy, D. J., and S. F. Vik. 1982. Artificial Reefs—A Second Life for Offshore Platforms? Belleair Bluffs, Florida: Aquabio.

Sheehy, D. J., and S. F. Vik. 1983. Recent advances in artificial reef technology. Pp. 957-960 in Proceedings of Oceans 83, August 29-September 1, 1983. Piscataway, New Jersey: Institute of Electrical and Electronic Engineers.

Sheehy, D. J., and S. F. Vik. 1988a. Extending mitigation banking beyond wetlands. Pp. 1242-1253 in L. R. King, ed., Proceedings of 11th International Conference of the Coastal Society, Ports and Harbors: Our Link to the Water, October 22-26, 1988, Boston, Massachusetts. Alexandria, Virginia: Coastal Society.

Sheehy, D. J., and S. F. Vik. 1988b. Mitigation planning planning for port development. Pp. 1470-1475 in Proceedings of Oceans '88. Piscataway, New Jersey: Institute of Electrical and Electronics Engineers.

Sheehy, D. J., and S. F. Vik. 1992. Developing prefabricated reefs: An ecological and engineering approach. Pp. 544-582 in G. W. Thayer, ed., Restoring the Nation's Marine Environment. College Park, Maryland: Maryland Sea Grant.

Shieh, C., Duedall, I. W., Kalajian, E. H., and Wilcox, J. R. 1989. Stabilization of oil ash for artificial reefs: An alternative to the disposal of oil ash waste. Environmental Professional 11(1):64-70.

Shisler, J. K. 1990. Creation and restoration of the coastal wetlands of the northeastern United States. Pp. 143-170 in J. A. Kusler and M. R. Kentula, eds., 1990, Wetland Creation and Restoration: The Status of the Science. Washington, D.C.: Island Press.

Sikora, W. B. 1989. Air Cushion Vehicles for the Transport of Drilling Rigs, Supplies, and Oil Field Exploration Operations in the Coastal Marshes of Louisiana: Final Report. Summit, New Jersey: C. A. Lindbergh Fund.

Simenstad, C. A., and R. M. Thom. 1992. Restoring wetland habitats in urbanized Pacific Northwest estuaries. Pp. 423-472 in G. W. Thayer, ed., Restoring the Nation's Marine Environment. College Park, Maryland: Maryland Sea Grant.

Simmers, J. W., R. G. Rhett, and C. R. Lee. 1986. Wetland Animal Bioassay of Saltwater Dredged Material. Environmental Effects of Dredging Technical Note EEDP-03-01. Vicksburg, Mississippi: U.S. Army Engineer Waterways Experiment Station.

Simmonds, J., S. Washburn, K. Hentz, and R. Harris. 1992. Development in the use of risk assessment to evaluate complex hazardous waste management facilities. Environmental Professional 14(3):228-237.

Skaggs, L. L., and F. L. McDonald, eds. 1991. National Economic Development Procedures Manual: Coastal Storm Damage and Erosion. Institute of Water Resources (IWR) Report 91-R-6. Fort Belvoir, Virginia: U.S. Army Corps of Engineers, Water Resources Support Center.

Smith, V. K. 1990. Natural resource damage assessments and the mineral sector: Valuation in the courts. Unpublished manuscript.

Soots, R. F., and M. C. Landin. 1978. Development and Management of Avian Habitat on Dredged Material Islands. Technical Report DS-78-18. Vicksburg, Mississippi: U.S. Army Engineer Waterways Experiment Station.

Steimle, F., W. Figley, and the Atlantic States Marine Fisheries Commission (ASMFC) Artificial Reef Advisory Committee. 1990. A Review of Artificial Reef Research Needs. Recreational Fisheries Report No. 7. Washington, D.C.: ASFMC.

Stone, R. B. 1985. National Oceanic and Atmospheric Administration (NOAA) Technical Memorandum NMFS OF-6: National Artificial Reef Plan. Washington, D.C.: NOAA.

Stout, D. J., and R. A. Streeter. 1992. Ecological risk assessment: Its role in risk management. Environmental Professional 14(3):197-203.

Stromberg, E. 1988. Environmental challenges faced by commercial ports in the United States Pp. 345-348 in Proceedings of the International Seminar on Environmental Impact Assessment of Port Development. London: International Maritime Organization.

Stroud, R. H., ed. 1992. Stemming the Tide of Coastal Fish Habitat Loss: Proceedings of A Symposium on Conservation of Coastal Fish Habitat, Baltimore, Maryland, March 7-9, 1991. Savannah, Georgia: National Coalition for Marine Conservation.

Suhayda, J. N., G. P. Kemp, R. S. Jones, and J. Peckham. 1991. Restoration of Wetlands Using Pipeline Transported Sediments. Paper presented at Gulf Coast Section South East Petroleum Managers 12th Annual Research Conference, December 2-5, 1991. Baton Rouge, Louisiana: Woodward-Clyde Consultants.

SWFWMD. 1992. Tampa Bay Surface Water Improvement and Management Plan. Brooksville, Florida: Southwest Florida Water Management District.

Thayer, G. W., ed. 1992. Restoring the Nation's Marine Environment. College Park, Maryland: Maryland Sea Grant.

REFERENCES

The Sounds Conservancy. 1990. Intertidal flats: Their value and legal status. TSC Coastal Publication No. 2. Essex, Connecticut: The Sounds Conservancy.

Thibodeau, F. R., and B. D. Ostro. 1981. The economic value of wetland systems. Journal of Environmental Management 12(1):19-30.

Thorhaug. A. 1990. Restoration of mangroves and segrasses—economic benefits for fisheries and mariculture. Pp. 265-281 in J. J. Berger, ed., Environmental Restoration: Science and Strategies for Restoring the Earth. Covelo, California: Island Press.

Titus, J. G., ed. 1988. Greenhouse Effect, Sea Level Rise and Coastal Wetlands. U.S. Environmental Protection Agency publication. Washington, D.C.: U.S. Government Printing Office.

Tschirhart, J., and T. D. Crocker. 1987. Economic valuation of ecosystems. Transactions of the American Fisheries Society 116(3):469-478.

Turner, M. G. 1989. Landscape ecology, the effect of pattern on process. Annual Review of Ecological Systems 20:171-197.

Turner, R. E., and D. F. Boesch. 1988. Aquatic animal production and wetland relationships: Insights gleaned following wetland loss or gain. Pp. 25-39 in Hooks, D. D., W. H. McKee, Jr., H. K Smith, J. Gregory, V. G. Burrell, Jr., M. R. DeVoe, R. E. Sojka, S. Gilbert, R. Banks, L. H. Stolzy, C. Brooks, T. D. Matthews, and T. H. Shear, eds. The Ecology and Management of Wetlands. Portland, Oregon: Timber Press.

Turner, R. E., and M. S. Brody. 1983. Habitat Suitability Index Models: Northern Gulf of Mexico Brown and White Shrimp. Report No. FWS/OBS-82/10.5. Washington, D.C.: U.S. Fish and Wildlife Service.

Turner, R. E., and D. R. Cahoon. 1988. Causes of Wetland Loss in the Coastal Central Gulf of Mexico, Volume II: Technical Narrative. Outer Continental Shelf (OCS) Study No. MMS 87-0120. New Orleans, Louisiana: Minerals Management Service.

USACE. 1984. Point Mouillee: Wetland Establishment in Connection with Disposal of Dredged Material. Detroit, Michigan: U.S. Army Corps of Engineers, Detroit District.

USACE. 1986. Dredged Material Beneficial Uses. Engineer Manual EM 1110-2-5026. Washington, D.C.: U.S. Army Corps of Engineers.

USACE. 1989a. Environmental Engineering for Coastal Protection. Engineer Manual EM 1110-2-1204. Washington, D.C.: U.S. Army Corps of Engineers.

USACE. 1989b. Environmental Engineering for Flood Control Channels. Engineer Manual EM 1110-2-1205. Washington, D.C.: U.S. Army Corps of Engineers.

USACE. 1989c. San Francisco Bay to Stockton navigation project. Monitoring program for created wetlands. Project summary for South Pacific Division, Environmental Contribution Program. Sacramento, California: U.S. Army Corps of Engineers, Sacramento, District.

USACE. 1990. Marsh establishment at Corpus Christi, Texas, 45-foot project mitigation site-wetland development. Document No. 900183, EH&A Job No. 11673 prepared by Espey, Huston & Associates. Galveston, Texas: U.S. Army Corps of Engineers, Galveston District.

USACE. 1991. Sand Bypassing System Selection. Engineer Manual EM 1110-2-1616. Washington, D.C.: U.S. Army Corps of Engineers.

USACE. 1992. Coastal Littoral Transport. Engineer Manual EM 1110-2-1502. Washington, D.C.: U.S. Army Corps of Engineers.

USACE. 1994. Shoreline Protection and Beach Erosion Control Study, Phase I: Cost Comparison of Shoreline Protection Projects of the U.S. Army Corps of Engineers. Prepared by Shoreline Protection and Beach Erosion Control Task Force. Fort Belvoir, Virginia: Institute for Water Resources, U.S. Army Corps of Engineers.

USACE, and Florida DNR. 1993. Hurricane Andrew Storm Summary and Impacts on the Beaches of Florida Special Report. Jacksonville and Tallahassee, Florida: U.S. Army Corps of Engineers, Jacksonville District, and Florida Department of Natural Resources.

USFWS. 1980. Habitat as a Basis for Environmental Assessment: Ecological Services Manual 101. Washington, D.C.: U.S. Fish and Wildlife Service.

Vanoni, V. A., ed. 1975. Sedimentation Engineering. New York: American Society of Civil Engineers.

Verhagen, H. J. 1990. Coastal protection and dune management in The Netherlands. Journal of Coastal Research 6:169-179.

Water Quality 2000. 1992. Phase II Challenge Report: Water Quality Problem Identification in the United States. Alexandria, Virginia: Water Quality 2000 Member Congress.

Weber, M., R. T. Townsend, and R. Bierce. 1990. Environmental Quality in the Gulf of Mexico. Washington, D.C.: Center for Marine Conservation and Environmental Protection Agency.

Wells, P. G., and J. Gratwick, eds. 1988. Canadian Conference on Marine Environmental Quality: Proceedings. Halifax, Nova Scotia, Canada: International Institute for Transportation and Ocean Policy Studies.

Wendt, P. H., D. M. Knott, and R. F. Van Dolah. 1989. Community structure of the sessile biota on five artificial reefs of different ages. Bulletin of Marine Science 44:1106-1122.

WES. 1978. Wetland Habitat Development with Dredged Material: Engineering and Plant Propagation. Technical Report DS-78-16. Vicksburg, Mississippi: Environmental Laboratory, U.S. Army Engineer Waterways Experiment Station.

WES. 1986. Field Guide for Low-maintenance Vegetation Establishment and Management. Instruction Report R-86-2. Vicksburg, Mississippi: Environmental Laboratory, U.S. Army Engineer Waterways Experiment Station.

WES. 1988. Environmental Effects of Dredging. Information Exchange Bulletin Volume D-88-5, November 1988. Vicksburg, Mississippi: U.S. Army Engineer Waterway Experiment Station.

WES. 1992. National Summary of Ongoing Wetlands Research by Federal Agencies. Vicksburg, Mississippi: U.S. Army Engineer Waterways Experiment Station.

Westman, W. E. 1991. Ecological restoration projects: Measuring their performance. Environmental Professional 13:207-215.

Wiens, H. J. 1962. Atoll Environment and Ecology. New Haven, Connecticut: Yale University Press.

Williams, J. 1990. Pescadero Marsh Natural Preserve Hydrological Enhancement Plan. San Francisco, California: Phillip Williams and Associates.

Williams, S. J., K. Dodd, and K. K. Gohn. 1990. Coasts in Crisis. U.S. Geological Survey Circular 1075. Washington D.C.: U.S. Government Printing Office.

Williams, J. G., and M. E. Tuttle. 1992. The Columbia River: Fish habitat restoration following hydroelectric dam construction. Pp. 405-422 in Thayer, G. W., ed., 1993. Restoring the Nation's Marine Environment. College Park, Maryland: Maryland Sea Grant.

Yozzo, D. J. 1991. Analytical Synthesis of the Marine Habitat Management Survey. Unpublished contract report to the Marine Board, National Research Council, Washington, D.C.

Zabawa, C.F. 1990. Shore Erosion Control Program. Presentation to the Committee on the Role of Technology in Marine Habitat Protection and Enhancement.

Zarba, C. 1989. National perspective on sediment quality. Pp. 38-46 in National Research Council, 1989. Contaminated Marine Sediments—Assessment and Remediation. Washington, D.C.: National Academy Press.

Zedler, J. B. 1984. Salt Marsh Restoration: A Guidebook for Southern California. California Sea Grant Report No. T-CSGCPO-009.

Zedler, J. B. 1992. Restoring cordgrass marshes in Southern California. Pp. 7-52 in G. W. Thayer, ed., Restoring the Nation's Marine Environment. College Park, Maryland: Maryland Sea Grant.

Zedler, J. B., and R. Langis. 1991. Comparisons of constructed and natural salt marshes of San Diego Bay. Restoration and Management Notes 9(1):21-25.

Zedler, J. B., and C. S. Nordby. 1986. The Ecology of Tijuana Estuary: An Estuarine Profile. Biological Report 85(7.5). La Jolla, California: California Sea Grant College Program.

REFERENCES

Zedler, J. B., C. S. Nordby, and B. E. Kus. 1992. The Ecology of Tijuana Estuary, California: A National Estuarine Research Reserve. Washington, D.C.: Office of Coastal Resource Management, Sanctuaries and Reserves Division, National Oceanic and Atmospheric Administration.

Zedler, J. B., and M. W. Weller. 1990. Overview and future directions. Pp. 405-413 in J. A. Kusler and M. E. Kentula, eds., Wetland Creation and Restoration. Covelo, California: Island Press.

Zentner, J. 1982. Development of regional wetland restoration goals: Coastal wetlands. Pp. 23-31 in M. Josselyn, ed., Wetland Restoration and Enhancement in California. La Jolla, California: California Sea Grant College Program.